"Most Reformed theologians have disagreed with some of the details and nuances of Dr. Lloyd-Jones's interpretation of baptism with the Holy Spirit. But as Park demonstrates, Lloyd Jones's doctrine was not a form of Pentecostalism so much as an adaptation of the doctrine of assurance as taught by one strand of Puritanism. While we may not align fully with Lloyd-Jones on this point, we still treasure his deeply Reformed experiential approach to Christianity and preaching, as well as his expectant longing for a mighty reviving work of God."

Joel R. Beeke, president, Puritan Reformed
Theological Seminary, Grand Rapids, MI

"Martyn Lloyd-Jones has been one of the major theological voices in not only the world in which he moved and had his being, namely, twentieth-century Evangelicalism in the British Isles and Ireland, but also throughout the entire Anglophone Evangelical world. While there have been some academic studies of this impact with regard to his preaching and other ecclesial issues, the subject of the sealing or baptism of the Spirit—a matter very dear to the Doctor's heart—has not been as thoroughly examined. This new study by Dongjin Park on this aspect of Lloyd-Jones's pneumatology is therefore most welcome. It explores the biblical and historical roots of his argument for this distinct work of grace as well as its differences with Pentecostal thought about the baptism of the Spirit, and it offers some helpful critique of Lloyd-Jones's thought. It is an important study for both its historical reflection and the contemporary significance of the Spirit's work for church life today."

Michael A. G. Haykin, chair and professor of church history,
The Southern Baptist Theological Seminary, KY

"This book represents an interesting and wide-ranging discussion of Lloyd-Jones's teaching on Revival/Spirit-baptism with particular reference to preaching. Extensive use is made of primary and secondary sources and for that reason alone the book is worth reading and evaluating."

Eryl Davie[illegible] hool of Theology

"Although Dr. Martyn Lloyd-Jones continues to be widely respected as one of the greatest preachers of modern times, there are some in the Reformed community who are critical of his understanding of the relationship between preaching and the baptism in the Holy Spirit. They maintain that his view on Holy Spirit baptism goes contrary to classic Reformation teaching and puts him in the camp of Pentecostals and charismatics. Dongjin Park disagrees with this criticism and attributes Lloyd-Jones's views to the fact that he was raised in a Welsh Methodist environment where the preaching was experiential and authenticated by frequent revivals during the eighteenth and nineteenth centuries. Park insists that Jones's views go back to a much older teaching of conversion and assurance of salvation that prevailed within the Reformed Puritan tradition until the mid-nineteenth century. I believe Park has succeeded splendidly."

Cornelis Pronk, emeritus pastor, Free Reformed Churches of North America, Brantford, Ontario

THE POWER *of* REVIVAL

Martyn Lloyd-Jones, Baptism in the Spirit, and Preaching on Fire

STUDIES IN HISTORICAL & SYSTEMATIC THEOLOGY

THE POWER *of* REVIVAL

Martyn Lloyd-Jones, Baptism in the Spirit, and Preaching on Fire

DONGJIN PARK

STUDIES IN HISTORICAL AND SYSTEMATIC THEOLOGY

LEXHAM ACADEMIC

The Power of Revival: Martyn Lloyd-Jones, Baptism in the Spirit, and Preaching on Fire
Studies in Historical and Systematic Theology

Lexham Academic, an imprint of Lexham Press
1313 Commercial St., Bellingham, WA 98225
LexhamPress.com

Print ISBN 9781683597261
Digital ISBN 9781683597278
Library of Congress Control Number 2023935086

Lexham Editorial: Todd Hains, Claire Brubaker, Katrina Smith
Cover Design: Joshua Hunt
Typesetting: Mandi Newell

CONTENTS

ABBREVIATIONS

KJV	King James (Authorized) Version
NASB	New American Standard Version
NA[28]	Nestle-Aland *Novum Testamentum Graece*. 28th ed. Stuttgart: German Bible Society, 2013
NIV	New International Version

FOREWORD

One can hardly imagine a topic more central to the life of the church in general and to the task of preaching in particular than the anointing of the Holy Spirit. Yet, inexplicably, many if not most contemporary discussions of preaching—whether popular or academic, liberal or conservative— focus instead on questions of exegesis, setting, or rhetorical method (if, indeed, they mention the Spirit at all). To be sure, these are also important considerations, but while God's Spirit can rescue the flounderings of an inarticulate or inadequately prepared preacher, no amount of eloquence, social sensitivity, or intellectual acumen will suffice if the Spirit is not present to bring home the message to its hearers with life and power. "God's word," writes John Calvin,

> ought indeed to be enough to engender faith in us, if our blindness and stubbornness did not prevent it. But ... the bare word profits nothing without the illumination of the Holy Spirit ... God's word is like the sun, for it shines on all to whom it is proclaimed, but it is without effectiveness among the blind. Now we are all naturally blind in this matter; that is why it cannot enter into our spirit unless God's Spirit, who is the inward Master, gives it access by His illumination.[1]

In practice, both pre-and post-Reformation concepts of preaching tend to focus instead on institutional forms of authorization, so as to determine who has the right to preach, when, and under what conditions. Again, these matters are not unimportant for the good ordering of the Christian community, but ordination itself is not a sufficient source of authority in the pulpit, even

1. John Calvin, Institutes of the Christian Religion: 1541 French Edition, trans. Elsie Anne McKee (Grand Rapids: Eerdmans, 2009), 188–90.

less so in the context of contemporary Western sensibilities that have little tolerance for institutional assertions of the right to be heard.

This is where David Martyn Lloyd-Jones can help us, as Dongjin Park so eloquently explains. Although some within his own confessional circle hinted at advancing senility as the cause for his emphasis on the anointing of the Holy Spirit, it was not intellectual impairment but deep spiritual insight combined with direct personal experience that led him to this view. True to his Reformed heritage, Lloyd Jones knew the importance of careful exegesis and orthodox theology. But he was equally convinced that, in the context of preaching, neither is sufficient of itself. Amidst the fervor of the Charismatic Renewal movement in the late 1960's and 1970's, it seemed to some that Lloyd Jones had simply capitulated to a neo-Pentecostal form of spirituality, thereby abandoning (perhaps even betraying) the more tempered, rational approach of historical Calvinism. On the contrary, this study shows that Lloyd Jones was inspired by traditions of Welsh revivalism, fully in line with the "experiential Calvinism" of classical Puritan spirituality. The example of famous preachers such as John Wesley, George Whitefield, Howell Harris, and Jonathan Edwards (each of whom relate pivotal encounters with the Holy Spirit), coupled with the experiential emphasis of Welsh Methodist spirituality, Welsh hymnody in particular, and the weighty responsibility of preaching itself, all prompted Lloyd Jones to seek the anointing of the Holy Spirit for his own life and ministry.

Still, as Park explains, it would be too simple to imagine Lloyd Jones arriving at a desire for the Spirit on the basis of theological convictions or historical precedent alone. Rather, having tasted "glory" for himself (on several occasions), we see him striving to explain the dynamic agency of the Holy Spirit in such a way that his listeners might experience it for themselves. Convinced of its absolute necessity, he desires revival both for individual believers and for the church as a whole. Yet here there is a curious irony: although he held that for preachers and congregants alike the power of God's Spirit is normally encountered in the context of preaching (as the Puritans had insisted), his own divine appointments were of a more private and personal nature. That discrepancy, Lloyd Jones might assure us, is simply due to the sovereignty of the Holy Spirit, who cannot be tied down to anyone, inalterable manner of proceeding. To our dismay, "the Spirit blows where it wills" (John 3:8), as a result of which even our most valiant attempts at precise definition end in frustration. The problem with preaching—and preachers—is that we get lost in words, whether the words of the biblical text, the words of our sermons, or the words that we use to describe spiritual experience. We argue, for instance, whether to speak of spiritual empowerment in terms of "anointing," "assurance," "unction," "doubling," "baptism," "sealing," or some other language, and whether it may be received once, just twice, or many times over. Here Lloyd Jones would surely insist that all such disagreements, whether concerning exact terminology or the proper manner of the Spirit's working, must take second place to actual experience of God's Spirit. It is only right that we strive for careful definition, but something ineffable invariably remains: because words by themselves cannot fully describe another person's encounter with God, we must find the meaning of those words in an encounter of our own. Admittedly, it requires great courage and spiritual yearning for us to abandon ourselves fully to God, risking the derision even of our fellow believers in our desire to drink more deeply of the Spirit. Yet as much as was the case in previous centuries for Lloyd Jones himself and the many saints whom he cites, it is this inner renewal, and the preaching to which it gives rise, that the church of our day needs most.

By way of conclusion, a more personal note seems appropriate. Over the course of several years, I was privileged to work with the author of this study in supervising both his MA thesis and PhD dissertation at McMaster Divinity College. It quickly became clear that his interest in David Martyn Lloyd Jones and the anointing of the Holy Spirit was not merely academic, but both personal and practical. As a committed disciple and preacher, Dr. Park showed keen interest in discovering the key to effective proclamation of the Christian gospel, less for his own sake than for the sake of the church and those who do not yet know Christ. My prayer, therefore, is that readers would approach this rich and insightful study in the same way as it was written, and to similar ends. Not, that is, as a merely intellectual adventure (although there is much here to satisfy historical and theological curiosity alike), but as an expression of personal engagement with the third Person of the Holy Trinity. *The Power of Revival: Martyn Lloyd-Jones, Baptism in the*

Spirit, and Preaching on Fire invites us to enter into Lloyd-Jones' journey of discovery for ourselves, and to be satisfied with nothing less. May God's own Spirit be the One to guide us in this way.

The Rev. Michael P. Knowles, ThD
George Franklin Hurlburt Chair of Preaching
McMaster Divinity College
Hamilton, Ontario, Canada

1

INTRODUCTION

Martyn Lloyd-Jones (1899–1981), one of the most influential Reformed preachers of the twentieth century, argues that true preaching is a most urgent need both for the church and for the world.[1] For him, preaching is the primary and peculiar task of the church as well as God's own method to lead people to the knowledge of the truth, namely, salvation. Although this is not always recognized, his homiletics has its roots in pneumatology,[2] and at the center of his pneumatology is his understanding of baptism with the Holy Spirit. Accordingly, his definition of true preaching is inextricably related to his doctrine of Spirit baptism. Preaching, according to Lloyd-Jones, consists of two elements: the sermon and the act of preaching itself. With respect to the former, true preaching is expository and doctrinal; as to the latter, preachers themselves require baptism with the Spirit. Lloyd-Jones was convinced that genuine Christian preaching should be accompanied by Spirit baptism since without a baptism of power, there will be no efficacy even in preaching that delivers sound doctrine from the Scriptures.

However, Lloyd-Jones's convictions regarding Spirit baptism are not confined to the area of preaching. Rather, Spirit baptism concerns a wide range of Christian spiritual experience, including assurance of salvation and empowerment for service.[3] In addition, what primarily arouses controversy over his convictions concerning Spirit baptism is the relation between regeneration and Spirit baptism rather than homiletics in particular. Lloyd-Jones suggests that baptism with the Spirit is the postconversion experience of an exceptional—that is, an immediate, direct, and overwhelming—work

1. Lloyd-Jones, *Preaching and Preachers*, 9.

2. Sargent, *Sacred Anointing*, xii.

3. Michael Eaton argues that the phrase "baptism with the Spirit" when used by Lloyd-Jones provides "a category of interpretation by which to understand the experience of a wide range of Christians" (*Baptism with the Spirit*, 238).

of the Spirit, as distinct from initial regeneration. By making such a clear distinction between rebirth and Spirit baptism, he maintains that though an individual can be a true believer, it is possible that the person still has not received baptism of the Spirit.

When *Joy Unspeakable: Power and Renewal in the Holy Spirit* (1984) and *Prove All Things: The Sovereign Work of the Holy Spirit* (1985) were posthumously published, both of which contained Lloyd-Jones's sermons specifically addressing Spirit baptism, harsh criticism arose from within the Reformed circles to which Lloyd-Jones had belonged. Critics claimed that these sermons deviated from Lloyd-Jones's earlier, more truly Reformed theology; they were evidence, it was said, of "a great man in decline, possibly suffering from a sort of theological Alzheimer's disease."[4] Such fierce opposition from the Reformed camp was not surprising in that the traditional Reformed position on Spirit baptism understands it as the initial experience that all Christians enjoy at the moment of conversion.

This book arises from a recognition that Lloyd-Jones's pneumatology, particularly as it relates to his homiletics, has not been fully explored, nor has the question of its relation with his Reformed theological heritage been sufficiently clarified. Since Lloyd-Jones passed away in 1981, only a few books and critical articles addressing either his doctrine on Spirit baptism or his homiletics have been published. There has been little comprehensive research that addresses his position on Spirit baptism in relation to preaching. A chronological review of some significant studies on his pneumatology and homiletics, as well as the relation between the two, will demonstrate the need for further research on this topic.

In 1989, Michael Eaton published *Baptism with the Spirit: The Teaching of Dr. Martyn Lloyd-Jones*, one of the most important studies on the subject to date. In this volume, Eaton explains various historical views on the subject of Spirit baptism. He divides them into two groups: those who view it as a nonexperiential event—sacramental interpretation, nonexperiential part of conversion, and nonexperiential postconversion event—and those who view it as experiential—associated with conversion, bestowal of holiness, power for service, gifts of the Spirit, and assurance of salvation. Positioning Lloyd-Jones's doctrine of baptism with the Spirit primarily as assurance of

4. Atherstone, Jones, and Kay, "Lloyd-Jones and the Charismatic Controversy," 114.

salvation—a sealing of salvation—within the latter category, Eaton argues that Lloyd-Jones's doctrine of baptism with the Spirit is entirely in harmony with the teachings of the Bible; it suggests "a category of interpretation by which to understand Christian experience."[5] The author identifies a wide range of phrases in both the Old Testament and New Testament indicating that baptism with the Spirit includes an experiential component. Since this volume concentrates specifically on Lloyd-Jones's teachings concerning Spirit baptism, Eaton's research helps not only to understand Lloyd-Jones's pneumatology but also to situate his doctrine of baptism in the Spirit historically and theologically. Above all, this book, though brief, reveals the inextricable connection in Lloyd-Jones's mind between baptism with the Spirit and preaching. Eaton points out that Lloyd-Jones has baptism with the Spirit in view when he exhorts preachers to seek for the power of the Spirit to rest on them. As further proof of this close relation, Eaton observes that most examples of Spirit baptism that appear in Lloyd-Jones's sermons are taken from the anecdotes of other preachers.[6]

Tony Sargent's *The Sacred Anointing: Preaching and the Spirit's Anointing in the Life and Thought of Martyn Lloyd-Jones*, which appeared in 1994, argues that Lloyd-Jones's homiletics cannot be comprehensively understood without sufficient appreciation for his doctrine of the Holy Spirit and in particular the pivotal position of "unction"—a technical term describing baptism of the Spirit connected with the act of preaching—in his pneumatology. Citing biblical exegesis, Puritan theology, and the historical context at that time,[7] Sargent explains why Lloyd-Jones adopted the conviction that preachers must be anointed by the Holy Spirit for their ministry to be effective. Whereas most other books and articles take a broader theological approach

5. Eaton, *Baptism with the Spirit*, 238.

6. Eaton, *Baptism with the Spirit*, 218. Eaton states, "In one sermon on Romans 8:16, for example, he relates incidents from Robert Bruce, John Preston, Thomas Horton, William Guthrie, Richard Sibbes, Edward Elton, Thomas Goodwin, George Whitefield, Gilbert Tennant, Jonathan Edwards, Mrs Jonathan Edwards, John Wesley, Howell Harris, Hugh Bourne, Christmas Evans, Edward Payson, Mere D'Aubigné, John McKenzie, Charles Finney, D. L. Moody, and Charles Spurgeon. Of these twenty-one names, one was a preacher's wife, one was primarily a historian (D'Aubigné), the other nineteen were preachers" (218).

7. Sargent argues that growing interest in the doctrine of the Holy Spirit due to the rise of Pentecostalism and the charismatic movement in Britain encouraged Lloyd-Jones to emphasize the need of the outpouring of the Spirit in the ministry of preaching, namely, through unction, though he did not align his views with Pentecostalism or the charismatic movement.

to Lloyd-Jones's teachings on the Holy Spirit and baptism of the Spirit in general, Sargent's work concentrates on the subject of unction. Moreover, this work takes a practical approach, addressing active preachers in order to help them adapt and apply Lloyd-Jones's methods and convictions to their own ministries of preaching.[8] Furthermore, as Sargent explains in the introduction, the purpose of his work is to define and illustrate Lloyd-Jones's own position[9] rather than to assess it critically.

In 1997, John Brencher completed a PhD dissertation at the University of Sheffield, published by Paternoster in 2002, titled, "David Martyn Lloyd-Jones 1899–1981 and Twentieth-Century Evangelicalism." In chapter 8 of his study, Brencher assesses from a historical point of view the acute debate over the relationship between Lloyd-Jones and the charismatic movement that emerged in Britain in the 1960s. The author describes him as "a sympathetic spectator"[10] rather than an active espouser of the renewal movement. As evidence, Brencher presents the fact that despite Lloyd-Jones's initially approving of Michael Harper's experience as demonstrating genuine evidence of Spirit baptism upon meeting him in 1963, he wrote seven years later to an acquaintance about the dangers and unscriptural nature of Harper's charismatic campaign.[11] Although it is plausible to evaluate Lloyd-Jones's opinion regarding Spirit baptism as being consistent with charismatic views apart from the question of speaking in tongues, Brencher argues that Lloyd-Jones's emphasis on a mighty outpouring of the Spirit, another expression of Spirit baptism, originates rather with eighteenth-century revivalism and reflects Lloyd-Jones's Calvinistic Methodist roots.

Assessing the controversy as a question of exegesis, Matthew Brook O'Donnell's article, "Two Opposing Views on Baptism with/by the Holy Spirit and of 1 Corinthians 12:13: Can Grammatical Investigation Bring Clarity?,"

---

8. Sargent, *Sacred Anointing*, xi. Sargent notes, "Our main objective is not to major so much on points of theological disagreement but to unearth helpful principles for preachers who desperately want to know more about being borne along in the power of the Holy Spirit as they preach to their congregations Sunday by Sunday" (34–35).

9. Sargent, *Sacred Anointing*, xii.

10. Brencher, "David Martyn Lloyd-Jones 1899–1981," 246.

11. Brencher cites Lloyd-Jones's letter to Douglas Johnson from 1970, in which he writes, "It is apparently a part of the Michael Harper movement but a particularly aggressive one. I fear that nothing can be done apart from helping people who are vaguely attracted and showing them the gross dangers and the thoroughly unscriptural character of the whole thing" (Iain Murray, *D. Martyn Lloyd-Jones: Letters 1919–1981* [Carlisle, PA: Banner of Truth Trust, 1994], 204).

from 1999, examines the controversy between John Stott and Martyn Lloyd-Jones over the interpretation of 1 Corinthians 12:13, which was one of the key verses in the Spirit baptism debate. In *Baptism and Fullness*, Stott argues that this verse signifies that the baptizer is Jesus Christ and the Spirit is an element that he uses for baptism.[12] On the basis of this interpretation, Stott claims that Spirit baptism means nothing other than regeneration. On the other hand, Lloyd-Jones argues in *Joy Unspeakable* that in this verse the baptizer is the Spirit, not Jesus Christ, in which case it is wrong to use the verse to argue that Spirit baptism is no different from regeneration.[13] O'Donnell applies a linguistic analysis to 1 Corinthians 12:13 to evaluate these two opposing views. He asserts that here the preposition ἐν in the phrase ἐν πνεύματι indicates "personal agency" (i.e., Lloyd-Jones's position) rather than "means" (i.e., Stott's position), specifically since the verb is in the passive voice (ἐβαπτίσθημεν). In addition, the word order of the verse, with the prepositional phrase ἐν πνεύματι placed before the verb, suggests the high possibility of interpreting it as the agent of the verb. Based on these grammatical grounds, O'Donnell concludes that Lloyd-Jones's interpretation of 1 Corinthians 12:13—"being baptized by the Spirit" (the Spirit as an agent)—has more grammatical support than Stott's—"being baptized with the Spirit" (the Spirit as a means).[14]

In chapter 7—"A Controversial Book *Joy Unspeakable*: The Baptism with the Holy Spirit"—of *Lloyd-Jones: Messenger of Grace*, published in 2008, Iain Murray addresses Lloyd-Jones's teachings on baptism with the Spirit. This chapter contains three significant points for the study of this topic. First, Murray differentiates Lloyd-Jones's position from that of the Pentecostal movement on such issues as the laying on of hands, delay of time, the sovereignty of God, speaking in tongues, and the question of a once-for-all crisis experience. Second, Murray points out inconsistencies in Lloyd-Jones's teachings on Spirit baptism. For instance, although Lloyd-Jones rejects the concept of a once-for-all crisis experience as the occasion for Spirit baptism, he sometimes describes it as lifting a Christian to another level all at once. Lloyd-Jones's explanation as to the difference between "baptism with the

12. Stott, *Baptism and Fullness*, 55–56.
13. Lloyd-Jones, *Joy Unspeakable*, 173–78.
14. O'Donnell, "Two Opposing Views," 334, 336.

Spirit" and "the filling of the Spirit" is that the former indicates an initial experience of Spirit baptism and the latter expression applies to subsequent experiences. Yet Lloyd-Jones's account that the difference between baptism and fullness is a matter of timing rather than of theological substance contains another inconsistency since he argues that even though baptism of the Spirit depends solely on the sovereignty of God, the filling of the Spirit is the responsibility of believers.[15] Lloyd-Jones sometimes illustrates the experience of Spirit baptism as being overwhelming, like a "sudden cloud-burst," but he also allows for the possibility of various degrees of intensity, including the example of a weak experience, which he likens to a "slight drizzle"[16] type of Spirit baptism. Last, Murray holds that Lloyd-Jones's doctrine of assurance (which Lloyd-Jones believes is the result of Spirit baptism) is not essentially different from that of the broader Reformed position, despite differences in its presentation.[17] This volume is of considerable significance in that it provides a balanced analysis of Lloyd-Jones's doctrine of baptism of the Spirit, relating it to his concern for the church of his time. However, since only one chapter deals with the subject, Murray's work needs further development.

"Lloyd-Jones and the Charismatic Controversy," written collaboratively by Andrew Atherstone, David Ceri Jones, and William Kay, appeared in 2011. This work has two main goals: (1) to clarify the relationship between Lloyd-Jones and emerging charismatic figures during the 1960s and 1970s, and (2) to review the various responses to Lloyd-Jones's published sermons, including posthumous ones about Spirit baptism. In the case of the former, the coauthors conclude that Lloyd-Jones's personal encouragement to the leaders of the charismatic movement was not confined to early figures, such as Michael Harper and Billy Richards in the 1960s, but lasted to the end of his life and included later church leaders from within Pentecostal and charismatic tradition such as Henry Tyler and Terry Virgo. With regard to the second issue, the authors examine in detail the diverse reactions to books such as *Preaching and Preachers*, *Romans: The Sons of God*, *God's Ultimate Purpose*, *Joy Unspeakable*, and *Prove All Things*, all of which include sermons on baptism of the Spirit. For some in the Reformed camp, such as Donald Macleod and Peter Masters, these

15. Murray, *Lloyd Jones: Messenger of Grace*, 136–39, 141.

16. Lloyd-Jones, *Joy Unspeakable*, 68.

17. Murray, *Lloyd Jones: Messenger of Grace*, 155.

volumes show that Lloyd-Jones's teachings were identical to those of charismatics or Pentecostals. Other scholars, including Iain Murray and Graham Harrison among them, attempt to defend him, arguing that Lloyd-Jones's doctrine on Spirit baptism was in harmony with the Reformed tradition. Still others, notably Peter Lewis and Christopher Catherwood, suggest that his sermons are good examples of rapprochement between Reformed and charismatic theological views.[18] This collaborative work offers a meaningful study of Lloyd-Jones's pneumatology because it takes a historical approach to the charismatic controversy surrounding Lloyd-Jones and his sermons without being bound to a particular theological viewpoint.

With the exception of Eaton's Baptism with the Spirit: The Teaching of Dr. Martyn Lloyd-Jones and Sargent's The Sacred Anointing: Preaching and the Spirit's Anointing in the Life and Thought of Martyn Lloyd-Jones, there has been little in-depth research into Lloyd-Jones's position on baptism of the Spirit and its relationship to preaching, even though some chapters in the volumes or several critical articles handling this topic have been published. Even Eaton's work is focused primarily on Lloyd-Jones's pneumatology, while Sargent concentrates on his homiletics. Thus, to date no study has offered a comprehensive investigation of both Lloyd-Jones's conviction on Spirit baptism and its close connection with his homiletics. In particular, as noted above, few studies on the subject have integrated exegetical, theological, and historical approaches. Accordingly, I trust that this book, which takes an in-depth and integrated approach, will make a significant contribution to the study of Martyn Lloyd-Jones's pneumatology and homiletics.

This book will demonstrate that Lloyd-Jones's pneumatology, particularly his doctrine of Spirit baptism, reappropriates a neglected dimension of Reformed theology that derives from classical Puritan spirituality, with its emphasis on experiential religion. The core of his doctrine on Spirit baptism is full assurance of salvation rather than speaking in tongues or the gifts of the Spirit, as are emphasized in Pentecostalism and the charismatic movement. Contrary to the assertions of his critics, Lloyd-Jones inherited an understanding of the doctrine of assurance from pietistic Puritanism of the sixteenth and the seventeenth centuries as well as from Welsh Calvinistic

18. Atherstone, Jones, and Kay, "Lloyd-Jones and the Charismatic Controversy," 115, 127–29, 143–46, 154–55.

Methodism in the eighteenth century, both of which embraced an experiential Calvinism. In addition, his doctrine of Spirit baptism is inextricably related to his theology regarding revival, which was his lifelong aspiration and concern. This aspect of his theology derives from the pneumatology of Calvinistic revivalism, prominently articulated by Jonathan Edwards in the eighteenth century and prevalent among Reformed pastors and preachers well into the mid-nineteenth century.

On these grounds, it appears that Lloyd-Jones's position on baptism with the Spirit is neither novel nor indebted to Pentecostal or charismatic doctrine. Rather, it should be regarded as a reappropriation of an older doctrine concerning assurance of salvation and revival that had prevailed within the Reformed tradition from the sixteenth until the mid-nineteenth centuries. This book will contribute both to a better understanding of Lloyd-Jones's pneumatology and homiletics and to a fuller appreciation of the role of the Holy Spirit in the ministry of preaching, on the basis of his example.

In order to analyze Lloyd-Jones's position on baptism with the Spirit and his conviction regarding its necessity for true preaching, this book employs an intellectual history approach. Such an approach deals with "the history of ideas" and "the people that have written and propagated them." It usually focuses on "the published writings of key intellectuals or authors and their ideas that have helped to shape the world."[19] This book adopts this approach because the main purpose of the research is to demonstrate that Lloyd-Jones's doctrine of Spirit baptism is a reappropriation of Reformed theology, particularly regarding the notions of assurance of salvation and revival, from the sixteenth until the mid-nineteenth centuries. Therefore, this book will trace the history of the doctrines of assurance and revival; while it will focus on the work of Lloyd-Jones himself, it will also discuss pietistic Puritans, the Welsh Calvinistic Methodists, Jonathan Edwards, and Reformed preachers of the mid-nineteenth century, all of whom propagated the same doctrines.

This book will concentrate mainly on the published sermons of Lloyd-Jones and his predecessors as sources for the history of the aforementioned doctrines. In his article "Sermon Literature and Canadian Intellectual History," Sid Wise asserts, "Sermon literature as a source for the history of ideas ... has been used extensively." As representative studies that use published sermons

19. Heath, *Doing Church History*, 36.

to trace the development of ideas, he suggests Christopher Morris's *Political Thought in England* and *Tyndale to Hooker* as well as William Haller's *The Rise of Puritanism*.[20] For instance, Haller's *The Rise of Puritanism* relies on the exploration of a large number of sermons to explore the intellectual development of early modern England. Haller turns to sermons and popular expositions of doctrine because he is convinced that "one could not understand Puritanism without knowledge of the teachings of the Puritan pulpit."[21]

Most obviously, this book will rely primarily on Lloyd-Jones's sermons and lectures regarding baptism of the Spirit. Yet because Lloyd-Jones himself often cites the sermons of the Puritans, Welsh Methodists, Jonathan Edwards, and Reformed preachers of the mid-nineteenth century, the scope of research will include these as well. In terms of his own sermon material, Lloyd-Jones preached about baptism of the Spirit on many occasions. His convictions on this subject stand out most prominently in his sermons on Ephesians 1:13–14 in *God's Ultimate Purpose*, Romans 5:5 in *Romans: Assurance*, and Romans 8:15–16 in *Romans: The Sons of God*.[22] The books *Revival*, *Joy Unspeakable: Power and Renewal in the Holy Spirit*, and *Prove All Things: The Sovereign Work of the Holy Spirit* also include sermons on the subject of Spirit baptism and its necessity for true preaching.[23] As for Lloyd-Jones's lectures, *God the Holy Spirit*, one of several volumes in a series on doctrine, and *The Puritans: Their Origins and Successors* and *Preaching and Preachers* will be the main sources for his views on baptism with the Spirit.[24]

An intellectual-history approach to Lloyd-Jones's sermons and lectures on Spirit baptism, tracing the sources of his theology by exploring his frequent citations of other writers and preachers, will demonstrate that his understanding of Spirit baptism stems from the Reformed doctrine related to assurance of salvation and revival that had been propagated from the sixteenth to the nineteenth centuries. At the same time, this approach will also show that Lloyd-Jones's doctrine of Spirit baptism is a thoughtful reappropriation

20. Wise, "Sermon Literature," 81.

21. Haller, *Rise of Puritanism*, ix.

22. Lloyd-Jones, *God's Ultimate Purpose*, 243–311; Lloyd-Jones, *Romans: Assurance*, 74–101; Lloyd-Jones, *Romans: The Sons of God*, 194–399.

23. Lloyd-Jones, *Revival*, 7–316; Lloyd-Jones, *Joy Unspeakable*, 15–280; Lloyd-Jones, *Prove All Things*, 15–158.

24. Lloyd-Jones, *God the Holy Spirit*, 234–54; Lloyd-Jones, *Puritans*, 1–23, 101–28, 191–214, 282–302, 348–71; Lloyd-Jones, *Preaching and Preachers*, 304–25.

of the older doctrines within the context of his own day rather than a simple repetition of their original content. I will also consider specific influences at play in this process of theological recontextualization in order to trace the development of the doctrines of salvation and revival that are behind Lloyd-Jones's more particular understanding of Spirit baptism. In this way, my adoption of an intellectual-history approach will provide sufficient evidence for the argument that Lloyd-Jones's position on the subject is neither novel nor identical to Pentecostal or charismatic doctrine.

The primary conclusion of this book is that rather than being original to him or indebted to Pentecostal or charismatic doctrine, Lloyd-Jones's position on baptism with the Spirit should be considered a redevelopment of older teachings on the assurance of salvation and revival that had been prevalent within the Reformed tradition from the sixteenth until the mid-nineteenth centuries.

2

—

BAPTISM WITH THE SPIRIT

Its Nature and Necessity for Preaching

From Lloyd-Jones's sermons and lectures on baptism with the Spirit, his teachings regarding this subject can be summarized as having six general characteristics. In his view, first, baptism with the Spirit is a subsequent experience of an exceptional work of the Spirit that is distinct from regeneration. He asserts that the work of the Holy Spirit can be divided into regular (or indirect) work and exceptional (or direct) work.[1] The regular work of the Spirit includes conviction, regeneration, and sanctification:[2]

> He [the Holy Spirit] has a number of functions which he serves; they include conviction, and particularly, of course, regeneration. But he also does the work of sanctifying us. It is the Spirit who sanctifies us through the truth. ... The Holy Spirit is in the church today and he does a regular work in it, though these are the days of small things. But we must not despise these days because, after all, what is happening is the work of the Holy Spirit. That is what I mean by his regular work. ... The Holy Spirit normally works through means. That is what I have in mind when I say that his work is "indirect." It is the Holy Spirit who has given us the Word, and his regular ministry, his ordinary (if one may use such a term with regard to the Holy Spirit) work is to deal with us through the Scriptures. He enlightens the mind,

---

1. Iain Murray disagrees with Lloyd-Jones's understanding of the work of the Spirit to regard indirect work of the Spirit as regular and to direct work of the Spirit as exceptional. Murray argues that the standard to divide regular and exceptional work of the Spirit is its intensity rather than its immediacy. See Murray, *Lloyd Jones: Messenger of Grace*, 162; Murray, *Pentecost Today?*, 31.

2. Lloyd-Jones, *Joy Unspeakable*, 66.

> gives us understanding, opens the Scriptures to us, uses the teacher or the preacher, and so on. Now that work is more or less indirect.[3]

In this manner, Lloyd-Jones argues that the regular work of the Spirit is usually accomplished indirectly, by means of God's written word in Scripture, rather than in the immediate experience of the Christian.

On the other hand, the exceptional work of the Spirit is related to assurance, witness, and ministry. Lloyd-Jones believes that baptism with the Spirit belongs to the category of the exceptional and direct work of the Spirit;[4] it greatly influences assurance of salvation, witness of the gospel, and church ministry. He suggests that such expressions as "poured out" (Acts 2:17) and "shed abroad" (Rom 5:5) both indicate tremendous profusion and describe the overwhelming nature of baptism with the Spirit. Concerning the directness of baptism with the Spirit, Lloyd-Jones takes Romans 8:16 as one scriptural example:

> Now there are many examples of this. Let me just take one, from Romans 8:16 where the apostle says, "The Spirit itself beareth witness with our spirit, that we are the children of God." ... Here the thing that is stressed is that the Spirit is bearing witness with our spirit. There is a witness in our spirit [Rom 8:15], but he now bears witness with that—together with that, right upon that; seals that and makes it absolutely certain to us. Occasionally he may use means, but speaking generally he does this without means.[5]

As an exceptional (i.e., overwhelming and direct) work of the Holy Spirit, baptism with the Spirit is "something which has been taught and recognized in the Christian church throughout the centuries and by men belonging to various and varied theological schools."[6] In his sermon "Filled with the Spirit," for example, he invokes John Owen (1616–1683), a representative Calvinistic Puritan, and John Wesley (1703–1791), an adherent of Arminianism, to support his argument that it transcends other theological distinctions. His citations

3. Lloyd-Jones, *Joy Unspeakable*, 66–67.
4. Lloyd-Jones, *Joy Unspeakable*, 66–67.
5. Lloyd-Jones, *Joy Unspeakable*, 70–71.
6. Lloyd-Jones, *Joy Unspeakable*, 72.

of statements from these two men exemplify the opposing theological camps. From Owen, Lloyd-Jones quotes:

> Now there are two ways whereby the Spirit worketh this joy in the hearts of believers: (1) He doth it immediately by Himself without the consideration of any other acts or works of His or the interposition of any reasonings or deductions and conclusions. As in sanctification He is a well of water springing up in the soul immediately exerting His efficacy and refreshment, so in consolation [which means assurance]. He immediately works the soul and the minds of men to a joyful rejoicing and spiritual frame, filling them with exultation and gladness. Not that this arises from our reflex consideration of the love of God, but rather gives occasion thereunto. When He sheds abroad the love of God in our hearts and so fills them with gladness by an immediate act and operation (as He caused John the Baptist to leap for joy in the womb upon the approach of the Mother of Jesus) then doth the soul even from hence raise itself to a consideration of the love of God whence joy and rejoicing doth also flow. Of this joy there is no account to be given but that the Spirit worketh it when and how He will. He secretly infuseth and distils it into the soul, prevailing against all fears and sorrows, filling it with gladness, exultations, and sometimes with unspeakable raptures of the mind.[7]

Likewise, Lloyd-Jones reports from Wesley: "This is something immediate and direct, not the result of reflection or argumentation. ... There may be foretastes of joy and peace, of love, and these not delusive but really from God long before we have the witness in ourselves."[8] Both of them, Lloyd-Jones maintains, refer to the exceptional characteristic of the baptism with the Spirit—"the immediacy, the directness, and the overwhelming character of the experience."[9]

In particular, for Lloyd-Jones, Spirit baptism is a postconversion experience of the Spirit, encountered subsequent to regeneration. Despite being a representative of the Reformed camp, he strongly objects to any assertion

---

7. Owen, *Of Communion with God*, 172–73, quoted in Lloyd-Jones, *Joy Unspeakable*, 72–73.
8. Wesley, *Works of the Reverend John Wesley* 1:95–100, quoted in Lloyd-Jones, *Joy Unspeakable*, 74.
9. Lloyd-Jones, *Joy Unspeakable*, 74.

that 1 Corinthians 12:13 ("For by one Spirit are we all baptized into one body, whether we be Jews or Gentiles, whether we be bond or free; and have been all made to drink into one Spirit")[10] describes an experience of baptism in the Spirit. He argues that the passage in question refers only to regeneration or engraftment into the body of Christ by the work of the Holy Spirit. Accordingly, he is convinced that one can be a Christian without being baptized with the Holy Spirit since Spirit baptism is a postconversion event. To teach baptism of the Spirit as regeneration, he even says, is little different from being guilty of quenching the Holy Spirit since such a teaching leads Christians to think that they no longer need to pursue the spiritual blessing that the Father promised (Acts 1:4).

Second, Lloyd-Jones argues that one of the main effects of baptism with the Spirit is to give a Christian a full assurance of salvation. He regards this unusual assurance as "the greatest and most essential characteristic of the baptism with the Spirit." He is convinced that there are three types of assurance for the Christian. The first type of assurance, the most commonly recognized form, is the one that the Christian attains "by deduction from the Scriptures," which is the lowest or simplest form.[11] The second form of assurance consists of being "strengthened as the Christian observes the change in his life corresponding with what Scripture says on the marks of the children of God; they 'love the brethren' (1 John 3:4), etc."[12] The third type, "the highest and the greatest form of certainty and assurance that one can ever have of the fact that one is a child of God," is an assurance that is given to the Christian directly by the action of the Holy Spirit himself.[13] Lloyd-Jones takes Romans 8:16 ("The Spirit himself beareth witness with our Spirit, that we are the children of God") as a proof that the greatest form of assurance is given as the result of baptism with the Spirit:

> Now this is neither our action, nor our deduction, but the immediate witness of the Spirit, and that is why it is both so absolute and so certain. What the Spirit does is this: he tells us in the most unmistakable

10. Biblical references follow the KJV because this is the translation that Lloyd-Jones consistently employed in his teaching and preaching.

11. Lloyd-Jones, *Joy Unspeakable*, 38, 90–92.

12. Murray, *Lloyd Jones: Messenger of Grace*, 128.

13. Lloyd-Jones, *Romans: The Sons of God*, 304; Lloyd-Jones, *Joy Unspeakable*, 93.

> manner that we are the children of God, that God loves us with an everlasting love, and that it was because he so loved us that Christ gave himself for us.[14]

There is an apparent distinction, he asserts, between saving faith and an assurance of faith; the latter is provided only to Christians who are baptized with the Spirit, though the former is given to all Christians:

> The Bible never says that we are saved by assurance, we are saved by faith. In other words, there are many Christian people who have come to see and to know that they are sinners, that they are under the wrath of God, that they are helpless and hopeless, and who are afraid of the judgement. ... They say, "I trust myself only to the Lord Jesus Christ." They believe the truth concerning him, they believe on him, and they rest on that. ... Now the Bible says that such people are Christians, but they are Christians who are not enjoying full assurance of salvation and of faith.[15]

Lloyd-Jones introduces Thomas Goodwin's (1600–1680) illustration to clarify the difference between saving faith and an assurance of faith:

> [Thomas Goodwin] describes a man and his little child, his son, walking down the road and they are walking hand in hand, and the child knows that he is the child of his father, and he knows that his father loves him, and he rejoices in that, and he is happy in it. There is no uncertainty about it all, but suddenly the father, moved by some impulse, takes hold of that child and picks him up, fondles him in his arms, kisses him, embraces him, showers his love upon him, and then he puts him down again and they go on walking together. That is it! The child knew before that his father loved him, and he knew that he was his child. But oh! this loving embrace, this extra outpouring of love, this unusual manifestation of it—that is the kind of thing. The Spirit bearing witness with our spirit, that we are the children of God.[16]

---

14. Lloyd-Jones, *Joy Unspeakable*, 93.
15. Lloyd-Jones, *Joy Unspeakable*, 40–41.
16. Lloyd-Jones, *Joy Unspeakable*, 95–96.

Furthermore, Lloyd-Jones is convinced that such full assurance is an integral part of sharing the gospel since without assurance no one can be an effective witness. In this regard, he believes that such great assurance leads a preacher to be equipped with authority and power:

> With this assurance comes the power. If we are uncertain about the word of God, as to what is true and what is not true, or if I am uncertain about my relationship to him and the truth of these things in my case, I shall, as we have seen, be an advocate, not a witness. But when a man is baptized with the Spirit or sealed with the Spirit, he knows; the Spirit is the certainty. That leads not only to certainty in the individual, it leads to power. It must do. It is when we are certain, that we speak with authority and power.[17]

To summarize, then, Lloyd-Jones asserts that as a direct work of the Holy Spirit to the spirit of a Christian, Spirit baptism provides that person with a full assurance of salvation; as a result, it leads that person to become an effective witness to the gospel, one who can speak with authority and power.

Third, baptism of the Holy Spirit is entirely dependent on the sovereignty of God. Lloyd-Jones asserts that this baptism is God's sovereign action, not the result of our own actions or effort. For him, there is little distinction between baptism of the Spirit and revival. He defines revival as a large number of people being baptized with the Holy Spirit simultaneously.[18] And he strongly opposes the assertion that one can produce revival merely if certain external requirements are brought to completion:

> You cannot get a revival whenever you like, or work one up. It is wrong to say that if you fulfil certain conditions, or do certain things a revival will come. So many have said that. I have known many who have taught and practised that, who have done everything that they have been instructed to do, but the revival has not come. The answer is that it is entirely his gift, and entirely in his hands. He is the Lord, he is sovereign, and as the Holy Spirit gives gifts to people according to

17. Lloyd-Jones, *Joy Unspeakable*, 157.
18. Lloyd-Jones, *Joy Unspeakable*, 51.

> his sovereign will, so the Son gives the gift, this baptism, according to his own sovereign will.[19]

One of the main factors for which Lloyd-Jones criticizes the charismatic movement is that the Spirit baptism that charismatics claim "lacked the primary marks of such sovereign movements of the Spirit as had awakened the church in the times past."[20] For him, baptism with the Spirit or revival is the Spirit's coming down, but for the charismatic movement, he argues, it is "more something *they* do or receive."[21]

Lloyd-Jones often cites David Morgan (1814–1883) as a good example of this characteristic of baptism of the Spirit. Morgan was a great instrument of God in the revival of 1859 in Wales. He was an ordinary man, a carpenter by trade, with little training as a preacher. One night in a certain meeting, however, he was baptized with the Holy Spirit. After that experience, he began to preach with great power and continued for the next two years. Subsequently, however, the remainder of his days reverted to a mere ordinary form of Christian experience. As Lloyd-Jones explains:

> He was in a meeting one night and was very moved, but he said to a friend later, "I went to bed that night as usual, David Morgan. I had felt power in the service but I went to bed at night David Morgan. But," he said, "you know when I woke up the next morning I realized I was a different man. I felt like a lion, I felt great power." He began to preach with tremendous power and it went on for two years. Then he said to this same friend, "One night I went to bed filled with this power that had accompanied me for two years, I woke up the next morning and found that I was David Morgan once more." And he continued to be David Morgan until he died about some fifteen years or so later.[22]

As in the case of Morgan, the Holy Spirit can give this baptism to a preacher and retrieve it from that person at will. Baptism of the Spirit is therefore not a permanent possession. Accordingly, Lloyd-Jones loves to exhort preachers

19. Lloyd-Jones, *Joy Unspeakable*, 52.
20. Murray, *David Martyn Lloyd-Jones: The Fight of Faith*, 693.
21. Murray, *David Martyn Lloyd-Jones: The First Forty Years*, 693; emphasis added.
22. Lloyd-Jones, *Joy Unspeakable*, 129.

to seek this baptism fervently and continually before they stand in the pulpit to preach:

> The power came, and the power was withdrawn. Such is the lordship of the Spirit! You cannot command this blessing, you cannot order it; it is entirely the gift of God. The examples I have given from the Scriptures indicate this. "Peter, filled with the Spirit." The Spirit filled him. He did the same to David Morgan; and then in His own inscrutable wisdom and sovereignty He took it from him. Revivals are not meant to be permanent. But at the same time I maintain that all of us who are preachers should be seeking this power every time we preach.[23]

Fourth, baptism of the Holy Spirit can be repeated many times. Lloyd-Jones takes as an example the experience of Peter. On the day of Pentecost, the apostles received baptism with the Spirit, and Peter was immediately enabled to preach with a great power from on high. But in Acts 4, when he stood before the Sanhedrin and was going to give an account, he "was filled with the Holy Spirit" (Acts 4:8) again. Lloyd-Jones asserts that it was another baptism with the Spirit to provide him with fresh power to deal with the current situation: "This 'accession of power,' or if you prefer it, this 'effusion of power' upon Christian preachers is not something 'once for all'; it can be repeated, and repeated many many times."[24] Furthermore, he is convinced that revival is a kind of repetition of what occurred on the day of Pentecost. For him, what happened on Pentecost in Acts 2 is not the event of "once and for all," which cannot be repeated. On the contrary, he is convinced, whenever revival has taken place, the church has come back to the original state described in Acts 2.[25] Lloyd-Jones states:

> Every one of them [revivals] seems to be a returning to what you can read in the book of the Acts of the Apostles. Every time the Church is thus revived, she seems to be doing what Isaac did, she is going back to something that had happened before, rediscovering it, and finding the ancient supply. There is nothing I know of that is more striking in the history of the Church than just that principle. Read the story

23. Lloyd-Jones, *Joy Unspeakable*, 324.
24. Lloyd-Jones, *Preaching and Preachers*, 325.
25. Lloyd-Jones, *Revival*, 199.

> of the great revivals with which God has visited the Church throughout the centuries, and you will find that it always seems to be almost precisely the same thing.[26]

Consequently, Sargent argues, Lloyd-Jones believes firmly that "Apostolic power for preaching the Gospel is still available within God's sovereignty today."[27]

Fifth, baptism with the Spirit simultaneously brings both preacher and congregation a sense of authority.[28] He notices a similar description from the journals of George Whitefield (1714–1770) and Howell Harris (1714–1773): "The Lord came down among us."[29] Such an expression, Lloyd-Jones believes, proves that baptism of the Spirit is accompanied by divine authority. He notes:

> Go back and read the history of the great revivals in the Church, and you will find that this power of the Holy Ghost and authority is always present ... As you read his [Howell Harris's] journals you find that he keeps on saying something like this: "Arrived at such and such a place; preached. Felt the old authority." ... He was never happy unless he was aware of "the authority." It was always the same message, but that was not enough without the authority. He knew that preaching, in a sense, was vain apart from "the authority." One cannot read the journals of Whitefield ... without finding exactly the same thing. I remember reading in the journals of Whitefield a statement which he makes of what happened while he was preaching in Cheltenham. This is how he expressed it, "The Lord came down amongst us." The authority![30]

The expression "The Lord came down among us" serves to describe experiencing the presence of God, leading the preacher to experience great boldness as a messenger of God. In this regard, Lloyd-Jones is convinced that baptism with the Spirit prompts not only power but also greater boldness

26. Lloyd-Jones, *Revival*, 28.
27. Sargent, *Sacred Anointing*, 51.
28. Lloyd-Jones, *Preaching and Preachers*, 324.
29. Sargent, *Sacred Anointing*, 16.
30. Lloyd-Jones, *Authority*, 86–87.

in preaching.[31] On the other hand, it brings the congregation a consciousness of God, leading a hearer to the conviction that "he is being addressed personally, and with authority greater than that of the human messenger."[32] Furthermore, baptism with the Spirit leads the congregation to become involved deeply in the message being proclaimed. Lloyd-Jones states:

> What about the people? They sense it at once; they can tell the difference immediately. They are gripped, they become serious, they are convicted, they are moved, they are humbled. Some are convicted of sin, others are lifted up to the heavens, anything may happen to any one of them. They know at once that something quite unusual and exceptional is happening. As a result they begin to delight in the things of God and they want more and more teaching. They are like the people in the Book of the Acts of the Apostles, they want "to continue steadfastly in the apostles' doctrine, and fellowship, and breaking of bread and in prayers."[33]

Thus, Lloyd-Jones believes that Spirit baptism leads a preacher to enjoy great boldness as a herald of God, just as it helps listeners to concentrate on and receive the message delivered by the preacher.

Sixth, baptism with the Holy Spirit provides preachers with the enormous power of the Holy Spirit. The primary purpose of baptism with the Spirit, Lloyd-Jones argues, is to give a preacher an endowment of the power of the Holy Spirit. He is assured that Spirit baptism is primarily connected with the empowerment of witness and service; it is not directly concerned with sanctification. As he clearly asserts:

> Go through Acts and in every instance when we are told either that the Spirit came upon these men or that they were filled with the Spirit, you will find that it was in order to bear a witness and a testimony. ... You will find that some would have you believe that this is mainly a matter concerned with moral qualities and character. But it is not. That is sanctification. That view is sheer, utter confusion. This [Spirit baptism] is not primarily concerned with moral qualities or character;

31. Sargent, *Sacred Anointing*, 35.
32. Murray, *Lloyd Jones: Messenger of Grace*, 32.
33. Lloyd-Jones, *Preaching and Preachers*, 324–25.

> this is primarily concerned with witness, testimony, and efficiency in operation.[34]

However, he admits that baptism of the Spirit, although indirect, plays a role as "the greatest possible encouragement to sanctification."[35] He illustrates:

> The moment a man is born again and this divine seed or principle enters into him, the life has started and there is this imperceptible growth. But let a man like that be baptized with the Holy Spirit, let the rain and the sunshine of the Spirit come upon him, let the love of God be shed abroad in his heart, and you will see him springing up into life and vigour and activity; his sanctification, everything about him, is stimulated in a most amazing and astonishing manner. But, it is an indirect connection, not direct and not the same thing.[36]

As it will be discussed in detail in the next chapter, Lloyd-Jones's position on Spirit baptism follows that of R. A. Torrey (1856–1928), who argues that its main concern is with power for service rather than sanctification, against Wesley's view of Spirit baptism as entire sanctification.

Lloyd-Jones often refers to this enduement of power of the Spirit on preachers in the act of preaching as "unction." For him, "unction" is a technical term that mostly applies when baptism with the Spirit is connected with preaching.[37] It can be used, however, interchangeably with "baptism with the Spirit," even though "unction" is the narrower term. He defines "unction" as follows:

> What is this? It is the Holy Spirit falling upon the preacher in a special manner. It is an access of power. It is God giving power, and enabling, through the Spirit, to the preacher in order that he may do this work in a manner that lifts it up beyond the efforts and endeavours of man to a position in which the preacher is being used by the Spirit and

34. Lloyd-Jones, *Joy Unspeakable*, 75–76.

35. Lloyd-Jones, *Joy Unspeakable*, 142.

36. Lloyd-Jones, *Joy Unspeakable*, 143–44.

37. Lloyd-Jones, *Joy Unspeakable*, 120. He says, "[Unction] I hasten to emphasize is the effect of the baptism with the Spirit upon the speech of men, by which I really mean preaching" (120).

> becomes the channel through whom the Spirit works. This is seen very plainly and clearly in the Scriptures.[38]

Since the two descriptions refer to the same experience, Eaton argues that Lloyd-Jones had "baptism with the Spirit" in mind when he repeatedly exhorted preachers to seek "unction" in preaching ministry.[39]

Lloyd-Jones divides the marks and signs of the experience of Spirit baptism into subjective (experiential) and objective (external) evidence. Evidence of the former includes an unusual sense of glory and presence of God, a sense of awe, an assurance of the love of God, joy and gladness, love of God, a desire to glorify Jesus Christ, and a deep understanding of the biblical truth. On the other hand, the change in facial appearance evident in Moses (Exod 34:29) and Stephen (Acts 6:15), together with power and liberty in speech—public preaching and personal conversation—are evidence of the latter.[40]

With respect to the question of how the blessing of Spirit baptism is given to Christians, Lloyd-Jones, on the basis of Scripture and church history, suggests that a Christian can experience this gift in a number of different ways, including the following: (1) while one is praying alone or in a group, (2) while one is reading the Bible, (3) while the word of God is being preached in a service, and (4) while one is meditating or mourning on one's spiritual life or the state of the church. In the last case particularly, Lloyd-Jones emphasizes that this blessing can come to the Christian apart from the word in a way of an immediate and direct impression on the Christian spirit by the Holy Spirit.[41]

Lloyd-Jones also deals with the most likely circumstances in which this blessing can be expected to take place: (1) when one has deeply mourned due to one's sin and sinfulness; (2) when one denies oneself to show one's obedience to God and to exalt his glory; (3) when one passes through a period of conflict and temptation under satanic attack; (4) when there are such great trials as illness, accident, and disease; (5) when one is needed to be consoled

---

38. Lloyd-Jones, *Preaching and Preachers*, 322.

39. Eaton, *Baptism with the Spirit*, 218.

40. Lloyd-Jones, *Joy Unspeakable*, 85–132.

41. Lloyd-Jones, *Joy Unspeakable*, 233–36. He says, "There is a danger that we may go too far and set a limit upon the freedom of the Spirit and his sovereignty in his determination of the way in which he grants this particular blessing. So I am asserting that this blessing may come to the believer apart from the word altogether, directly and immediately" (237).

and empowered before facing the season of crisis and adversity; and (6) when one is on one's deathbed.[42]

So far, we have covered the general characteristics of Spirit baptism as well as the subjective and objective marks of the experience according to Lloyd-Jones. Additionally, we have discussed how the blessing is given and when it can be expected to happen. Yet the most important question still remains: What is the relation between baptism of the Spirit and preaching? Eaton provides a significant insight concerning the relation between the two. He points out the close connection between them in Lloyd-Jones's sermons on this subject:

> It is interesting to note that the vast majority of illustrations that come in his sermons on the baptism with the Spirit are stories taken from the lives of preachers. He constantly makes the point that the baptism with the Spirit is not only for special Christians or for preachers but is for every Christian. Yet when he comes to illustrate his teaching concerning the baptism with the Holy Spirit he is almost invariably drawn to tell of incidents from the lives of great preachers.[43]

As a good example, Eaton suggests one of Lloyd-Jones's sermons on Romans 8:16,[44] which contains twenty-one names to illustrate the experience of Spirit baptism. Intriguingly, of all these names, nineteen are those of preachers:

> In one sermon on Romans 8:16, for example, he relates incidents from Robert Bruce, John Preston, Thomas Horton, William Guthrie, Richard Sibbes, Edward Elton, Thomas Goodwin, George Whitefield, Gilbert Tennant, Jonathan Edwards, Mrs. Jonathan Edwards, John Wesley, Howell Harris, Hugh Bourne, Christmas Evans, Edward Payson, Merle D'Aubigné, John McKenzie, Charles Finney, D. L. Moody, and Charles Spurgeon. Of these twenty-one names, one was a preacher's wife [Mrs. Jonathan Edwards], one was primarily a historian (D'Aubigné), the other nineteen were preachers.[45]

42. Lloyd-Jones, *Joy Unspeakable*, 239–43.
43. Eaton, *Baptism with the Spirit*, 218.
44. Lloyd-Jones, *Romans: The Sons of God*, 338–55.
45. Eaton, *Baptism with the Spirit*, 218.

As Eaton says, Lloyd-Jones asserts that "the baptism with the Spirit is always associated primarily and specifically with witness and testimony and service."[46] In particular, he emphasizes the effect of baptism with the Spirit on preaching. As the general characteristics of baptism with the Spirit indicate, it brings the preacher full assurance, great boldness, divine authority, and power from on high. In this regard, Lloyd-Jones is convinced that baptism with the Holy Spirit is obligatory for efficacy in the ministry of preaching. Also, he is assured that it is an essential element of genuine Christian preaching. He believes there to be two elements in preaching: the sermon—the content that is being delivered—and the act of preaching itself.[47] Of these two elements, preaching is the more important because "demonstration of the Spirit and of power" (1 Cor 2:4) occurs in the act of preaching. Lloyd-Jones is convinced, Eaton argues, that "what made the 'second element' (the act of preaching) in preaching all that it ought to be, was the baptism with the Spirit coming upon preachers of the gospel."[48]

Lloyd-Jones identifies one of the causes of the decline of the churches in England as widespread ignorance and indifference to the work of the Holy Spirit, particularly baptism of the Spirit, in the ministry of preaching. He deplores modern preaching's failure to "recognize that the first work of the Holy Spirit is to convict of sin and to humble men in the presence of God." According to Murray, he was convinced that "any preaching which soothes, comforts and pleases those who have never been brought to fear God, is not preaching which the Spirit of God will own." His method of preaching was to return to "a principle once regarded as imperative for powerful evangelistic preaching ... that before men can be converted they must be convinced of sin"[49] by the work of the Spirit as the Convincer. Also, he argues, the tendency of pulpit ministry from the 1850s onward to place all emphasis on a preacher's academic education and ability, rather than on his anointing with the Spirit, eventually emptied the churches.[50] Therefore, for Lloyd-Jones, the most urgent need of the church is to recover not only genuine

46. Lloyd-Jones, *Joy Unspeakable*, 75.
47. Lloyd-Jones, *Preaching and Preachers*, 69.
48. Eaton, *Baptism with the Spirit*, 218.
49. Murray, *David Martyn Lloyd-Jones: The First Forty Years*, 206.
50. Lloyd-Jones, *Joy Unspeakable*, 121–22.

Christian preaching in general but baptism with the Spirit in particular, since it provides a preacher with authority and power from on high and leads him to become the channel through whom the Holy Spirit can work.

3

REFORMED AND PENTECOSTAL PERSPECTIVES

Similarities and Differences with Lloyd-Jones on Spirit Baptism

The rise of Pentecostalism and the charismatic movement in the twentieth century has brought about two significant changes in the discussion of pneumatology. First, it has raised a remarkable interest in the doctrine of the Holy Spirit, which some scholars previously described as the Cinderella of theology or as subordinate to Christology.[1] Second, it has triggered a theological debate on Spirit baptism regarding whether it takes place at the moment of conversion or is a subsequent experience of the Spirit, distinct from regeneration. The controversy between Lloyd-Jones and John Stott on this point must be situated within the historical context of the emerging charismatic movement in Britain in the 1960s.

In the early 1960s, the Reverend Michael Harper, one of John Stott's curates at All Souls Church, and other Anglican ministers not only were influenced by "the wave of charismatic renewal" that was spreading among evangelicals in the United States but also experienced Pentecostal phenomena themselves. In 1963, Harper invited Pentecostal and charismatic leaders from the United States to meet at All Souls. The American leaders emphasized experiencing Spirit baptism and speaking in tongues, which caused division among the staff team and confusion among the congregation at All Souls. This situation prompted Stott to deal with the seemingly urgent topic

1. In this regard, Gregg Allison argues, "As a result of Pentecostalism, the charismatic movement, and the third wave evangelicalism, the doctrine of the Holy Spirit has been elevated to its appropriate place among Christian doctrines" (*Historical Theology*, 449).

in a lecture at the Islington Clerical Conference in January 1964.[2] The lecture was published as a booklet titled *The Baptism and Fullness of the Holy Spirit* in July of the same year.[3] In his lecture, Stott asserted that baptism of the Spirit is "not a second and subsequent experience, enjoyed by some Christians, but the initial experience enjoyed by all"; it cannot be repeated or lost because of its character as an initiatory experience.[4]

Lloyd-Jones read the booklet in the summer of 1964 and thought Stott's argument led Christians to self-contentment with their present spiritual condition; it tended to suffocate any aspiration for a great work of the Holy Spirit, discouraging any effort to pray for revival.[5] Almost immediately, he began to preach a series of sermons on baptism of the Spirit, beginning on November 15 of that year, which were later compiled and published under the titles *Joy Unspeakable* and *Prove All Things*. In these sermons he claims that baptism with the Spirit is the subsequent experience of an extraordinary work of the Spirit distinct from the unconscious work of the Spirit in regeneration; such baptism, which is entirely dependent on the sovereignty of God and can be repeated many times, gives the Christian a full assurance of salvation and divine power to witness to the gospel. Therefore, he emphasizes the urgent need for Spirit baptism for two reasons: first, it leads believers to "enjoy the full blessings of the Christian salvation"; second, it is one of the most effectual ways to transform the contemporary church from spiritual inertia into a revived church.[6] In particular, he argues that baptism with the Spirit is an essential element of genuine Christian preaching and is obligatory for the efficacy of preaching since it clothes a preacher with authority and power from on high and leads the preacher to become the channel through whom the Holy Spirit works.[7]

In fact, understanding Spirit baptism as a postconversion experience rather than as an initiatory experience at the moment of conversion has a long history, dating back to as early as the sixteenth century with pietistic

2. Atherstone, Jones, and Kay, "Lloyd-Jones and the Charismatic Controversy," 116–17.

3. The second edition, titled *Baptism and Fullness: The Work of the Holy Spirit Today*, was published in 1975 with slight revision.

4. Stott, *Baptism and Fullness*, 23.

5. Murray, *Lloyd Jones: Messenger of Grace*, 131.

6. Lloyd-Jones, *Joy Unspeakable*, 33.

7. Lloyd-Jones, *Preaching and Preachers*, 305.

Puritanism, and continues to be prominent in the Pentecostal and the charismatic movement today. Besides, the doctrine of Spirit baptism—a subsequent experience of the Spirit—entails too many dimensions to be described as a single definite concept. For pietistic Puritans, it was considered to be an assurance of salvation. For the Wesleyans, it was mainly related to sanctification. Pentecostals hold that its primary purpose is to empower the Christian.[8] Yet, the undeniable common factor in the history of the doctrine of Spirit baptism is that in most cases it has been suggested as an effective way to overcome nominal and superficial Christianity as well as to awaken the church from spiritual lethargy by seeking a powerful encounter with the Holy Spirit. Lloyd-Jones's doctrine of baptism with the Spirit is in line with such views.

In the following discussion, I will explore the history of the doctrine of Spirit baptism since it is helpful to locate Lloyd-Jones's position within the larger context of Christian pneumatology. Then I will offer evidence that there is a fundamental discrepancy between Lloyd-Jones's doctrine of Spirit baptism and Pentecostal doctrine, which stems from the theological origin of Lloyd-Jones's doctrine, that is, the old Reformed tradition. I will argue that his doctrine should be considered a reflective reappropriation of the old Reformed doctrines within the circumstances in which Lloyd-Jones lived, rather than as a mere repetition of their original contents.

In the sixteenth and the seventeenth centuries, pietistic English Puritans such as Richard Sibbes (1577–1635) and Thomas Goodwin understood Spirit baptism as conveying assurance of salvation or as the direct witness of the Spirit. Salvation, they were convinced, was experienced in two stages. They called the first stage "saving faith," which meant the experience of becoming a Christian, or conversion. But, they argued, there exists a second experience of the Spirit distinct from conversion that they called "assurance of salvation." For them, full assurance of salvation was given as the result of the immediate witness of the Spirit to the heart of the Christians that "All of your sins are forgiven" or "You are my lovely Child." In this regard, Goodwin states:

> When we say that assurance is an immediate testimony, the meaning is not that it is without the Word. ... It is the Spirit applying [directly] the Word to the heart. ... God says unto a man's soul "I am thy salvation,"

8. Dunn, *Baptism in the Holy Spirit*, 1–2.

> and as Christ said on earth to some few, "Thy sins are forgiven thee," so from Heaven is it spoken by his Spirit … that a man's sins are forgiven him, and he is owned by the whole trinity to be God's child.[9]

For pietistic Puritans, Romans 8:16 ("The Spirit itself beareth witness with our spirit, that we are the children of God," KJV) describes two kinds of witness that assure Christians of their salvation: the witness of "our spirit" and the witness of "the Spirit." According to their interpretation, the former acts as an indirect witness, through a Christian's *conscience*, while the latter is the direct witness of the Spirit, to the Christian's *heart*, of God's everlasting love, the Christian's forgiveness, and the Christian's sonship.[10] Goodwin says that the direct witness of the Spirit "will make a man differ from himself in what he was before in that manner almost as conversion doth before he was converted." He insists that the full assurance of both salvation and God's eternal love, given by the direct testimony of the Spirit, is "the promise of the Spirit as a sealer" (Eph 1:13) that is allowed for the Christians in New Testament times. Therefore, for those who lack it, he exhorts: "Sue this promise out, wait for it, rest not in believing only, rest not in assurance by graces only; there is a further assurance to be had."[11]

For Sibbes, both the distinction between saving faith and full assurance and his teachings on the witness of the Spirit arose from his pastoral concern.[12] From his pastoral experience, he found that many Christians remained in a spiritual state that compelled their obedience to God's commandments but without delighting in them, suffering from fear toward God. He wanted to encourage them to strive for the advancement of their faith and assurance. Moreover, he was convinced that genuine assurance not only resulted in "a greater desire of sanctification and heavenly-mindedness" but also furnished a Christian with "spiritual mettle."[13] His concern for the direct witness of the Spirit was to prompt "an experiential, behavioral, and character-modifying realization of the depth of the love of God"[14] in Christians' day-to-day living.

9. Goodwin, *Exposition on Ephesians*, in *Works* 1:250, 260.
10. Packer, *Quest for Godliness*, 183–87.
11. Goodwin, *Exposition on Ephesians*, 247–48, 251.
12. Beeke and Jones, *Puritan Theology*, loc. 21977.
13. Sibbes, *Fountain Sealed*, in *Works* 5:443, 447–48.
14. Beeke and Jones, *Puritan Theology*, loc. 21993.

Interestingly, John Wesley, the founder of Methodism, had the same experience that the pietistic Puritans explained as "the direct witness of the Spirit" at Aldersgate Street in 1738.[15] Three decades later, Wesley described the crucial experience at Aldersgate as follows: "The Spirit Himself bore witness to my spirit that I was a child of God, gave me an evidence thereof: and I immediately cried, 'Abba, Father.'"[16] In his later days, Wesley came to differentiate between "faith of a servant (weak faith)" and "faith of a son (strong faith)." The former signified the faith of those who were justified but had not yet received the witness of the Spirit, whereas the latter described those who were justified and had the witness of the Spirit as well.[17]

However, for Wesley and the early Methodists of the eighteenth century, unlike the Puritans, Spirit baptism as a postconversion experience was mainly understood in relation to entire sanctification. Wesleyans argued that there were two aspects of sanctification: the gradual aspect (process) and the instantaneous aspect (crisis); the latter was a second work of grace after conversion, which could be described as Spirit baptism.[18] For instance, John Fletcher (1729–1785), designated as the successor of Wesley, began to explain Christian perfection more specifically in terms of "being baptized with the Holy Spirit," relating it to Pentecostal experience.[19] When Wesley spoke of Christian perfection, he emphasized progressive stages of growth, using the human metaphors of infancy, childhood, adolescence, and adulthood. He argued that each stage has its own perfection, even though one is in the stage of infancy.[20]

Donald Dayton argues that the holiness movement in the nineteenth century brought about significant changes in the idea of Spirit baptism. First, a

---

15. He recorded the unforgettable experience as follows: "In the evening I went very unwillingly to a society in Aldersgate-Street, where one was reading Luther's preface to the Epistle to the Romans. About a quarter before nine, while he was describing the change which God works in the heart through faith in Christ, I felt my heart strangely warmed. I felt I did trust in Christ, Christ alone for salvation: And assurance was given me, that he had taken away *my* sins, even *mine*, and saved *me* from the law of sin and death" (Wesley, *Journal of John Wesley*, 64; emphasis original).

16. Wesley, *Wesley's Standard Sermons* 2:350.

17. Wesley, *Bicentennial Edition of the Works* 3:497.

18. In matters relating to the order of the crisis and the process, Wesley understood that the crisis always comes first, followed by the process (Dayton, *Theological Roots of Pentecostalism*, 48).

19. Smith, "How John Fletcher Became," 72.

20. Wesley, *Bicentennial Edition of the Works* 2:105.

growing emphasis was placed on "the instantaneous character of the second blessing as a second work of grace." Second, there was an increasing tendency to put less emphasis on the teleological aspect of entire sanctification that Christians must finally reach[21] and consequently to understand it as being experienced at a much earlier point in a Christian's life. Third, there was a gradual change of emphasis from purity to power as an accompanying effect of Spirit baptism.

In particular, these changes became more apparent through R. A. Torrey's teachings on baptism of the Spirit. Torrey was a leading evangelist in the late nineteenth and early twentieth centuries in America. He defines baptism of the Spirit as "the Spirit of God coming upon the believer, taking possession of his faculties, imparting to him gifts not naturally his own but which qualify him for the service to which God has called him." He argues that Spirit baptism is a work of the Spirit that is separate and distinctive from regeneration; its main purpose is to endow the believer with power for service, rather than to impart sanctification. Not only does he specifically describe seven steps in the process of receiving baptism—accepting Jesus as Lord, renouncing sin, water baptism, obedience, real and intense desire, asking, and believing—but he also lists the reasons for losing spiritual power: separation from God, incoming of sin, self-indulgence, greed for money, pride, neglect of prayer, and neglect of the word. Torrey thinks that such an experience as baptism with the Spirit brings a new power that never existed before into a Christian's service and thoroughly transforms its character. Baptism with the Spirit, he argues, furnishes those who receive it with "new liberty and fearlessness in testimony for Christ."[22]

Torrey's teaching on Spirit baptism is regarded as foundational for Pentecostalism, excepting the issue of speaking in tongues as physical proof of Spirit baptism. In his *A Theology of the Holy Spirit*, F. D. Bruner names Torrey as "the most influential figure in the pre-history of Pentecostalism" and "a kind of John the Baptist figure for later international Pentecostalism." Three salient features of the Pentecostal position on Spirit baptism, Bruner asserts, are "its subsequence—its difference from or its coming after initiation, baptism, or conversion[;] its evidence—speaking in tongues[;]

21. Dayton, *Theological Roots of Pentecostalism*, 68–69.
22. Torrey, *Person and Work of the Holy Spirit*, 20, 31–53, 57–67, 101–3.

and its conditions—the requirements for its attainment."[23] "All believers," Pentecostals argue, "are entitled to and should ardently expect and earnestly seek the promise of the Father, the baptism in the Holy Spirit and fire, according to the command of our Lord Jesus Christ."[24] They are convinced Spirit baptism is accompanied by "the enduement of power for life and service, the bestowment of the gifts."[25]

This brief review of the history of the doctrine of Spirit baptism reveals that discussion in different camps at different periods has emphasized various experiential aspects, and in particular the effectiveness of an exceptional work of the Spirit after rebirth as assurance of salvation, entire sanctification, and/or empowerment for service. Lloyd-Jones's doctrine of baptism of the Spirit follows a similar trajectory in a broad sense in that he understands Spirit baptism as an extraordinary postconversion experience. The consistent tendency to regard baptism of the Spirit as a postconversion experience is itself evidence that in the history of the church, not a few Christians have enjoyed a definite experience of the Spirit and his spiritual blessings after their rebirth. From this point of view, it is worthwhile to reflect on Myer Pearlman's statement:

> We admit that these two operations of the Holy Spirit [conversion and Spirit baptism] are not differentiated in the Scriptures with mathematical precision; but there are general indications of this distinction; and that distinction has been confirmed by the experience of spiritual Christians in many Churches, who teach and testify to the fact that in addition and subsequent to spiritual regeneration there is a baptism of power for Christians.[26]

The traditional Reformed position, however, has been to consider Spirit baptism an initiatory experience of regeneration, as the apostle Paul demonstrates clearly in 1 Corinthians 12:13 ("For by one Spirit are we all baptized into one body, whether we be Jews and Gentiles, whether we be bond or free; and have been all made to drink into one Spirit"). From this perspective,

---

23. Bruner, *Theology of the Holy Spirit*, 45, 61.

24. "The Baptism of the Holy Spirit," Assemblies of God 16 Fundamental Truths, accessed October 31, 2022, https://ag.org/Beliefs/Statement-of-Fundamental-Truths#7.

25. Bruner, *Theology of the Holy Spirit*, 61.

26. Pearlman, *Heavenly Gift*, 26.

Reformed theologians have discerned little difference between Lloyd-Jones's teachings and the Pentecostal position. As a representative figure, Donald Macleod strongly opposes Lloyd-Jones's teachings on the topic in his book *The Spirit of Promise*, issued in 1986, five years after Lloyd-Jones's death. Macleod holds a traditional Reformed position regarding Spirit baptism as the initial experience that all Christians enjoy at the moment of conversion, rejecting Lloyd-Jones's opinion of it as a subsequent experience of only some Christians. More specifically, Macleod criticizes Lloyd-Jones's doctrine as to the sealing of the Spirit by reviewing his exegesis of Ephesians 1:13 grammatically and contextually: "In whom ye also trusted, after that ye heard the word of truth, the gospel of your salvation: in whom also after that ye believed, ye were sealed with that holy Spirit of promise." He concludes that the sealing of the Spirit as described in this verse does not imply a subsequent act of the Spirit that leads believers to enjoy a full assurance of salvation, as Lloyd-Jones argues. Rather, he claims, it is the Holy Spirit himself who is given to every Christian when they are regenerated. Macleod's critiques of Lloyd-Jones's doctrine on the sealing of the Spirit provide valuable insight into how Lloyd-Jones's teachings on Spirit baptism are evaluated in the perspective of Reformed theology.

In addition, Lloyd-Jones took criticism from the Reformed camp on the issue of cessationism since he manifestly opposes the cessationists' position in his sermon "Gifts That Authenticate" in *Prove All Things*, asserting that "the Scriptures never anywhere say that these things were only temporary—never!"[27] Naturally, he never forgot to emphasize the necessity of testing the spirits:

> Why must we not accept uncritically everything that claims to be a manifestation of the power of the Holy Spirit? The answer is, first and foremost, that the Scriptures themselves warn us against uncritically accepting everything that is put before us. This is for the simple reason that there is such a being and person as the devil, that there are such entities as evil spirits, foul and malign spirits.[28]

27. Lloyd-Jones, *Prove All Things*, 31.
28. Lloyd-Jones, *Prove All Things*, 58.

Despite Lloyd-Jones's attempt to maintain a balance regarding the gifts of the Spirit, Peter Masters, for instance, a Reformed commentator, asserts that Lloyd-Jones "demolishes his (Reformed) mentors and forebears on the matter of the doctrine of the Spirit." Masters states:

> From all the bombardments and sniping directed at them throughout this book [*Prove All Things*], one would never guess that these cessationists are the very people from whom the Doctor learned all his theology, and to whom he owed all his ministerial influence. He, after all, lived and preached as the successor of the Puritans, the Matthew Henryites, the Warfieldites, and so on. It was because he learned from them, drew his scriptural views from them, and perpetuated and reproduced them (in the best sense) that so many people appreciate his work today. In the light of this it is rather jarring to note the ferocity with which Dr Lloyd-Jones demolishes his mentors and forebears on the matter of the doctrine of the Spirit.[29]

However, even though Lloyd-Jones's doctrine of Spirit baptism seems to follow the classic double paradigm or two-stage view of Pentecostalism as he rejects the cessationists' position, is it plausible to argue that his doctrine of the Spirit is little different from the Pentecostal stance? According to Murray, Lloyd-Jones was irritated by the fact that some identified his doctrine of Spirit baptism with Pentecostalism, since he was mainly concerned with full assurance of salvation, not speaking in tongues. In the concluding years of his life, Lloyd-Jones spoke personally to Murray: "I was against Pentecostalism and still am. My doctrine of the baptism of the Spirit is that it gives full assurance. I have never been satisfied with any speaking in tongues that I have heard. ... It is very unfair to put the label Pentecostal on me." Likewise, he wanted to distinguish his view on Spirit baptism as "the older experimental view of full assurance" of English Puritans from "those later Pentecostal views which had only a superficial similarity."[30]

In fact, Lloyd-Jones clearly objects to the Pentecostal position of glossolalia as an initial physical evidence of Spirit baptism:

---

29. Masters, "Opening the Door," 24–26.
30. Murray, *David Martyn Lloyd-Jones: The Fight of Faith*, 691–92, 695.

> Now what is the teaching in the Scripture with regard to speaking in tongues? In the first place, speaking in tongues is not the invariable accompaniment of the baptism of the Spirit. I put it like that because there is teaching which has been current for a number of years and still is today, which says that speaking in tongues is always the initial evidence of the baptism with the Spirit. It therefore goes on to say that unless you have spoken in tongues you have not been baptized with the Holy Spirit. Now that, I suggest, is entirely wrong. In 1 Corinthians 12:30 the Apostle asks, "Have all the gifts of healing? Do all speak with tongues?" Again in 1 Corinthians 14:5 he says, "I would that ye all speak with tongues, but rather that ye prophesied." And when he says that he would that they all spake in tongues, he is clearly saying that they all did not. That, it seems to me, should be sufficient in and of itself.[31]

Likewise, he opposes the Pentecostal position that baptism of the Spirit is given through the laying on of hands. This blessing, he argues, takes place "as the result of the Spirit coming or falling upon" individuals and larger groups rather than as the result of the laying on of hands:

> This whole idea of giving the gift by the laying on of hands has been restored by the Pentecostal movement in this present century, but until then you do not find it. You find rather what seems to have been the norm in the New Testament itself—namely, that the Spirit has "fallen upon" people in the various ways I have tried to describe to you. ... That seems to have been the way and the method of the Spirit throughout the centuries. ... If the Lord has acted throughout the centuries in the manner we have been considering, why should it suddenly become common that people can lay hands on others and give the gift of the Spirit; especially when you bear in mind the psychological danger and the power of suggestion and hysteria and various other possibilities?[32]

For Lloyd-Jones, the issue of the laying on of hands is closely connected with the issue of the sovereignty of God in relation to the blessing of Spirit baptism. As Murray points out, Lloyd-Jones implies that Spirit baptism—the

31. Lloyd-Jones, *Prove All Things*, 144.

32. Lloyd-Jones, *Joy Unspeakable*, 191–92.

highest degree of assurance of salvation—is awarded to faithful Christians after waiting many years, sometimes even at their deathbed.[33] Lloyd-Jones even argues: "You can live a good life, surrender yourself, do all you are told to do, but still you are not baptized with the Spirit. Why not? It is he who does it. It is in his control. He is the Lord. He is a sovereign Lord and he does it in his own time and in his own way." In Lloyd-Jones's view, Spirit baptism is not something "we do," but that "we receive," and not that "we work it up," but "it happens to us."[34] The essence of Spirit baptism, for him, is that its timing and manner are entirely dependent on God's sovereign will. Accordingly, he cannot accept the Pentecostal/charismatic position that the gift of Spirit baptism can be conveyed through the laying on of hands whenever one wants to do so. He argues that the office of an apostle has ceased: "The uniqueness of this great position! It cannot be repeated. There have been no apostles since those early days and any claim to be an apostle is a claim that runs directly contrary to the New Testament teaching concerning what is meant by the term."[35] However, he does not deny the possibility that a man can have received "a definite and a special commission" to give Spirit baptism by laying his hands on the basis of the case of Ananias, who is nonapostle, laying his hands on Saul.[36]

Last, there is a fundamental discrepancy between Lloyd-Jones's doctrine of Spirit baptism and Pentecostal doctrine in that he does not regard it as a once-for-all crisis experience, as Pentecostals traditionally assert. They carefully distinguish the gift (i.e., baptism in the Spirit in Acts) and the gifts (i.e., the gifts in 1 Cor 12–14). The gift, they argue, takes place only once; only after one is baptized with the gift, one can enjoy the gifts. Bruner illustrates well the relation between the gift and the gifts in classic Pentecostal perspective:

> Pentecostals wish, however, to distinguish carefully between the two phenomena—the gift and the gifts—as the experiences, respectively, of Acts and Corinthians. For the gift occurs only once, while the gifts should be experienced continually. But the gifts cannot occur

33. Murray, *Lloyd Jones: Messenger of Grace*, 137.
34. Lloyd-Jones, *Joy Unspeakable*, 50, 77–78.
35. Lloyd-Jones, *Romans: The Gospel of God*, 49.
36. Lloyd-Jones, *Joy Unspeakable*, 188–91.

> at all—or they cannot occur fully—until one has the gift of the Holy Spirit, i.e., until one is baptized in the Holy Spirit with the initial glossolalic evidence. Only when the Holy Spirit permanently, personally, and fully enters the believer's life does the believer become eligible for the full equipment of the spiritual gifts.[37]

Therefore, for Pentecostals, Spirit baptism, the once-for-all event, leads the believer to a higher level of Christian life in power and service. For Lloyd-Jones, however, baptism of the Spirit is never a single event causing perpetually transformative change. Contrary to the Pentecostal view, it can come and go in God's sovereign will, and it can be repeated many times.

Murray, however, points out Lloyd-Jones's inconsistency on this matter since in one of his sermons Lloyd-Jones speaks of those "who are suddenly lifted to another level, and go on living on the mountain tops of the Christian life."[38] The sermon Murray quotes from is "The Nature of the Blessing," one of Lloyd-Jones's sermons in *Spiritual Blessing: The Path to True Happiness*. In the sermon, he says:

> As we have seen with John Bunyan, John and Charles Wesley, and George Whitefield, they saw that something was wrong. They began to be dissatisfied with the Christian life they had been living. They said, "When I really look at the New Testament and then at myself or when I sing those hymns, I see the disparity. When I stop and think about what I am singing, I know the words are not true of me and I am being a hypocrite. I am not singing my own experience." So they began to seek and to search, and sometimes went on doing so for a long time, but nothing seemed to happen. Then almost without exception they said that suddenly everything became clear to them. Something happened within them, something was done to them. And out of the darkness and the despair, and the sense of hopelessness and futility, they obtained great joy and peace. ... Remember, I am not talking about conversion, but about Christian people living under the law *who are suddenly lifted to another level, and go on living on the mountain tops of the Christian life and the Christian faith*. I am just trying to show what is

37. Bruner, *Theology of the Holy Spirit*, 130.
38. Murray, *Lloyd Jones: Messenger of Grace*, 139.

> possible to us as Christians. The tragedy is that so many of us, having entered on the Christian life, remain content with forgiveness and the first beginnings, and live a kind of moral life using Christian terminology. But it is a life of failure and frustration, lacking this great power and principle of assurance that characterizes New Testament Christians.[39]

As Murray points out, Lloyd-Jones frequently depicts the experience of Spirit baptism as transforming Christians, especially preachers, into a higher state of being. For instance, he interprets John Wesley's Aldersgate experience as his being baptized with the Spirit; he argues that the baptism transformed an ineffectual preacher into one of the most powerful evangelists of his day. According to Lloyd-Jones, George Whitefield and Howell Harris also underwent the same experience. If, as he argues, the experience of Spirit baptism was critical in changing these men into preachers accompanied by enormous power, it is understandable how this could be construed as identical to the once-for-all crisis experience of Pentecostal theology. However, Murray tempers his critique with other distinctions that warrant consideration.

It should be noted that at some points Lloyd-Jones's presentation of Pentecostalism does not represent the nuances within the Pentecostal tradition. First, Lloyd-Jones's understanding of the Pentecostal position on Spirit baptism as a one-time event has a tendency to disregard its dynamic aspect. Pentecostals do not believe that once baptized with the Spirit, the believer is always filled with the Spirit. Instead, as Anthony Palma, a Pentecostal theologian, argues: "The widely accepted Pentecostal view is that of 'one baptism, many fillings.'"[40] Pentecostals affirm that a Christian who has already received Spirit baptism should seek ongoing fillings of the Spirit.

Second, as William Kay, a Welsh Pentecostal scholar, points out, Lloyd-Jones objects to the Pentecostal approach to "see charismatic gifts as normative"[41] for the event of Spirit baptism. However, Pentecostals do not strictly tie spiritual gifts to Spirit baptism. For them, the main result of Spirit baptism

---

39. Lloyd-Jones, *Spiritual Blessing*, 66–67; emphasis added.

40. Palma, *Holy Spirit*, loc. 2864. Myer Pearlman also emphasizes a continuous aspect of Spirit baptism while distinguishing "the initial filling when a person is for the first time baptized with the Holy Spirit" and "fillings or anointings for special occasions" (Pearlman, *Knowing the Doctrines of the Bible*, loc. 5305).

41. Kay, "Martyn Lloyd-Jones's Influence," 285.

is to empower for witness and service. Concerning the relation between Spirit baptism and spiritual gifts, although they believe that the baptism is the gateway for Christians into the gifts of the Spirit,[42] they acknowledge the sovereignty of God in terms of disposal of the gifts. Pearlman, an early Pentecostal theologian, states: "God is sovereign in the matter of the bestowal of gifts; He is the One to decide as to the kind of gift that shall be imparted. He may impart a gift without human intervention at all, and even without the person's asking."[43]

Even though Lloyd-Jones's understanding of Spirit baptism shares common factors with the Pentecostal position, such as that it is a postconversion experience, that it is an empowerment to witness and service, and the present existence of the gifts of the Holy Spirit, there exists a considerable difference between the two, which stems from the theological origin of Lloyd-Jones's stance. His doctrine of baptism with the Spirit originates from an older doctrine regarding assurance of salvation and revival that prevailed within the Reformed tradition from the sixteenth until the mid-nineteenth centuries rather than corresponding to Pentecostal doctrines. In this regard, Murray evaluates Lloyd-Jones's doctrine of Spirit baptism as follows: "While ML-J differed from his own Reformed tradition on the presentation of the doctrine of assurance, he did not differ from that tradition on its true nature."[44]

Nevertheless, even though it derives from the Reformed tradition, the uniqueness of Lloyd-Jones's doctrine of baptism with the Spirit should not be disregarded. Eaton argues: "Lloyd-Jones' interpretation of 'the baptism with the Spirit' provides a category of interpretation by which to understand Christian experience."[45] As Eaton suggests, for Lloyd-Jones, baptism with the Spirit is a theological concept to categorize the exceptional postconversion experiences of the Spirit, such as full assurance of salvation, special anointings on preaching, and revivals, which are found in the Scriptures as well as in the history of the church. As we saw earlier, he uses the same terminology for Spirit baptism as Pentecostals. This appears to have been the main

42. Menzies and Horton, *Bible Doctrines*, loc. 1858.

43. Pearlman, *Knowing the Doctrines of the Bible*, loc. 5560.

44. Murray, *Lloyd Jones: Messenger of Grace*, 155.

45. Eaton, *Baptism with the Spirit*, 238.

reason for the criticism he received from the Reformed circle to which he belonged. However, his category of Spirit baptism is not limited to merely systematizing the doctrine in the Scripture, but attempts to encompass the exceptional experiences of the Spirit that Christians, in particular preachers, enjoy as well as the extraordinary works of the Spirit that appear during times of revival.

The distinctiveness of Lloyd-Jones's concept of baptism with the Spirit is not confined to his using the terminology as a category to define extraordinary postconversion expressions. More importantly, his doctrine should be regarded as a reflective reappropriation of the older doctrines within the circumstances of the twentieth century in which he lived, rather than as simple repetition of their original substance. In other words, particular influences have been at play in the process of theological recontextualization. The following two chapters, therefore, will explore probable factors that contributed to forming Lloyd-Jones's doctrine of baptism with the Spirit. After considering these factors in the formation of his position, I will argue that the theological foundations for his doctrine of Spirit baptism—assurance of salvation and revival—are inherited from the English Puritans, the Welsh Calvinistic Methodists, and Jonathan Edwards (1703–1758), all of whom are grouped within the old Reformed tradition.

4

—

LLOYD-JONES'S DOCTRINE OF SPIRIT BAPTISM

Contributing Factors, Part 1

In the next two chapters (3–4), I will examine the following five key factors that helped shape Lloyd-Jones's doctrine of baptism with the Spirit: (1) Lloyd-Jones's upbringing as a Welsh Calvinistic Methodist, (2) his personal experience of baptism of the Spirit, (3) his public experience of baptism of the Spirit in connection with his ministry, (4) his interpretation of baptism with the Spirit in the New Testament, and (5) the history and theology of revival in Britain as well as in New England in the eighteenth century. This will be done with consideration of the general characteristics of Spirit baptism that were explored in chapter 1. This examination will show that all the factors played significant roles in forming Lloyd-Jones's doctrine of Spirit baptism, providing him with biblical, historical, theological, and experiential evidence to validate his argument concerning the general characteristics of Spirit baptism. In this chapter, we will review the first three factors: (1) Lloyd-Jones's upbringing as a Welsh Calvinistic Methodist, (2) his personal experience of baptism of the Spirit, and (3) his public experience of baptism of the Spirit in connection with his ministry. The remaining two factors will be discussed in chapter 4.

LLOYD-JONES'S UPBRINGING AS A WELSH CALVINISTIC METHODIST

Murray opens the first chapter ("A Welshman Now!") of *David Martyn Lloyd-Jones: The First Forty Years 1899–1939*, which describes Lloyd-Jones's childhood in Llangeitho, Wales, with a telling quotation: "The fundamental elements in our personality and temperament are not changed by conversion and by rebirth. The 'new man' means the new disposition, the new understanding, the new orientation, but the man himself, psychologically, is essentially what he was before."[1] With this notion, Murray implies that Lloyd-Jones's background as a Welshman is one of the significant keys to understanding him as a theologian, preacher, and pastor. In like manner, Catherwood argues Lloyd-Jones was Welsh "not just nationally but spiritually."[2] In particular, "Calvinistic Methodist spirituality"[3] deeply affected him from his childhood.

Llangeitho, where Lloyd-Jones spent his early years, is not far from where Howell Harris and Daniel Rowland (1713–1790), both leaders of the Welsh Methodist revival in the eighteenth century, preached the gospel.[4] In his biography of Lloyd-Jones, Murray introduces two crucial events in Llangeitho that tremendously affected him. The first one was the Llangeitho Association meetings of 1913, which celebrated the bicentenary of Daniel Rowland's birth. Lloyd-Jones acknowledges its lifelong influence as follows:

> The other truly important event in 1913 was that our Chapel had invited the Summer Association of the Calvinist Methodists to Llangeitho. As I have already said, the reason for this was the bicentenary of Daniel Rowland's birth. This Association had a deep impact on me. I had never seen or heard open-air preaching before, but because of the number of people expected, the main meetings were held in a field at the bottom of, and to the left side of, the hill which leads down into Llangeitho from the direction of Tregaron. A stage had been erected, with a pulpit at the front for the preacher and seats for the leading ministers behind him. And then the congregation of about four to five thousand sat on benches facing the preacher. ... That Association had a deep effect upon me, and possibly the most important thing it did was to create in me an interest in the Calvinistic Methodist Fathers which has lasted until today.[5]

The second significant event happened just a few weeks after the first. As he stood in the playground, S. M. Powell, Lloyd-Jones's history teacher, handed

1. Murray, *David Martyn Lloyd-Jones: The First Forty Years*, xvi.
2. Catherwood, "Afterword," 275.
3. Randall, "Martyn Lloyd-Jones and Methodist Spirituality," 104.
4. Lloyd-Jones, *Joy Unspeakable*, 12.
5. Murray, *Life of Martyn Lloyd-Jones*, 18–19.

him a booklet on Howell Harris's ministry to read. This book, the first work he read regarding the history of Calvinistic Methodism, led him to "gain a distinctive view of the majesty and power of God."[6] In this regard, Murray says, "If his father chose Llangeitho for small business reasons, the providence of God had a much bigger reason in it."[7]

Murray points out that Lloyd-Jones's pursuit of the spirituality of the Welsh Methodists persisted from the beginning of his ministry to the end of his life. On Lloyd-Jones's first ministry at Sandfields, Murray observes: "For sheer stimulus and enjoyment there were no volumes which he prized more highly than *Y Tadau Methodistaidd* which relate (in Welsh) the lives of the fathers of Welsh Calvinistic Methodism. They were constantly in his hands in the early years."[8] Lloyd-Jones's comments in his later years regarding his principles for finalizing decisions demonstrate the tremendous influence the Welsh Methodists had on him.

> First, my understanding of the Scripture and, second, my reading of the Calvinistic Methodist revival of the eighteenth-century. These things governed me and when anything presented itself to me, if it did not fit into that framework, I had no difficulty over my duty. When I saw something which was so different from the high spirituality and the deep godliness of the Methodist Fathers I did not have a struggle over whether to follow it or not.[9]

In particular, with respect to Lloyd-Jones's distinctive pneumatology, Sargent and Eaton agree that it originated from the Welsh Calvinistic Methodism characteristic of the eighteenth-century revival. Sargent argues that Lloyd-Jones's interest in the experience of the Spirit certainly traces back to his background in Welsh Calvinistic Methodism.[10] Eaton also states: "The combination of the two words 'Calvinistic' and 'Methodism' perfectly expressed his background and the source of his distinctive view of the Spirit."[11] Accordingly,

6. Murray, *Life of Martyn Lloyd-Jones*, 46.
7. Robinson, *Logic on Fire*.
8. Murray, *David Martyn Lloyd-Jones: The First Forty Years*, 156.
9. Murray, *David Martyn Lloyd-Jones: The First Forty Years*, 195.
10. Sargent, *Sacred Anointing*, 43.
11. Eaton, *Baptism with the Spirit*, 136.

his religious background is a probable factor behind the formation of his convictions regarding Spirit baptism.

What, then, is Welsh Calvinist Methodism and its spirituality? It was born out of the eighteenth-century revival in Wales that was led by Harris, Rowland, and William Williams (1717–1791).[12] As David Ceri Jones points out, the birth of this movement can be traced back to 1735. This was a crucial year for the movement since Harris and Rowland went through "a similar spiritual awakening" independently in that year. Jones states:

> During spring 1735, Howell Harris, a twenty-one-year-old schoolmaster from Trefeca near Brecon, passed through a protracted evangelical conversion experience; at roughly the same time, Daniel Rowland, a slightly older curate in the parish of Nantcwnlle, near Llangeitho in Cardiganshire, experienced a similar spiritual awakening. These unconnected events set in motion two religious awakenings, fused together a couple of years later to create the Welsh Methodist movement.[13]

Jones describes "a protracted evangelical conversion experience" because Harris's conversion process took almost three months. According to his personal record, his conviction of sin began when he attended the Parish Church at Talgarth on March 30, 1735. During the service, his heart was struck by the minister's announcement regarding the next week's Communion service: "If you are not fit to come to the Lord's Table, you are not fit to come to Church, you are not fit to live, nor fit to die."[14] After passing through a severe inner struggle, he was convinced that his sin was forgiven when he attended a Communion service on May 25, 1735. Harris describes the historic moment as follows:

> At the table, Christ bleeding on the cross was kept before my eyes constantly; and strength was given to me to believe that I was receiving pardon on account of that blood. I lost my burden: I went home leaping for joy; and I said to a neighbor who was sad, "Why are you sad?"

12. Eveson, *Travel with Martyn Lloyd-Jones*, 25.
13. Jones, "'Glorious Morn'?," 98.
14. Harris, *Brief Account*, 10.

> I know my sins have been forgiven. … Oh, blessed day! Would that I might remember it gratefully evermore.[15]

Only three weeks after the conversion experience, Harris underwent a further spiritual experience that occurred when he was secretly praying in the tower of the church at Llangasty on June 18, 1735. Harris records:

> Suddenly I felt my heart melting within me like wax before a fire, and love to God for my Savior. I felt also not only love and peace, but a longing to die and to be with Christ. Then there came a cry into my soul within that I had never known before—Abba, Father! I could do nothing but call God my Father. I knew that I was His child, and He loved me and was listening to me. My mind was satisfied and cried out, Now I am satisfied! Give me strength and I will follow Thee through water and fire.[16]

In this unforgettable experience, Richard Bennett says, "the love of God was shed abroad in [Harris's] heart and he received the Spirit of adoption, teaching him to cry 'Abba, Father.'"[17] After this extraordinary experience, fired up with evangelistic zeal, he led spiritual awakenings in south and mid-Wales.[18]

Around the same time, Rowland also underwent a transformative conversion experience through the ministry of Griffith Jones (1684–1761). John Owen describes the life-changing event as follows:

> [Griffith Jones] came to Llanddewibrevi, which is between four and five miles from Llangeitho. And as his preaching was very powerful, energetic, and awakening, a great many people went to hear him. Rowlands was also induced to go. His appearance at this time was very vain, full of conceit and levity. So large was the assembly, that there was no room for them to sit down; and in the midst of them, just opposite the preacher, stood Rowlands, evidently conceited and full of himself, and his countenance shewing no small measure of contempt. His appearance was such as to draw the attention of Mr. Jones while

15. Bennett, *Early Life of Howell Harris*, 26.
16. Lloyd-Jones, *Puritans*, 290.
17. Bennett, *Early Life of Howell Harris*, 27.
18. Jones, Schlenther, and White, *Elect Methodists*, 11–12.

> he was preaching, and so much so, that he suspended his discourse, and offered up a very earnest and affecting prayer for the vain young man that stood before him, beseeching God in an especial manner to make him a suitable instrument for turning many from darkness into light. This prayer, it has been said, produced an amazing effect on the mind of Rowlands. His appearance when returning home was quite different from what it was when he went there. The proud gait had disappeared, and the vain talk was no longer heard. With the head and face towards the ground, he seemed very thoughtful. It was thus that his great change commenced. He was not afterwards the same man: nor was his preaching the same.[19]

The experience, Jones says, "revolutionized Rowland's life and infused his ministry with a new tone and sense of urgency."[20] Following his evangelical conversion, his preaching ministry awakened a large number of people who did not mind traveling to Llangeitho to listen to his sermons.

In 1737, two years after Harris and Rowland had their similar spiritual awakenings, they met for the first time at Defynnog. For historians, the meeting was the beginning of Welsh Calvinistic Methodism. The Welsh Methodist movement came to join the English Methodist movement, which was led by George Whitefield and the Wesley brothers, even though it later separated from the Wesley brothers due to theological differences between Calvinism and Arminianism.

What, then, is the spirituality of Welsh Calvinistic Methodism? The essence of the movement is to seek a balance between the theology of Calvinism and experiential Christianity. White argues that Welsh Calvinistic Methodism was "the first version of the Protestant [Calvinistic] faith which was intrinsically Welsh and was not imported from outside the country."[21] All three of the most important figures in the movement, the fathers of Welsh Calvinistic Methodism—Rowland, Harris, and Williams—held Calvinistic convictions. According to Evans, the Welsh Calvinistic Methodists were "conscious of and dependent upon the Reformed heritage and made great use of its rich expression in the Puritan authors of the previous century." What

19. Owen, *Memoir of the Rev. Daniel Rowlands*, 55.
20. Jones, Schlenther, and White, *Elect Methodists*, 12.
21. White, "Eighteenth-Century Revival and Welsh Identity," 95.

made the Welsh Calvinistic Methodism unique is that it pursued an experiential Christianity based on Reformed theology. They believed that the biblical truth was "meant for the heart as well as the brain." Thus, they insisted on "personal dealings with God on the basis of biblical teaching, in the categories of sin and atonement, regeneration and sanctification, faith, hope and love." The emphasis on the experiential aspect of Christian life prompted them to set up religious societies (experience meetings) to foster the converts' experiences by sharing in them with each other under the supervision of leaders.[22]

Another uniqueness of the Welsh Methodist movement is that it had a legacy of successive revivals. Revival was "God's visitation of a community with unusual power attending gospel preaching and resulting in conversions over a wide area, giving sustained reforming effects on a personal and social level."[23] In this regard, Jones states, "Revival was one of the fundamental elements of their Christianity."[24] Their continuing revival experiences led the Welsh Methodists to the unshakable conviction that, first, the prosperity of God's work entirely depends on his initiative and power, and second, God's people should pray earnestly for outpouring of the Spirit in times of religious declension.[25]

It should be noted that the distinctive features of spirituality attributable to Welsh Calvinistic Methodism, especially with its emphasis on experiential Christianity based on Reformed theology and the earnest pursuit of revival, greatly influenced Lloyd-Jones's ministry as well as his pneumatology. The following section will concentrate on Lloyd-Jones's own understanding of the Welsh Calvinistic movement, which is reflected in his several lectures on the movement and its significant figures. Representatively, in his lecture "William Williams and Welsh Calvinistic Methodism," Lloyd-Jones summarizes the characteristics of Welsh Calvinistic Methodism as follows: great preaching, assurance of salvation and joy, a succession of revivals, a great emphasis on experience, and stress on prayer.[26] It is noteworthy that these features are exactly what Lloyd-Jones emphasizes as the elements needed

22. Evans, "'Power of Heaven,'" 9–11. White argues that powerful preaching and the society were two significant driving forces of Welsh Calvinistic Methodism ("Revival and Renewal," 3).

23. Evans, "'Power of Heaven,'" 7.

24. Jones, *Grym y Gair a Fflam y Ffydd*, 297.

25. Evans, "'Power of Heaven,'" 13.

26. Lloyd-Jones, *Puritans*, 202–10.

in contemporary churches. Also, such characteristics as assurance of salvation, a succession of revivals, and a great emphasis on experience are closely related to the characteristics of baptism with the Spirit. This implies that his doctrine of Spirit baptism was significantly influenced by his own interpretation and understanding of Welsh Calvinistic Methodism. Accordingly, we will examine each of these three features that are closely related to his Spirit-baptism doctrine. This review will demonstrate that his study of Welsh Calvinistic Methodism not only was a valuable historical and theological source to form his doctrine of Spirit baptism, but also gave him conviction that what the church in his days needed to restore could be found in Welsh Calvinistic Methodism.

ASSURANCE

Lloyd-Jones argues that the Welsh Methodists sought further assurance coming from the direct witness of the Spirit that they were the children of God, rather than being satisfied only with the assurance based on deduction from Scripture or evidence of new life.[27] They considered Romans 8:15–16 ("For ye have not received the spirit of bondage again to fear; but ye have received the Spirit of adoption, whereby we cry, Abba, Father. The Spirit itself beareth witness with our spirit, that we are the children of God") and Galatians 2:20 ("I am crucified with Christ: nevertheless I live; yet not I, but Christ liveth in me: and the life which I now live in the flesh I live by the faith of the Son of God, who loved me, and gave himself for me") significant texts for these foundational principles.

William Williams, a Welsh Methodist poet and hymnist, uses the term "doubling of the Spirit" to explain the direct witness of the Spirit. For instance, he exhorts long-time members in the church to ask themselves according to Romans 8:16, "Has this testimony ['we are the children of God'] which you have in your own spirit been doubled by the Holy Spirit?" Lloyd-Jones explains the term "doubled" that Williams uses as follows:

> That is the term he used—doubled. In other words, that was William's view of "the Spirit himself also beareth witness with our spirits that we are the children of God" (Rom 8:16). Our spirit tells us this, "the

27. Lloyd-Jones, *Puritans*, 198–99.

> Spirit of adoption, whereby we cry, Abba, Father." But the Spirit, as it were, doubles it, seals it, guarantees it, gives an extra, an overplus on top of it, confirms it. That is the term which he uses with regard to these older converts.[28]

The Welsh Methodists' teaching on "doubling of the Spirit," Lloyd-Jones also argues, was consistent with their own experience. As examples, he introduces the cases of Rowland and Harris:

> This comes out very clearly in the case of Daniel Rowland, who having come to see the doctrine of justification by faith as he had heard it preached by Griffith Jones at Llanddewi Brefi, still did not have certainty about it. But one day when he was reading the litany at the communion service in his own church in the village of Llangeitho, suddenly the Spirit came and did this doubling; and he knew. And it was from then on that he began to preach in that amazing way and with that amazing power. ... The same thing is very clear in the case of Howell Harris. Howell Harris, being convicted of sin on the Sunday before Good Friday 1735, got an assurance at Whitsun. But it was only three weeks later that he had this doubling by the Spirit, and that was the thing that made him an evangelist. They taught this, and they taught people to expect this, not to be satisfied with anything else.[29]

According to Lloyd-Jones, the same pattern was found in both Rowland and Harris: First, they were converted, but they were short of assurance of their salvation. Later, they enjoyed full assurance through the doubling of the Spirit. It should be noted, however, that the pattern Lloyd-Jones suggests in these two figures—conversion and the doubling of the Spirit—is his interpretation after studying the life and ministry of these two Welsh Methodists.

The important fact, nevertheless, is that the Welsh Methodists' teaching on doubling of the Spirit differs little from Lloyd-Jones's own teaching on baptism with the Spirit. Both teachings underscore the direct witness of the Spirit to believers' spirits that they are children of God. There is no difference between the doubling of the Spirit and baptism with the Spirit in that

28. Lloyd-Jones, *Puritans*, 199–200.

29. Lloyd-Jones, *Puritans*, 200.

such direct witness of the Spirit gives birth to a full assurance of salvation as the highest form of assurance.

Most of all, on the basis of the Welsh Methodists' experience of the doubling of the Spirit and their personal experience of dramatic change subsequent to this event, Lloyd-Jones is convinced that baptism of the Spirit leads preachers to be transformed into powerful instruments of God. To Lloyd-Jones, the representative figure is Harris. Lloyd-Jones argues that Harris was converted on May 25, 1735, when he attended a Communion service in the parish church at Talgarth. Three weeks after the conversion, on June 18, 1735, Lloyd-Jones asserts, he received the crucial experience—baptism with the Spirit—while he was praying secretly in the tower of the church at Llangasty.[30]

The experience of baptism with the Spirit, Lloyd-Jones argues, is the key to understanding both Harris and spiritual revival. According to Lloyd-Jones, that Spirit baptism happened after Harris had already converted affirms that baptism with the Spirit is not the same as regeneration. The experience of Spirit baptism was for him to receive the sealing of the Spirit, or the Spirit of adoption. At that moment, the love of God was shed abroad—poured out—in his heart, leading him to cry, "Abba, Father." It was the baptism of power that transformed Harris into an effective evangelist.

> It is from that moment that this man began to be the flaming Evangelist. ... As a result of this experience he felt a compassion for souls and a sorrow for all people who were in sin. It was this experience which led to his evangelistic activity. ... There is always this distinction between receiving forgiveness of sins and receiving the Holy Ghost; in other words, the difference between what happened to him on Whit Sunday 1735 and what happened to him on June 18th in the same year. This is the only explanation of this man.[31]

In the history of revival, Evan Roberts (1878–1951), an accredited candidate for the Calvinistic Methodist ministry and the leading figure in the Welsh Revival in 1904–1905,[32] also provided Lloyd-Jones with a good example of the connection between the extraordinary experience of shedding abroad

30. Lloyd-Jones, *Puritans*, 285–86.
31. Lloyd-Jones, *Puritans*, 292.
32. Randall, "Martyn Lloyd-Jones and Methodist Spirituality," 110.

God's love—the sealing of the Spirit—and the empowering of one's ministry. In his expository sermon on Ephesians 3:18–19, Lloyd-Jones introduces the case of Roberts:

> An instance of [an overwhelming experience of God's love] is found in the accounts of the Revival which took place in Wales in 1904–6 and which is associated with a man called Evan Roberts. Evan Roberts had an experience of this nature which not only proved to be the turning point in his life but also a crucial moment in the story of that Revival. He stood up in a meeting in a chapel, and suddenly this love of God so came upon him that he literally fell to the ground. Many present thought that he was actually dead. What had happened was that he had had a realization of this overwhelming love of God.[33]

As Lloyd-Jones says, this event was a crucial moment in the Welsh Revival, and he believed that the experience of assurance transformed Roberts into a powerful instrument of God to arouse a great spiritual awakening in Wales. In short, the Welsh Calvinistic Methodists' doctrine and their crucial experiences of the so-called the doubling of the Spirit offered Lloyd-Jones theological and historical sources for his doctrine of Spirit baptism.

EMPHASIS ON EXPERIENCE

Lloyd-Jones defines Methodism as "experiential religion and a way of life," not as "a theological movement." As evidence for his definition, he notes that Welsh Calvinistic Methodism did not have a confession of faith until the nineteenth century.[34] As discussed above, the Welsh Methodists' emphasis on the doubling of the Spirit for full assurance shows well that they considered the experiential elements of religion significant. They sought personal and direct knowledge of assurance that their sins were forgiven, which came by an immediate work of the Spirit.[35] In this matter of assurance, Lloyd-Jones argues, Welsh and English Methodism were fully in agreement.[36]

---

33. Lloyd-Jones, *Unsearchable Riches of Christ*, 213.

34. Lloyd-Jones, *Puritans*, 195. As he indicates, its first confession of faith—the Confession of Faith of the Calvinistic Methodist in Wales—was drawn up in 1823.

35. Lloyd-Jones, *Puritans*, 196.

36. Contrary to Lloyd-Jones, however, White argues that there existed a different opinion regarding assurance among the Welsh Methodists. White states, "Harris came to believe that

To prove the complete agreement concerning assurance among the Welsh and the English Methodists, Lloyd-Jones introduces a compelling anecdote regarding the first meeting between George Whitefield and Harris in 1739:

> Many have probably read the account of the first meeting between Whitefield and Harris in Cardiff in 1739. The first question that George Whitefield put to Howell Harris was this: "Mr. Harris, do you know that your sins are forgiven?" He did not ask him, "Do you believe that sins can be forgiven?" for various reasons, but, "Do you *know* that your sins are forgiven?" And Harris was able to say that he had rejoiced in this knowledge for several years. This again was a point that was common to all of them—assurance of salvation, assurance of sins forgiven.[37]

As the anecdote shows, the Methodists, whether Welsh or English, believed that even though Christians had intellectual knowledge and belief concerning their salvation through Jesus Christ, they should seek earnestly to experience and realize their salvation and the great love of God toward them through the direct witness of the Spirit—the doubling or sealing of the Spirit. Lloyd-Jones argues that they had a great aspiration for "a direct knowledge of God, not to believe things about God—they had already got that." This led them to seek for an even fuller assurance of salvation.[38]

Another feature of the Welsh Methodists related to experiential inclination was their emphasis on "the place of feelings in our Christian experience." They desired to feel Christ in their hearts, not satisfied only with understanding orthodoxy.[39] In his lecture, as a good example, Lloyd-Jones cites the lyrics of what he esteemed as one of the greatest of William Williams's many hymns:

> Speak, I pray Thee, gentle Jesus!
> O, how passing sweet Thy words,
> Breathing o'er my troubled spirit

---

those who experienced conversion should feel full certainty of their faith, but Daniel Rowland and William Williams, on the other hand, were concerned that this demanded too much of some of the members, especially the new converts" (White, "Revival and Renewal," 5).

37. Lloyd-Jones, *Puritans*, 196; emphasis added.
38. Lloyd-Jones, *Puritans*, 196.
39. Lloyd-Jones, *Puritans*, 196.

Peace which never earth affords!
All the world's distracting voices,
All the enticing tones of ill,
At Thy accents mild, melodious,
Are subdued, and all is still.
Tell me Thou art mine, O, Saviour,
Grant me an assurance clear,
Banish all my dark misgivings,
Still my doubting, calm my fear.
O, my soul within me yearneth
Now to hear Thy voice divine;
So shall grief be gone for ever,
And despair no more be mine.[40]

Lloyd-Jones says: "There are endless hymns by him on that theme in the Welsh hymn-book. He wanted to 'feel' these things. He believed, but he was not satisfied with that; he wanted to know."[41] As Williams's hymn shows, the Welsh Methodists, not content with intellectual understanding of Christ, sought further to experience him in their hearts and in their lives.[42]

Along the same lines, Lloyd-Jones refers to the Methodists' meetings to describe the importance of experience in relation to faith.

> They met together in little groups or classes. ... The main thing they did was to state their experiences to one another, and to examine one another's experiences, and to discuss them together. They told of the Lord's dealings with them, what had happened to them since they last met, of anything remarkable that had occurred to them, and so on. This was the main element in these societies ... this great emphasis on experience, and on assurance, on this felt element. They were primarily experience meetings. Indeed I think we are justified in using this term, that the thing that characterized Methodism was this pneumatic

40. Lloyd-Jones, *Puritans*, 197. The hymn is translated by Richard Morris Lewis (1847–1918), a Welsh scholar and litterateur.

41. Lloyd-Jones, *Puritans*, 197.

42. Intriguingly, according to Elizabeth Catherwood, Lloyd-Jones's eldest daughter, one of two books that Lloyd-Jones read on his deathbed was the Welsh hymn book (Catherwood and Catherwood, *Martyn Lloyd-Jones: The Man and His Books*, 33–34).

> element. Over and above what they believed was this desire to feel and to experience the power of the Spirit in their lives.[43]

The Welsh Methodists' emphasis on experience in religion encouraged their members to attend regular experience meetings in groups to nourish a "felt-Christ" experience by sharing it with each other.[44] The Methodist leaders divided these meetings into "general society" gatherings and "private society" gatherings, the latter of which were attended by more of an inner group. Only those who could say yes to the question "Does God's Spirit at all times bear witness with your spirit that you are a child of God?" were allowed to join the private society meetings.[45]

Citing the Welsh Methodists' tremendous emphasis on experience, Lloyd-Jones underscores the experiential element of religion, which is likewise evident in his teaching on baptism with the Spirit. For Lloyd-Jones, baptism with the Spirit is essentially experiential. He argues: "The baptism of the Holy Spirit is always something clear and unmistakable, something which can be recognized by the person to whom it happens and by others who look on at this person."[46] He regards the baptism experience as "the highest, the greatest experience which a Christian can have in this world."[47] Expounding Galatians 4:6 ("And because ye are sons, God hath sent forth the Spirit of his Son into your hearts, crying, Abba, Father"), he explains baptism of the Spirit in the following terms:

> Looking at the argument in the Epistle to the Galatians chapter 4 in greater detail, we find that the word which is translated "crying, Abba, Father" is most interesting. The Greek word for "crying" is extremely old. Its original meaning is the "croaking of a raven." It was used to express any kind of elemental cry that came out of the heart, something that is not always characterized by dignity or felicity of expression; it goes much deeper than that! It is the heart cry of a child, a cry that results from a relationship, the cry of a child who is pleading

43. Lloyd-Jones, *Puritans*, 200.
44. Randall, "Martyn Lloyd-Jones and Methodist Spirituality," 107.
45. Eifion Evans, *Daniel Rowland and the Great Evangelical Awakening in Wales* (Edinburgh: Banner of Truth Trust, 1995), 183–85.
46. Lloyd-Jones, *Joy Unspeakable*, 52.
47. Lloyd-Jones, *God's Ultimate Purpose*, 270.

> with his father. It is most interesting and helpful to note that this selfsame word is used with regard to our blessed Lord Himself. In the fourteenth chapter of Mark's Gospel we find that our Lord used this same expression when he was in the garden of Gethsemane, and prayed saying, "Abba, Father, all things are possible unto thee; take away this cup from me: nevertheless not what I will, but what thou wilt" (v. 36). … So the Apostle tells us in the fourth chapter of Galatians that as the result of the work of Christ and this baptism of the Spirit we also are given the Spirit that was in Christ, and He makes us also cry "Abba, Father." We have become certain of God as Father, we know Him as Father. We no longer believe in God as Father theoretically, it is the cry of the heart, an elemental, instinctive cry that comes welling up from the depths. That is the result of the sealing of the Spirit.[48]

In short, baptism of the Spirit leads Christians to experience and realize vividly what they have already believed intellectually, which is exactly what the Welsh Calvinistic Methodists aspired to.

But what factors in his own day led Lloyd-Jones to accentuate the same experiential elements as the Welsh Methodists did? He was convinced that the lethargy prevalent in contemporary churches was largely due to believism, which only focused on "taking it by faith" while disregarding the empirical aspects of Christian faith. Lloyd-Jones says, "if you have never felt anything, if you have never had any experience, I say it is not faith, it is mere intellectual assent, and intellectual belief." He emphasizes that such an attitude "accounts for so much of dead orthodoxy, and is such a grievous hindrance to revival."[49] Thus, the only effective remedy for all-pervading spiritual inertia in the contemporary church, he strongly believed, was baptism with the Spirit. Such baptism, he argues, provides a Christian with "the personal, subjective, experimental consciousness of the individual." He says, "What the Holy Spirit does is make real to us the things which we have believed by faith, the things of which we have had but a kind of indirect certainty only. The Holy Spirit makes these things immediately real."[50] Spirit baptism, for him,

48. Lloyd-Jones, *God's Ultimate Purpose*, 272–73.
49. Lloyd-Jones, *Revival*, 87.
50. Lloyd-Jones, *Joy Unspeakable*, 85.

makes real to Christians what they previously believed by faith; it leads them to a more direct certainty of their salvation and sonship in relation to God.

A SUCCESSION OF REVIVALS

In his lecture "William Williams and Welsh Calvinistic Methodism," Lloyd-Jones emphasizes an element in Welsh Calvinistic Methodism that distinguishes it from seventeenth-century Puritanism. This is the revival aspect. As he points out, one of the significant characteristics of Welsh Calvinistic Methodism was its continuing legacy of revivals. For the Welsh Calvinistic Methodists, revival was "a visitation from on High, an outpouring of the Holy Spirit,"[51] which is very different from holding evangelistic campaigns that are humanly organized meetings intended or designed to produce mass conversions. In his book *Welsh Calvinistic Methodism*, William Williams of Swansea (1817–1900), a Welsh Methodist minister, argues that the revivals in Wales should not be identified as something produced by revival meetings or revivalists. The Welsh revivals, he said, took place "not as the result of any predetermined and special effort to produce them, but in the ordinary means of grace, and were frequently unexpected by the great mass of the congregation."[52] He illustrated as follows how the revivals of Wales usually occurred:

> When the congregation had assembled together to hold the usual service, and while that service was proceeding in the usually quiet manner, the preacher would suddenly find himself under some unusual influence—felt at liberty to relinquish the string of his discourse, and to utter words which were not on his paper, and thoughts which had not occurred to him in his study. Some of the oldest brethren and sisters would soon recognize the sound. John would remark to his brother Simon, "It is the Lord!" and possibly follow the glad announcement with the shout, "Gogoniant! [Glory!]" to which Simon would respond with "Diolch iddo byth! [Thanks be to him!]" Presently the whole congregation was ablaze. Christians shouted for joy that their good Lord had again visited them, while numbers who had been so far indifferent to their souls' salvation would send forth the distressing cry, "What shall we do to be saved?" It was no transient feeling.

51. Lloyd-Jones, *Puritans*, 203, 205.
52. Williams, *Welsh Calvinistic Methodism*, 151.

> It would be present at the next service, and the next afterwards, and for months to come. It would spread to the adjoining districts, perhaps over the whole country, and possibly over the greater part of Wales.[53]

The Welsh revivals were a series of unexpected visitations of the Lord to his people with his sovereignty and extraordinary power. According to Lloyd-Jones, at least fifteen major revivals occurred in Wales from 1760 to 1860.[54] Williams, for example, describes a succession of revivals that took place in 1779, 1791, and 1818 in Wales.[55]

Most of all, the Welsh Methodists believed that the revivals in Wales were a direct recurrence of what had happened on the day of Pentecost. Williams says, "As it was on the day of Pentecost, when the disciples were all with one accord in one place, suddenly there came a sound from heaven as of a mighty rushing wind, and it filled all the house where they were sitting, it has often happened in Wales."[56] In *Daniel Rowland and the Great Evangelical Awakening in Wales*, Eifion Evans asserts that Rowland and Harris found a biblical foundation to understand the great awakening in Wales in the day of Pentecost in Acts 2. He writes:

> It was important for the leaders to come to a biblical understanding of this work of God in their midst. The most obvious parallel was the Spirit's outpouring on the Day of Pentecost, and the contemporary writers repeatedly drew on the second chapter of Acts for an adequate base for their theology of the revival. Thus in Williams Pantycelyn's view, the days of heavenly authority in Wales were "like the time of the Apostles, when the Spirit descended from on high on a handful of people. ... As it was then, so it was here now."[57]

The Welsh Methodists' belief in revival as the recurrence of the Pentecost was closely related to their cyclical view of revival. Since the day of the Pentecost, they believed, the church had gone through decline and revival cyclically. This meant that decline in the church was inevitably followed by

53. Williams, *Welsh Calvinistic Methodism*, 151–52.

54. Lloyd-Jones, *Puritans*, 4.

55. Williams, *Welsh Calvinistic Methodism*, 153–62.

56. Williams, *Welsh Calvinistic Methodism*, 151.

57. Evans, *Daniel Rowland*, 74.

a great awakening through the outpouring of the Spirit on the church. Eryn White summarizes well William Pantycelyn's conviction concerning cyclical revival for the preservation and revitalization of the church:

> Pantycelyn considered the whole history of Christianity as a continuous cycle of renewal and decline. He describes the pattern in *Ateb Philo-Evangelius*, referring to three hundred years of commitment and growth in the Early Church following the first Pentecost. Then, when the Emperor Constantine espoused Christianity, although Christians gained a greater measure of freedom, there followed a period of sluggishness which, in Pantycelyn's view, set the basis for "all the heresies of the Roman Catholic Church." During the fifteenth century there was an outpouring of the Spirit on individuals, including Wycliff, Hus, and the Waldensians, which paved the way for the Protestant Reformation. Again, said Williams, "after establishing a church, lukewarmness came in like a flood" and, likewise after the Act of Toleration in 1689, apathy appeared hand in hand with religious freedom, until "around the year 1738 the light broke out like the dawn in many religions of the world." That revival was again followed by dissension and darkness, namely the Division in Welsh Methodism in 1750. However, writing in 1736, Williams could take heart in a new revival following some years of stagnation. As can be expected this is history written from a Protestant slant, but also emphasized is the belief that apathy seems to follow revival inevitably and that some are fired spiritually during the heat of revival only to cool afterwards. Undoubtedly Pantycelyn had seen this for himself amongst members of the Methodist movement.[58]

How, then, did the history of the revivals in Wales influence Lloyd-Jones's doctrine of Spirit baptism? It convinced Lloyd-Jones that both baptism with the Spirit and true revival are dependent on the sovereignty of God; human efforts or human-made organization cannot give birth to it. In this regard, he differentiates a revival from an evangelistic campaign: "An evangelistic campaign is the Church deciding to do something with respect to those who are outside. A revival is not the Church deciding to do something and doing

58. White, "Revival and Renewal," 4.

it. It is something that is done to the Church, something that happens to the Church. The two things are essentially different."[59] With regard to baptism of the Spirit, he argues the same thing: it is something that happens to Christians, not something that happens as the result of what they do.[60] Accordingly, he asserts that nothing so directly manifests the sovereignty of God as revival.[61]

Also, for Lloyd-Jones the history of the Welsh revivals clearly demonstrates that revival is a return to the life of the church in Acts: "[Revival] is in a sense a repetition of the day of the Pentecost. It is something happening to the Church that inevitably and almost instinctively makes one look back and think again of what happened on the day of Pentecost as recorded in Acts 2."[62] As Williams of Pantycelyn believed, Lloyd-Jones was also firmly assured that a series of revivals in the history of the church was a gracious intervention of the living God to preserve and revitalize his church. Lloyd-Jones states:

> The graph of the church's history is one of up and down, up and down. That in itself proves that the church is not a human institution. If it were it would long since have perished and disappeared. It is the church of the living God. It is solely due to the fact that she is His and that He has graciously intervened from time to time for her preservation that she is alive.[63]

For Lloyd-Jones, the history of revival in Wales offers a historical resource to support his belief that "God has really kept His work alive and has advanced it most of all by these unusual, exceptional, signal manifestations of His glory and of His power."[64] In particular, that such Spirit-empowered preachers as Rowland and Harris and their powerful preaching ministries were a key element in the Welsh revival in the eighteenth century[65] encouraged Lloyd-Jones's conviction that God uses preaching as his primary means to awaken

59. Lloyd-Jones, *Revival*, 99–100.
60. Lloyd-Jones, *Joy Unspeakable*, 49–50.
61. Lloyd-Jones, *Puritans*, 19.
62. Lloyd-Jones, *Revival*, 100.
63. Lloyd-Jones, *Puritans*, 18.
64. Lloyd-Jones, *Puritans*, 17.
65. White, "Revival and Renewal," 3.

a slumbering church. He was convinced of the urgent need for baptism with the Spirit in preaching ministry.

So far, we have reviewed Lloyd-Jones's understanding regarding significant characteristics of Welsh Calvinistic Methodism. Lloyd-Jones, as a Welshman, was convinced that the features and spirituality of the Welsh Methodists were necessary for the revival of the church in his days. As will be discussed in detail at the conclusion of the next chapter, his understanding of both the eighteenth-century Welsh revival and the Welsh Calvinistic movement, together with the history and theology of revival in Britain and New England in the eighteenth century, played the most significant role in forming his doctrine of Spirit baptism.

LLOYD-JONES'S PERSONAL EXPERIENCE OF THE SPIRIT

In *Joy Unspeakable*, Lloyd-Jones challenges his congregation by raising a question at the end of his sermons as to whether they have had an experience of baptism with the Spirit. For instance, in the sermon "The Sealing of the Spirit," he asks:

> Have you been sealed with the Spirit? Has the Spirit testified with your spirit that you are a child of God? I do not mean that you deduce it from your sanctification or from your reading of the Scripture or prayer or services or any of these others. ... I am asking, has he himself authenticated, attested, sealed it to you; let you know beyond any doubt or uncertainty that you are a child of God, and a joint-heir with Christ?[66]

In "Receive the Spirit," another sermon regarding Spirit baptism, he again asks:

> The great question I'd like to leave with you is this—did you receive the Holy Ghost when you believed? Have you received him up to date? Have you been baptized with the Holy Spirit? That is the question. We all of us either have or have not, and we know exactly which it is. Has the love of God been shed abroad in your heart? Does the Spirit "bear

66. Lloyd-Jones, *Joy Unspeakable*, 161–62.

> witness with your spirit that you are a child of God?" I am not talking about deducing evidence, but the Spirit himself directly, immediately letting you know that you are a child of God.[67]

From his forthright questions, it can be assumed that Lloyd-Jones himself personally experienced baptism with the Holy Spirit. Without this individual experience, he could not have posed the question "Have you been baptized with the Holy Spirit?" to the listeners with such boldness. According to Lloyd-Jones's testimonies and Murray's biography, it is obvious that Lloyd-Jones had crucial experiences of the Holy Spirit in 1925–1926 and in 1949.

EXPERIENCES OF SPIRIT BAPTISM IN 1925–1926

Lloyd-Jones's experiences of Spirit baptism in 1925 and 1926 were closely related to his process of conversion and his obedience to God's calling to preaching ministry. In 1916, he began his career as a medical student at St. Bartholomew's Hospital—generally referred to as Bart's—in London, one of the leading hospitals of England. There Lloyd-Jones built up his medical career as a promising young physician. In 1921, when he was only twenty-one years old, he gained the degrees of MRCS (member of the Royal College of Surgeons), LRCP (licentiate of the Royal College of Physicians), and MBBS (bachelor of medicine and bachelor of surgery). Two years later, in 1923, he not only earned a London University MD (doctor of medicine) degree but also became chief clinical assistant to Thomas Hoder, one of the most competent physicians of the day as well as a doctor to the royal family. His career as a talented young physician reached a pinnacle when he gained his MRCP (member of the Royal College of Physicians) in 1925.[68]

Alongside Lloyd-Jones's externally successful life as a young promising physician, he went through spiritual change, gradually but dramatically. During his days at Bart's, he came to a realization of being thoroughly sinful from the Scripture and his experiences.[69] He gives his testimony regarding the realization of his own sin as follows:

---

67. Lloyd-Jones, *Joy Unspeakable*, 195–96.
68. Eveson, *Travel with Martyn Lloyd-Jones*, 37, 41–42.
69. Murray, *Life of Martyn Lloyd-Jones*, 49.

> [God] brought me to know that I was dead, "dead in trespasses and sins," a slave to the world, and the flesh, and the devil, that in me "dwelleth no good thing," and that I was under the wrath of God and heading for eternal punishment. He brought me to see that the real cause of all my troubles and ills, and that of all men, was an evil and fallen nature which hated God and loved sin. My trouble was not only that I did things that were wrong, but that I myself was wrong at the very centre of my being.[70]

Murray says that it took him many days to come to the knowledge of his sinfulness. Accordingly, Lloyd-Jones records no date for his conversion since it was "progressive."[71]

After his conversion, the feeling that God was calling him to ministry was becoming stronger. He fell into a severe struggle over whether he should give up his medical career to obey God's calling. During these agonizing days, his first overwhelming experience of the Spirit took place in his little study room at home on Easter in 1925. Murray describes the event as follows:

> Martyn now found himself in the throes of an intense struggle over whether or not he was right to abandon medicine. ... On the other hand, he knew what it was to have experiences which rendered all questions of position and self-interest utterly insignificant. One such experience occurred at Easter 1925 in the small study which he shared with Vincent at their Regency Street home. Alone in that room on that occasion he came to see the love of God expressed in the death of Christ in a way which overwhelmed him. Everything which was happening to him in his new spiritual life was occurring because of what had first happened to Christ. It was solely to that death that he owed his new relationship to God. The truth amazed him and in the light of it he could only say with Isaac Watts,
>
> Were the whole realm of nature mine,
> That were a present far too small;

70. Murray, *Life of Martyn Lloyd-Jones*, 49.
71. Murray, *Life of Martyn Lloyd-Jones*, 49.

Love so amazing, so divine,
Demands my soul, my life, my all.[72]

Another remarkable experience of the Spirit happened in his research room at Bart's in 1926, though there is no specific description of the event in Murray's biography. However, at the end of Lloyd-Jones's life, he testified concerning these two unforgettable moments: "I must say that in that little study at our home in Regency Street, and in my research room next to the post-mortem room at Barth's, I had some remarkable experiences. It was entirely God's doing. I have known what it is to be really filled with a joy unspeakable and full of glory."[73] That he uses the expression "filled with a joy unspeakable and full of glory" may suggest that he regarded these two experiences as baptism with the Holy Spirit, since he frequently cites 1 Peter 1:8 ("you rejoice with joy unspeakable and full of glory") as one of the key verses to describe spiritual blessing. Such overwhelming experiences of God's love eventually led him to commit himself to this divine calling, putting an end to the struggle.

Sargent argues that it was a sealing of the Spirit on Lloyd-Jones that gave him authority and power for his upcoming ministry in 1927 in Wales.[74] For Lloyd-Jones, as Sargent states, it was Spirit baptism that set him apart for his ministry as a preacher. Lloyd-Jones's understanding of the sealing of the Spirit as being "solemnly set apart for the fulfilment of a charge and authenticated by intelligible signs"[75] likely came from his personal experience. He appears to connect these specific experiences with his preaching ministry when he writes: "Whatever authority I may have as a preacher is not the result of any decision on my part. It was God's hand that laid hold of me, and drew me out, and separated me to this work."[76]

---

72. Murray, *David Martyn Lloyd-Jones: The First Forty Years*, 85.

73. Murray, *David Martyn Lloyd-Jones: The First Forty Years*, 101.

74. Sargent says, "Was it not providential that at such a critical time in DML-J's life he should be so singularly blessed? Cannot this be interpreted as the Lord's seal and anointing on him for what was to lie ahead? Is not this the reason for the success which was to meet him when he returned to his home country?" (*Sacred Anointing*, 31).

75. Lloyd-Jones, *Joy Unspeakable*, 156. In his sermon "The Sealing of the Spirit," this is what Lloyd-Jones quotes from Bishop Westcott's comment on John 6:25–27, agreeing with Westcott's definition on sealing.

76. Lloyd-Jones, *God's Ultimate Purpose*, 92.

EXPERIENCES OF SPIRIT BAPTISM IN 1949

Another crucial experience of the Holy Spirit occurred in the summer of 1949, when Lloyd-Jones suffered from depression both due to his poor health and from the temptation to question the regard of a lifelong friend who had provided great support for a long time. He came to believe the suspicion toward his friend came from his carnal pride, which the devil was using to attack his soul. He could still confess what his carnal pride was that cast him into an agony of spirit more than three decades later: "It was a terrible thing, it was the thing that revealed to me ultimately the pride of the human heart. I knew I was a sinner without any hope at all, but I never realized the depth of the pride of the human heart. Eventually, I saw it was nothing but pride. Carnal, devilish pride. And I was humbled to the ground." At that time, he was staying at a nursing home near Bristol for the treatment of his persistent catarrh (sinus problems), and he spent nearly two weeks by himself in his private room. The inner agony lasted for the first few days, and nothing could lead him to spiritual relief, including the Scriptures or A. W. Pink's books, which often gave him spiritual help.[77] At the very moment of his complete desperation, baptism with the Spirit recurred. Murray describes the moment:

> Then one morning he awoke soon after six a.m. in "a complete agony of soul" and even feeling a sense of evil in the room. He once spoke of the well-known episode in the life of Luther in terms which he could have applied to his own experience in Bristol, "He was deeply conscious of the devil's presence in his room and he could not get away from him." Then, as he started dressing, and at the very moment when his eye caught just a word in a sermon of Pink's which lay open beside his bed—the word "glory"—instantly, "like a blaze of light," he felt the very glory of God surround him. Every doubt and fear was silenced. The love of God was "shed abroad" in his heart. The nearness of heaven and his own title to it became overwhelming certainties and, at once, he was brought into a state of ecstasy and joy which remained with him for several days.[78]

77. Murray, *David Martyn Lloyd-Jones: The Fight of Faith*, 207–8.
78. Murray, *David Martyn Lloyd-Jones: The Fight of Faith*, 208–9.

Lloyd-Jones was convinced that what he experienced was the direct work of the Holy Spirit to bear witness with his spirit regarding his sonship (Rom 8:16).[79] For him, it was another experience of Spirit baptism. In the 1970s, during a meeting of the Westminster Fraternal, Lloyd-Jones referred to the remarkable experience cited in Murray's biography and used the term "the baptism with the Holy Spirit" to describe it.[80] He discovered that his unusual experience was similar to those of, for example, William Guthrie (1620–1665), Thomas Goodwin, Robert Bruce (1554–1631), John Flavel (1627–1691), and Christmas Evans (1766–1838) in two respects: (1) "the sense of light and glory" and (2) "the suddenness and the unexpectedness with which the assurance came."[81] As a result, he often cited these ministers' testimony regarding their experiences while preaching about Spirit baptism, whereas he was very secretive concerning his own experience. The reason he was reticent about his unusual experience was that true spiritual experience, he believed, was a secret transaction between the triune God and a believer too sacred and transcendent to describe, let alone to boast or talk about glibly.[82] Also, he was convinced that a preacher did not need to introduce his personal experience directly to the congregation since the preacher's primary task was to instruct them about the general knowledge of Spirit baptism.[83]

Intriguingly, another remarkable experience of the Spirit happened to Lloyd-Jones in the same year when he visited Pant-y-Neuadd, Wales. Murray describes the second experience as follows:

> It was on this visit to Pant-y-Neuadd that Dr. Lloyd-Jones had a second experience akin to that described above. The Davies' farmhouse was busy with visitors and he had retired early one Saturday evening. Alone in their bedroom, he was reading the Welsh hymns of William Williams in the Calvinistic Methodist hymn book when he was again given such a consciousness of the presence and love of God as seemed to exceed all that he had ever known before. It was a foretaste of glory.[84]

79. Murray, *David Martyn Lloyd-Jones: The Fight of Faith*, 209.
80. Sargent, *Sacred Anointing*, 51.
81. Murray, *David Martyn Lloyd-Jones: The Fight of Faith*, 209.
82. Lloyd-Jones, *Romans: The Sons of God*, 367–68.
83. Murray, *Life of Martyn Lloyd-Jones*, 430.
84. Murray, *David Martyn Lloyd-Jones: The Fight of Faith*, 210.

Murray analyzes how the experiences in 1949 affected Lloyd-Jones's life and ministry. First, these spiritual experiences "deepened his conviction both about his own superficiality as well as the superficiality of much evangelical religion." They led him to confess: "I was brought to the end of myself in a way that had never happened before. I really saw the depths of sin and that man's ultimate problem is his pride." He was convinced that the decline of the church today was due to its superficiality concerning a conviction of sin that produces a sense of confidence before God rather than unworthiness.[85]

Second, following the experiences in 1949, Murray argues, there was "a degree of change in the content (of his preaching)," though "not a change in doctrine but of emphasis."[86] In his biography, Murray records a personal conversation with Lloyd-Jones regarding the experiences of 1949. Lloyd-Jones told Murray that they led him to a real turning point, confessing to Murray that he "had been becoming too intellectual, too doctrinal and theological." The experiences of 1949, Murray argues, increased Lloyd-Jones's awareness of the affective dimensions of Christian spirituality, resulting in a greater emphasis on the love of God in his ministry; he felt a greater need for preaching that transformed the hearts of listeners as well as their minds.[87] Sargent likewise maintains that, after the experiences of 1949, "his preaching became less cerebral and more experimental."[88]

Last, Lloyd-Jones believed the crucial experience of the Spirit in 1949 was given by God to humble and strengthen him for further ministry ahead. Murray notes when the event took place, Lloyd-Jones was "on the threshold of exercising a profound influence upon a younger generation." For instance, from September 19–21, 1949, he spoke on "The Biblical Doctrine of Man" at the inaugural Welsh Inter-Varsity Fellowship Conference, which "shaped Inter-Varsity thought in Wales for the next decade."[89] Murray says:

> But, more than all this, was the humbling and the strengthening which he received for the long years ahead. He had learned more of what it means to enjoy the love of God. Dr. Lloyd-Jones had not been

85. Murray, *David Martyn Lloyd-Jones: The Fight of Faith*, 217–18.
86. Murray, *David Martyn Lloyd-Jones: The Fight of Faith*, 218.
87. Murray, *Life of Martyn Lloyd-Jones*, 281.
88. Sargent, *Sacred Anointing*, 51.
89. Murray, *David Martyn Lloyd-Jones: The Fight of Faith*, 214, 220–21.

> praying for assurance, or for the Holy Spirit, when he was so unforgettably helped at Bristol and at Bala [the places where his previous experiences with the Holy Spirit took place], but such dealings of God with those called to serve Him are not uncommon.[90]

Thus, the crucial experiences of the Spirit given to Lloyd-Jones in 1949 in preparation for upcoming ministry appear to have convinced him that baptism with the Spirit can be renewed or refreshed repeatedly whenever a Christian is faced with a particularly challenging situation and needs to be prepared for it.

PUBLIC EXPERIENCE OF THE SPIRIT IN CONNECTION WITH LLOYD-JONES'S MINISTRY

In *Preaching and Preachers*, Lloyd-Jones argues that when baptism of the Spirit takes place in the act of preaching, it is first to be recognized in the consciousness of the preacher, and then the listeners should sense it immediately.[91] With respect to a preacher's consciousness, Lloyd-Jones cites 1 Thessalonians 1:5 to prove this contention:

> "Our gospel came not unto you in word only," says Paul, "but also in power and the Holy Ghost, and much assurance." Who knew the assurance? Paul himself. He knew something was happening, he was aware of it. You cannot be filled with the Spirit without knowing it. He had "much assurance." He knew he was clothed with power and authority. How does one know it? It gives clarity of thought, clarity of speech, ease of utterance, a great sense of authority and confidence as you are preaching, an awareness of a power not your own thrilling through the whole of your being, and an indescribable sense of joy.[92]

As for the listeners' awareness of the event, he continues:

> What about the people? They sense it at once; they can tell the difference immediately. They are gripped, they become serious, they are convicted, they are moved, they are humbled. Some are convicted

---

90. Murray, *David Martyn Lloyd-Jones: The Fight of Faith*, 221.
91. Lloyd-Jones, *Preaching and Preachers*, 324.
92. Lloyd-Jones, *Preaching and Preachers*, 324.

> of sin, others are lifted up to the heavens, anything may happen to any one of them. They know at once that something quite unusual and exceptional is happening. As a result they begin to delight in the things of God and they want more and more teaching. They are like the people in the Book of the Acts of the Apostles, they want "to continue steadfastly in the apostles' doctrine, and fellowship, and breaking of bread and in prayers."[93]

Importantly, Lloyd-Jones's description of the experience both of the preacher and the listeners stems not only from the Scriptures and the history of the church, but also from Lloyd-Jones's own experiences in his preaching ministry. Though Lloyd-Jones rarely spoke of his own experiences because of his tendency toward reticence regarding them, during his lifelong ministry both in Wales and London many people testified that they experienced the unusual anointing of the Holy Spirit through his preaching. In this regard, Murray says, "What they witnessed of the effects of unction and authority under his ministry is in full harmony with the records of powerful preaching throughout church history."[94]

PUBLIC EXPERIENCE IN ABERAVON (1927–1938)

The Bethlehem Forward Movement Presbyterian Church, in which Lloyd-Jones began his first ministry in 1927, was located in a poor district of Sandfields, Aberavon, in Wales. At that time, the mining village suffered from the economic effects of the beginning of the Great Depression, social unrest, and poverty.[95] Almost 90 percent of the residents did not attend worship in any place.[96] The villagers were paying more attention to the messengers of Marxism-Leninism than the preachers in the churches.[97]

For the first half year of his ministry in Aberavon, there seemed to be no change. However, beginning with the conversion of E. T. Rees, the church secretary, who used to immerse himself in socialism and was a passionate member of the Labour Party, the number of converts steadily increased.

---

93. Lloyd-Jones, *Preaching and Preachers*, 324–25.
94. Murray, *Lloyd Jones: Messenger of Grace*, 32.
95. Sargent, *Sacred Anointing*, 53.
96. Murray, *David Martyn Lloyd-Jones: The First Forty Years*, 118.
97. Sargent, *Sacred Anointing*, 53.

During this time, many unbelievers were transformed into Christians, and many professing Christians, including Bethan Lloyd-Jones, his wife, were genuinely converted.[98] In *Memories of Sandfields*, Bethan describes how she was converted through Lloyd-Jones's preaching:

> In those early years at Aberavon, I rejoiced to see men and women converted—drunkards, evil livers—all manner of types and backgrounds and all different ages! I rejoiced to see them and I envied them and sometimes wished, when I saw their radiant faces and changed lives, that I had been a drunkard or worse, so that I could be converted! I never imagined that I needed to be converted, having always been a Christian or that I could get any more than I had already! In those first two years, God graciously used Martyn's morning sermons to open my eyes and to show me myself and my needs. I came to know my sins forgiven and the peace of God in my heart.[99]

Like Bethan, many people were profoundly converted during the ministry of Lloyd-Jones, even though they were already church members. Also, the number of those who came to salvation from outside the church increased remarkably. In 1930, for instance, when church membership increased by 88, 70 members came from outside the church.[100] During Lloyd-Jones's eleven and a half years of ministry in Aberavon, the church membership grew from 93 to 530; the average attendance at worship was 850.[101] One old man in the congregation who had experienced the revival of 1904 in Wales called out, "Why, this is revival! The power of the Spirit is greater here than in 1904."[102] Likewise, Murray argues that what happened at Sandfields was a repetition of a true revival. The report of J. C. Griffith-Jones, South Wales correspondent of the *News Chronicle*, a secular paper, describes at full length "the unusual nature of what was happening in Aberavon"[103] through Lloyd-Jones's ministry:

---

98. Bethan Lloyd-Jones, *Memories of Sandfields*, 5.
99. Bethan Lloyd-Jones, *Memories of Sandfields*, 5.
100. Murray, *Life of Martyn Lloyd-Jones*, 132.
101. Jung, "Evaluation of the Principles," 6.
102. Murray, *Life of Martyn Lloyd-Jones*, 137.
103. Murray, *David Martyn Lloyd-Jones: The First Forty Years*, 217, 224.

Into this desperate little world came the young physician-minister, preaching, living the gospel of old-new hope. He shocked the locality out of its despair. This world had failed them; there was another world. Men listened amazed. Here was one who practiced the gospel that he preached with such tremendous conviction. ... The little church filled. Under the previous pastor it had not been a dead letter by any means, but now it awakened to a galvanic new life. Not only in Port Talbot, but all around the district, the word went forth that surprising things were happening at the "mission hall" on the sand dunes. Curious, skeptical, doubting, hoping, believing, people flocked to the church. It was no passing wonder. Today, years after the first revelation of new power, the congregations still overflow the church. Every meeting is a "big meeting." More than 500 members, the faithful augmented by "hard cases," sinners whom others considered, and who regarded themselves, as beyond redemption, irretrievably lost. ... No whist drives, bazaars or worldly side-shows, no dramas except the great drama of salvation. A working-class (and unemployed) membership raising £1,000 a year for church work. Crowded prayer meetings, a crowded "seiat" (church meeting) in mid-week, a crowded brotherhood meeting on Saturday, of all nights, when men discuss the problems of spiritual salvation and the pastor sums up the discussion. Sandfields now shares the glad tidings with all Wales. The "physician of souls," who shuns publicity, draws thousands to hear his message in all parts of the Principality. ... The doctor's [Lloyd-Jones'] sermons penetrate the innermost secrets of the heart. Spellbound, but sorrowful, men sometimes go back into the world after hearing the message, saying: "It is terrific. We ought to take that road, but it is too hard, too completely revolutionary." ... As preaching it was mesmeric in its appeal: as a message of hope to a world that has tried everything but Christianity, it was electrical. An awe-inspiring new force has arisen in the life of Wales.[104]

Sargent also concludes that the unusual fruitfulness in Wales was due to the extraordinary outpouring of the Spirit on Lloyd-Jones's preaching:

104. Murray, *David Martyn Lloyd-Jones: The First Forty Years*, 224–25.

> It seems quite evident, on reading a selection of his early sermons, hearing the testimonies of a reporter [J. C. Griffith-Jones] ... as well as considering what took place in terms of church growth, coupled with the fascinating accounts of conversion recorded by Bethan Lloyd-Jones, that his ministry was attended with great power, even from the earliest days. The evidence surely leads to the conclusion that an unusual unction was on DML-J's preaching and that this, in part, is the explanation for its remarkable fruitfulness.[105]

Lloyd-Jones never named what he and the congregation had experienced in Aberavon as "revival," since for him it was only a "shower" rather than the "rain" he felt was needed in the area. Nevertheless, from the experience of "a glimpse of glory"[106] in the ministry of Sandfields, he came to be more assured that the greatest need of the church was genuine preaching accompanied by the mighty outpouring of the Spirit, which leads hearers' hearts and lives to be profoundly transformed through the word of God, as the New Testament attests.

PUBLIC EXPERIENCE IN WESTMINSTER CHAPEL (1938–1968)

In his letter to the congregation of Westminster Chapel informing them of his retirement after having completed thirty years as the minister of the chapel, sent on May 30, 1968, Lloyd-Jones testified that there had been many occasions of baptism with the Spirit, which they felt and recognized during his preaching: "What things we have experienced! To a preacher nothing is so wonderful as to feel the unction of the Holy Spirit while preaching, and to hear of souls being brought under conviction of sin, and then experiencing the new birth. Thank God, that has often been our experience."[107] Confirming his testimony, many people who heard Lloyd-Jones's sermons in the chapel testified to their experience of the unusual baptism during their services. For instance, James Packer, a colleague and theologian who regularly attended evening worship at the chapel as a student in London during the winter of 1948–1949, describes "the thunder and lightning"— baptism with the

105. Sargent, *Sacred Anointing*, 33.
106. Murray, *David Martyn Lloyd-Jones: The First Forty Years*, 225.
107. Murray, *D. Martyn Lloyd-Jones*, 215.

Spirit—which occurred while he was preaching. He describes the impression he received during the days as follows:

> In some way there was in the Doctor's preaching thunder and lightning that no tape or transcription ever did or could capture—power I mean, to mediate a realization of God's presence. ... Nearly forty years on it still seems to me that all I have ever known about preaching was given me in the winter of 1948–49, when I worshiped at Westminster Chapel with some regularity. Through the thunder and lightning, I felt and saw as never before the glory of Christ and of his gospel as modern man's only lifeline and learned by experience why historic Protestantism looks on preaching as the supreme means of grace and of communion with God.[108]

In particular, Packer witnessed that the energy in Lloyd-Jones's preaching was not only "animal energy" but also "God-given liveliness," that is, "the anointing of God's Holy Spirit upon the preacher."[109]

Tom Allan, then a Scottish soldier, who went to Westminster Chapel to attain spiritual help during the Second World War, also affirms the unction that accompanied Lloyd-Jones's preaching.

> There was a thin congregation. A small man in a collar and tie walked almost apologetically to the platform and called the people to worship. I remember thinking that Lloyd-Jones must be ill and that his place was being taken by one of his office-bearers. This illusion was not dispelled during the first part of the service, though I was impressed by the quiet reverence of the man's prayers and his reading of the Bible. Ultimately, he announced his text and began his sermon in the same quiet voice. Then a curious thing happened. For the next forty minutes I became completely unconscious of everything except the word that this man was speaking—not his words, mark you, but someone behind them and in them and through them. I didn't realize it then, but I had been in the presence of the mystery of preaching, when a man is lost in the message he proclaims.[110]

---

108. Packer, "David Martyn Lloyd-Jones," 119.
109. Packer, "David Martyn Lloyd-Jones," 118.
110. Murray, *Lloyd Jones: Messenger of Grace*, 29–30.

Allan, who later became a preacher himself, was immersed in "the mystery of preaching" while hearing Lloyd-Jones. Intriguingly, Lloyd-Jones himself often used the term "the mystery" to describe the mystical elements of preaching. He says, "To me preaching is a great mystery; it is one of the most mysterious things of all, and that is why I find it eludes any kind of analysis."[111] His preaching, such as that Allan experienced in Westminster Chapel, had inexplicable dimensions that do not belong to natural oratorical gifts and effective speaking.

Murray understands "the mystery of preaching" as "the presence of the Spirit of God" that exists in preaching that brings about authority, power, and boldness, as Jesus and his disciples' preaching shows.[112] Sinclair Ferguson, a Reformed theologian, is another witness who felt the presence of the Spirit while hearing Lloyd-Jones's preaching in the chapel: "There were occasions in his preaching where he must have thought if we go one step further, we must be beginning to experience what happens in revival, when people are so bowed down under the sense of the presence of God."[113]

According to Murray's biography, the presence of the power of the Holy Spirit in Lloyd-Jones's preaching does not seem to have been confined to Westminster Chapel. For instance, Murray includes Stacy Wood's description of what happened in the congregation when Lloyd-Jones preached at the Scots Church in Paris in 1959.

> The Church was crowded. The Doctor's text was, "Strait is the gate and narrow is the way that leadeth unto Life and few there be that find it." In an extraordinary way, the presence of God was in that Church. I personally felt as if a hand were pushing me through the pew. At the end of the sermon for some reason or the other the organ did not play, the Doctor went off into the vestry and everyone sat completely still without moving. It must have been almost ten minutes before people seemed to find the strength to get up and, without speaking to one another, quietly leave the Church. Never have I witnessed or

111. Murray, *Lloyd Jones: Messenger of Grace*, 30.

112. Murray, *Lloyd Jones: Messenger of Grace*, 30–31.

113. Robinson, *Logic on Fire*.

experienced such preaching with such fantastic reaction on the part of the congregation.[114]

Undoubtedly, his powerful preaching under the anointing of the Spirit greatly affected the lives of many Christians. In his biography, Murray records one such case in the 1950s, that of Ralph M. Hettrick, a pastor of a church in Washington, DC, who visited Westminster Chapel to hear Lloyd-Jones's sermon during his sabbatical. He describes how Lloyd-Jones's preaching turned his life around:

> After the singing had stopped the doctor began leading in the morning prayer. Never in my life had I heard a public prayer like that prayer. Then the message. What can I say? It was part of his series on the 73rd Psalm. Later I discovered his text that Sunday had been planned for the Sunday previous but that he was not able to finish it. He began dealing with verses 22 and 23, "So foolish was I, and ignorant. I was as a beast before thee. Nevertheless, I am continually with thee: thou have holden me by my right hand." Every part of the message was directed to me. I had traveled across the United States from the west coast, boarding a ship to take me to England. I had been traveling for more than five weeks. I was in a backslidden state and my heart was full of fear. My spiritual condition made me fearful that God would finally disown me and I would find myself lost and without hope. It was as though the Lord had been in detailed conversation with the doctor concerning my condition. Everything seemed to fit. I was weakened, greatly humbled and yet thrilled to think that God knew where I was (even if I didn't), and that He was again at work in my soul. As I reflect today on that November 29, 1953 experience at Westminster Chapel, I have deep appreciation and gratitude to God for His leading me to hear that particular message. It was a life-changing happening. God's timing was perfect, as is everything He does. There is no way of my conveying what the ministry of Dr. Lloyd-Jones has meant to me. It turned my life around. I'm sure this same acknowledgement could come from hundreds of others.[115]

---

114. Murray, *David Martyn Lloyd-Jones: The Fight of Faith*, 377.
115. Murray, *Life of Martyn Lloyd-Jones*, 313–14.

In short, the experiences in Westminster Chapel strengthened Lloyd-Jones's conviction that true preaching is not the act of a human but primarily the act of God; the preacher is an instrument or a channel through whom the Holy Spirit works with the truth in the Bible. In this regard, Lloyd-Jones's definition of "unction of the Spirit"—a "preacher is being used by the Spirit and becoming the channel through whom the Spirit works"—was confirmed by the experience of both Lloyd-Jones and his congregation in the ministry of Westminster Chapel.[116] Lloyd-Jones was convinced that the preacher should yearn for baptism with the Spirit to be used by the Spirit of the truth, which without fail fills the preacher with authority, power, and boldness from on high. Such apostolic preaching anointed with the Spirit could lead listeners not only to be convicted of sin but to a new life.

116. As a good example, Faith Linton, one of the regular worshipers at Westminster Chapel during Lloyd-Jones's ministry, stated: "It was as if I lost all count of time and space. The eternal truth that I hungered for so deeply was being revealed, and I was caught up body, mind, and spirit in the sublime experience of receiving, finding, understanding, knowing. ... *ML-J was only an instrument*. What I experienced was the power of the Word and a deep, intensive, quickening work of the Holy Spirit" (Murray, *David Martyn Lloyd-Jones: The Fight of Faith*, 266; emphasis added).

5

LLOYD-JONES'S DOCTRINE OF SPIRIT BAPTISM

Contributing Factors, Part 2

This chapter will explore the remaining two key factors that helped to form Lloyd-Jones's doctrine of baptism with the Spirit: (4) his interpretation of baptism with the Spirit in the New Testament and (5) the history and theology of revival in Britain and New England in the eighteenth century. Then it will examine which among the five factors played the most significant role in shaping Lloyd-Jones's doctrine of Spirit baptism.

BAPTISM OF THE SPIRIT IN THE NEW TESTAMENT

The key to understanding Lloyd-Jones's conviction concerning baptism with the Spirit is his belief that it is rooted in both Scripture and the history of the church, especially the history of revival. For instance, in his own preaching about this subject, he states, "I propose therefore to look first at the scriptural teaching, then to view the subject from the historical standpoint, and finally to make some comments."[1] Accordingly, in these following two sections, I will investigate examples of baptism with the Holy Spirit in Scripture as well as cases in the history of revival in the eighteenth century, all of them suggested by Lloyd-Jones as illustrations of baptism with the Spirit.

In his lectures and sermons, Lloyd-Jones cites various cases of baptism with the Spirit, most of which are found in the New Testament. Regarding his biblical interpretation, Lloyd-Jones differentiates his approach from that

1. Lloyd-Jones, *Preaching and Preachers*, 305.

of literal fundamentalists.[2] While such an approach is not unsophisticated in its own way, nonetheless he reads the biblical text in a simple and straightforward manner, assuming that its theological content and apparent purpose can be applied directly to readers in his own day with little reference to its original social, historical, or even literary context.

The examples of Spirit baptism I present here demonstrate different aspects of Lloyd-Jones's understanding of the subject. The comments here regarding his interpretation of Spirit baptism in the New Testament will be introductory and general. His exegetical work on the core verses related to his doctrine of Spirit baptism, such as Romans 8:15–16 and Ephesians 1:13–14, will be dealt with in chapter 7.

THE EXPERIENCE OF JESUS

Lloyd-Jones presents the experience Jesus himself had when he was baptized at the Jordan River as a good example of what baptism with the Spirit means. First, Lloyd-Jones argues, this text clearly shows that at the moment when the Holy Spirit came down on Jesus in the form of a dove, he was baptized with the Spirit so as to preach the gospel in Nazareth (Luke 4:18–19). He explains:

> I refer to the way in which the Holy Ghost descended upon Him as He was coming up out of the river Jordan after John the Baptist has baptized Him. The Spirit came upon Him in the form of a dove. He Himself explained afterwards what this meant, when He spoke in the Synagogue in His home town of Nazareth as recorded in Luke 4:18ff. "The Spirit of the Lord is upon me, because He hath anointed me to preach the gospel to the poor ..." What I am concerned to emphasize is that He says that what had happened to Him there at the Jordan was that He was anointed by the Spirit to preach this Gospel of salvation, "to preach the acceptable year of the Lord."[3]

2. In an interview with Aneirin Talfan Davies in 1970, Lloyd-Jones identified himself as "a conservative evangelical" rather than "a fundamentalist," stating: "I think our [conservative evangelicals'] attitude is a little more intelligent. I mean, I have very little sympathy with the man [a fundamentalist] who just holds up a Bible and says, 'I believe this from cover to cover, every comma and full stop,' and all the rest of it. There's been a little bit too much of that and a refusal to use one's mind and to recognize figures of speech and so on. I think their danger has been to be literalistic, in a wrong sense. That would be the main difference, I think, between us" ("Dr. Lloyd-Jones Interview with Aneirin Talfan Davies," https://www.youtube.com/watch?v=tt-_pLjSA98).

3. Lloyd-Jones, *Preaching and Preachers*, 306.

He asserts that the case of Jesus's baptism with the Spirit proves that he could not have exercised his public ministry as an incarnated man on earth if he had not received this special baptism.[4] The point of Jesus's Spirit baptism, he argues, is that if not even Jesus could proclaim the gospel without receiving this endowment of the Spirit, how much more for any human preacher is baptism of the Spirit absolutely necessary for the ministry of preaching.

Second, Lloyd-Jones argues, Jesus's experience of baptism with the Spirit at the Jordan was "the sealing of the Spirit," which served to authenticate him as Son of God by an obvious sign and set him apart for his ministry as the Messiah, filling him with the Holy Spirit in fullness. In his sermon "The Sealing of the Spirit," Lloyd-Jones argues that Jesus's baptism with the Spirit also represented the sealing of the Spirit:

> [Jesus] insisted, you remember, that John the Baptist should baptize him, and as they stood in the Jordan the Holy Spirit descended upon him in the form of a dove, and, we see in John 1:33, it remained on him. "And a voice came from heaven, saying, This is my beloved Son, in whom I am well pleased." Now that is the sealing, the authentication. Jesus of Nazareth, the carpenter suddenly steps forward, begins to teach, and everybody says, "Who is this?" Then God answers the question. God seals him, and authenticates him. He says: "This is my son; the Spirit is sent upon him." ... Sealing means "solemnly set apart for the fulfilment of a charge and authenticated by intelligible signs." That is what happened there to our Lord.[5]

We should note that for Lloyd-Jones, "the baptism with the Spirit" and "the sealing of the Spirit" can be used interchangeably. He says, "I am not concerned about the terminology with regard to 'sealing' with the Spirit or 'baptism' with the Spirit. ... It is the experience itself that matters most."[6] He argues that the terminology depends on the context in which it occurs. On the one hand, when a text deals with the matter of witness and testimony, the term "baptism" is used. On the other hand, when the text speaks of believers' certainty of being heirs of God's eternal inheritance, the term "sealing" is

4. Lloyd-Jones, *Preaching and Preachers*, 307.
5. Lloyd-Jones, *Joy Unspeakable*, 157.
6. Lloyd-Jones, *God's Ultimate Purpose*, 279.

used.[7] Therefore, as much as Jesus was sealed with the Spirit at the Jordan, a Christian should desire to be authenticated "by intelligible signs that we are indeed the children of God, heirs of God, and joint-heirs with our blessed Lord and Saviour Jesus Christ."[8]

THE EXPERIENCE OF THE DISCIPLES IN ACTS

In his sermon "Blessed Assurance" in *Joy Unspeakable*, Lloyd-Jones deals with some objections from Stott to using the book of Acts to support his doctrine of Spirit baptism. Among Stott's objections are that (1) any doctrine should be based only on the teaching of Jesus and that of the Epistles, not on the history in Acts; (2) Acts deals with exceptional times in the history of the church, so it cannot be applied to today's church; and (3) there is no exhortation for believers to be baptized with the Spirit in the Epistles.[9]

As for the first objection, Lloyd-Jones says, "You should never pit one section of Scripture against another." He argues that pitting Scripture against Scripture is a characteristic of higher criticism and that one should accept both Acts and the Epistles without allowing one to depreciate the other. For the second objection, he states straightforwardly: "It is always wrong to say that any teaching in Scripture had nothing to do with us, that it was exceptional. What we read in the whole of the Scripture must be applied to ourselves. It is a kind of pattern or standard or norm of what we should expect individually and in the case of the Christian church." To support the validity of this argument, he suggests that a revival of religion is "the church returning to the book of Acts." Therefore, it is wrong to say that since Acts describes an exceptional time in the history of the church, it cannot be presented as a norm or a pattern for a later age. On the contrary, the churches and Christians described in Acts are suggested as the norm or standard for the church as well as for individual Christians today. Finally, he asserts that the Epistles do not need to exhort believers to be baptized with the Spirit since they were already baptized with the Spirit. Furthermore, he says, it is impossible to understand the teachings of the Epistles without presupposing

7. Lloyd-Jones, *Joy Unspeakable*, 157.

8. Lloyd-Jones, *God's Ultimate Purpose*, 248.

9. Lloyd-Jones, *Joy Unspeakable*, 34–36. To review Stott's view, see page 21, 37–40, and 59 in *Baptism and Fullness*.

the history described in Acts. Likewise, he firmly rejects any attempt "to differentiate between the teachings of Acts and the epistles."[10]

For Lloyd-Jones, the book of Acts is a critical resource for the doctrine of Spirit baptism, even though he also finds numerous illustrations regarding Spirit baptism in the Epistles. First, with respect to baptism with the Spirit for Jesus's disciples, Lloyd-Jones regards Acts 1:8 ("But ye shall receive power, after that the Holy Ghost is come upon you: and ye shall be witnesses unto me both in Jerusalem, and in all Judaea, and in Samaria, and unto the uttermost part of the earth") as the most significant passage. Lloyd-Jones argues that this passage points forward to the Spirit's coming on Pentecost in Acts 2. As such, the passage indicates that baptism with the Spirit is not related to regeneration because the apostles had already been regenerated before they were baptized with the Holy Spirit on Pentecost. Rather, what they received was a baptism of power to transform them into powerful witnesses.

> There on the Day of Pentecost we have seen the apostles filled with this power, and seen also that the real object of "the baptism with the Spirit" is to enable men to witness to Christ and His salvation with power. The Baptism with the Holy Spirit is not regeneration—the apostles were already regenerate—and it is not given primarily to promote sanctification; it is a baptism of power, or a baptism of fire, a baptism to enable one to witness. ... It is not regeneration or sanctification; this is power, power to witness.[11]

For Lloyd-Jones, Acts 1:8 is obvious evidence that Spirit baptism is a post-conversion experience distinct from regeneration. In addition, he argues, the Samaritan converts (Acts 8), Saul (Acts 9), Cornelius (Acts 15), and the Ephesian disciples (Acts 19) are good examples of Spirit baptism as an experience subsequent to regeneration.[12]

Second, Lloyd-Jones argues that the disciples' reception of power, which he describes as baptism of the Spirit, was refreshed repeatedly "whenever they had some very special situation to deal with." He presents Peter

10. Lloyd-Jones, *Joy Unspeakable*, 34–37.
11. Lloyd-Jones, *Preaching and Preachers*, 308.
12. Lloyd-Jones, *God's Ultimate Purpose*, 251–53.

(Acts 4:8), Stephen (Acts 7:55), and Paul (Acts 13:9) as examples of this repetition.[13] For instance, in Acts 4, Peter was standing with John on trial before the Sanhedrin as they were asked, "By what power, or by what name, have ye done this?" (Acts 4:7). The text records what happened to Peter at that moment: "Then Peter, filled with the Holy Ghost, said unto them ..." (Acts 4:8). Lloyd-Jones interprets this phrase as another Spirit baptism for Peter at this crucial moment.

> How do you interpret that? Why does it say, "Then Peter, filled with the Holy Spirit?" You might argue, "But was he not filled with the Holy Ghost on the Day of Pentecost as the other men were?" Of course he was. What then is the point of repeating it here? There is only one adequate explanation of this. It is not just a reminder of the fact that he had been baptized with the Spirit on the Day of Pentecost. There is no purpose in the use of this expression unless it means that he received a fresh accession of power. He was in a critical position. Here he was on trial with John, indeed the Gospel and the entire Christian Church were on trial, and he needed some new, fresh power to witness positively and to confute the persecutors—some new, fresh power, and it is given him. So the expression is used, "Peter filled with the Holy Ghost." This was another filling for this special task.[14]

According to Lloyd-Jones's interpretation, the cases of Stephen and Paul are little different in that another baptism of the Spirit was given to them to deal with their special task. For Stephen, it took place right before being martyred; for Paul, it occurred at the moment when he resisted Elymas. Accordingly, Lloyd-Jones was convinced that Spirit baptism was repeated for the disciples, especially when they encountered some significant situation to cope with.

THE EPISTLES

Lloyd-Jones's interpretation of baptism of the Spirit in the Epistles can be summarized in three categories: (1) the sealing of the Spirit, (2) assurance, and (3) demonstrations of the Spirit and of power. In the following section,

13. Lloyd-Jones, *Preaching and Preachers*, 309–11.
14. Lloyd-Jones, *Preaching and Preachers*, 309.

I will review Lloyd-Jones's understanding of the key verses related to each category.

The Sealing of the Spirit

The key verse for the sealing of the Spirit is Ephesians 1:13, which has given rise to sharp exegetical disputes as to whether it refers to a conversion experience or a postconversion one in conjunction with the controversy over the nature of Spirit baptism. Lloyd-Jones takes the translation of the KJV, "in whom also *after that ye believed*, ye were sealed with that Holy Spirit of promise," as theologically correct, though not literally precise.[15] The prevalent teaching in evangelical circles, he argues, is that the sealing of the Spirit is "something that happens immediately, inevitably, inexorably to all who believe." He himself insists, on the other hand, that it is "something subsequent to believing, something additional to believing,"[16] as the KJV reads.

To support his argument, he draws on such sources (all from the Reformed tradition) as Thomas Goodwin, John Owen, Charles Simeon (1759–1836), and Charles Hodge (1797–1878).[17] He maintains that each of these men taught that there exists "a sharp distinction between believing (the act of faith) and the sealing of the Spirit"; there may be such an interval between the two that a believer does not still know the sealing of the Spirit, though the person has been regenerated and possesses the Spirit.[18] Therefore, he concludes, "It is surely obvious that the godly men who gave us the Authorized Version held that view, because they deliberately introduced the word *'after.'*"

---

15. Lloyd-Jones, *Joy Unspeakable*, 149; emphasis added. He states, "We are well aware of the fact that the Authorized translation here is not literally accurate. ... The better translation is 'believing,' or 'having believed.' ... Now both those translations are correct and the authorities are divided between the two" (*Joy Unspeakable*, 149).

16. Lloyd-Jones, *God's Ultimate Purpose*, 249–50.

17. See Lloyd-Jones, *Joy Unspeakable*, 149. In his sermon "The Sealing of the Spirit," Lloyd-Jones quotes the comment of Charles Hodge on this matter. He states, "Charles Hodge referring to this Authorized translation says, 'This is more than a translation; it is exposition of the original,' and he is undoubtedly right" (*Joy Unspeakable*, 149).

18. Lloyd-Jones, *God's Ultimate Purpose*, 249. It should be noted that Lloyd-Jones misunderstood John Owen's position on this matter. Owen interpreted the sealing of the Spirit in Eph 1:13 as the Spirit himself rather than a particular act of the Spirit. He clearly states: "The effects of this sealing are gracious operations of the Holy Spirit in and upon believers but the sealing itself is the communication of the Spirit unto us." See Owen, *Works of John Owen* 4:400.

Assurance ("the Witness of the Spirit")

According to Lloyd-Jones, a significant result of the sealing of the Spirit is to experience the "shedding abroad of God's love" in a believer's heart. His biblical grounds for this assertion come from texts such as Romans 5:5: "And hope maketh not ashamed; because the love of God is shed abroad in our hearts by the Holy Ghost which is given unto us." Also, he argues that Galatians 4:6, "And because ye are sons, God hath sent forth the Spirit of his Son into your hearts, crying, 'Abba, Father,'" presents the same expression to illustrate the effect of the sealing. Expounding the verse, he explains what happens when a Christian receives baptism of the Spirit as follows:

> So the Apostle tells us in the fourth chapter of Galatians that as the result of the work of Christ and this baptism of the Spirit we also are given the Spirit that was in Christ, and He makes us also cry "Abba, Father." We have become certain of God as Father, we know Him as Father. We no longer believe in God as Father theoretically, it is the cry of the heart, an elemental, instinctive cry that comes welling up from the depths. That is the result of the sealing of the Spirit.[19]

In his view, baptism of the Spirit is a spiritual experience of an exceptional, immediate, and overflowing work of the Spirit that leads Christians to full assurance of their salvation, adoption, inheritance, and the everlasting love of God toward them.

"The witness of the Spirit" is Lloyd-Jones's other preferred term, which comes from Romans 8:16 ("The Spirit itself beareth witness with our spirit, that we are the children of God") and describes the full assurance given by the immediate work of the Spirit. Lloyd-Jones explains, "The Spirit itself beareth witness with our spirit" as the direct witness of the Spirit to a believer's heart: "Now this is neither our action, nor our deduction, but immediate witness of the Spirit, and that is why it is both so absolute and so certain. What the Spirit does is this: he tells us in the most unmistakable manner that we are the children of God, that God loves us with an everlasting love, and that it was because he so loved us that Christ gave himself for us."[20]

19. Lloyd-Jones, *God's Ultimate Purpose*, 273.

20. Lloyd-Jones, *Joy Unspeakable*, 93.

Furthermore, Lloyd-Jones is convinced that such full assurance is a non-negotiable requirement for bearing witness to the gospel since without assurance no one can be an effective witness. In this regard, he believes that this great assurance leads a preacher to be equipped with authority and power.[21] In other words, for him, there is a close connection between full assurance and "demonstrations of the Spirit and of power" in preaching.

Demonstrations of the Spirit and of Power

Regarding baptism with the Spirit in relation to preaching, Lloyd-Jones considers the apostle Paul's confession in 1 Corinthians 2:3–5 as a significant statement.[22] Lloyd-Jones notes that Paul always longed to emphasize a thorough dependence on the power of the Holy Spirit, as he confesses in 1 Corinthians 2:4: "And my speech and my preaching was not with enticing words of man's wisdom, but in demonstration of the Spirit and of power."

> Here is a man who was greatly gifted, who had exceptional natural powers; but he deliberately determined not to use them in a carnal manner. He "determined not to know any thing among them, saving Jesus Christ, and Him crucified"; he then deliberately eschewed the manner of the Greek rhetoricians, both as to content and style, with which he was so familiar. As he says later to these same Corinthians he became "a fool for Christ's sake," in order that it might be clear that the power was not his but God's, and that their whole position should not be based upon "the wisdom of men but upon the power of God."[23]

Lloyd-Jones states that Paul's emphasis on a "demonstration of the Spirit and of power" in preaching can be found in 1 Corinthians 4:18–20; 2 Corinthians 4:1–7; 10:3–5; 12:9–10; Colossians 1:28–9; and 1 Thessalonians

21. For instance, he states: "With this assurance comes the power. If we are uncertain about the word of God, as to what is true and what is not true, or if I am uncertain about my relationship to him and the truth of these things in my case, I shall, as we have seen, be an advocate, not a witness. But when a man is baptized with the Spirit or sealed with the Spirit, he knows; the Spirit is the certainty. That leads not only to certainty in the individual, it leads to power. It must do. It is when we are certain, that we speak with authority and power" (Lloyd-Jones, *Joy Unspeakable*, 157).

22. Lloyd-Jones, *Preaching and Preachers*, 311.

23. Lloyd-Jones, *Preaching and Preachers*, 311–12.

1:5.[24] From all of these passages he asserts that Paul was strongly convinced that it is "the demonstration of the Holy Spirit and of power" that made the ministry of preaching effective.[25] For instance, expounding 1 Thessalonians 1:5, he argues:

> The Apostle is reminding the Thessalonians of how the Gospel had come to them, which many think was his first letter to a church. It is a most important chapter indeed as the definitive and controlling statement concerning preaching and evangelism. He reminds them that the Gospel had "come" to them; "not in word only." It had come "in word," and he reminds them of the content of the word in verses 9 and 10, but it was "not in word only, but also ..." It is this "also," this addition of the power of the Holy Ghost that ultimately makes preaching effective. This is what produces converts and creates Churches, and builds up Churches—"power," "Holy Ghost," and "much assurance."[26]

Proof of the connection between Spirit baptism and powerful preaching is not confined to Paul's Epistles. Lloyd-Jones cites 1 Peter 1:12 ("Unto whom it was revealed, that not unto themselves, but unto us they did minister the things, which are now reported unto you by them that have preached the gospel unto you with the Holy Ghost sent down from heaven; which things the angels desire to look into") as another case of demonstrations of the Spirit and of power in preaching.

> The apostle Peter says exactly the same thing. He talks in 1 Peter 1:12 about the "things, which are now reported unto you by them that have preached the gospel unto you with the Holy Ghost sent down from heaven; which things the angels desire to look into." It is "with the Holy Ghost sent down from heaven" that the gospel is preached with assurance and conviction, with authority and with power.[27]

So far, we have reviewed Lloyd-Jones's interpretation of cases of Spirit baptism in the New Testament. What should be emphasized is that he

24. Lloyd-Jones, *Preaching and Preachers*, 312–14.
25. Jung, "Evaluation of the Principles," 210.
26. Lloyd-Jones, *Preaching and Preachers*, 313–14.
27. Lloyd-Jones, *Authority*, 86.

strongly believes that the history of the church, particularly the history of revival, affirms his interpretation regarding Spirit baptism in the New Testament. He argues that the experiences of the disciples and the church in the New Testament have been repeated in periods of revival: "The long history of the Church shows repeatedly that what we find in the New Testament has characterized the Church always in periods of revival and reformation."[28] Lloyd-Jones was deeply influenced by the history and theology of revival in Britain and New England in the eighteenth century. The theology of revival of Jonathan Edwards and the journals of preachers such as George Whitefield, John Wesley, and Howell Harris not only provided great inspiration but also exerted great influence on his understanding of this subject. That the general characteristics of Spirit baptism are found commonly in Edwards's revival theology and in the journals of these other great preachers convinced him that his understanding of Spirit baptism was correct, theologically and historically.

THE HISTORY AND THEOLOGY OF REVIVAL IN BRITAIN AND NEW ENGLAND IN THE EIGHTEENTH CENTURY

JONATHAN EDWARDS'S THEOLOGY OF REVIVAL

For Lloyd-Jones, the most influential figure of the eighteenth century regarding the topic of revival is Jonathan Edwards, whom Lloyd-Jones loves to call "preeminently the theologian of revival."[29] In *Preaching and Preachers*, he expresses how much he has been influenced by Edwards's work concerning revival.

> I can simply testify that in my experience the help that I derived in my early years in the ministry from reading the sermons of Jonathan Edwards was immeasurable. And, of course not only his sermons, but also his account of that Great Awakening, that great religious Revival that took place in America in the eighteenth century, and his great *The Religious Affections*.[30]

---

28. Lloyd-Jones, *Preaching and Preachers*, 315.
29. Lloyd-Jones, *Puritans*, 361.
30. Lloyd-Jones, *Preaching and Preachers*, 176.

In his lecture "Jonathan Edwards and the Crucial Importance of Revival," Lloyd-Jones suggests several reasons Edwards was worthy to be given the title "the theologian of revival." First, during his lifetime he experienced several revivals and actively participated in the Great Awakening:

> The thing that stands out in the life of [Edwards] was the remarkable revival that broke out under his ministry in Northampton, beginning at the end of 1734, and in 1735, and then later his participation with others in the so-called Great Awakening in connection with the visit of George Whitefield and others in 1740. Those are the salient facts in the life of this great man.[31]

Second, Edwards felt compelled to defend the idea that "the outpouring of the Spirit" was a true work of the Holy Spirit, standing against criticisms and misunderstandings regarding these revivals. He devoted much of his time and his intellectual gifts to writing works intended to defend and promote revival: *Faithful Narrative of a Surprising Work of God* (1737), *The Distinguishing Marks of a Work of the Spirit of God* (1741), *Some Thoughts Concerning the Revival* (1743), *Religious Affections* (1746), and *Humble Attempt to Promote Explicit Agreement and Visible Union of God's People in Extraordinary Prayer* (1748). In this regard, Lloyd-Jones esteems Edwards as "pre-eminently the expert" in revival. Because of his experience of the outpourings of the Spirit and his ceaseless efforts to theologically support them, Lloyd-Jones argues that "the element of the Holy Spirit is more prominent in Edwards than in any other of the Puritans." He placed emphasis on "a direct and immediate influence of the Spirit, and in sudden and dramatic conversion."[32]

Another reason for Lloyd-Jones to consider Edwards as the predominant theologian of revival was that he always sought to maintain a balance between the commands "Do not quench the Spirit" (1 Thess 5:19) and "Everything must be done decently and in order" (1 Cor 14:40). Lloyd-Jones says:

> [Edwards] was always fighting on two fronts right through his life. ... There were some who were totally opposed to the revival. They were orthodox men who held the same theology as Edwards. They were Calvinists, but they disliked revival. They disliked the emotional

31. Lloyd-Jones, *Puritans*, 350.
32. Lloyd-Jones, *Puritans*, 350, 362.

> element, they disliked the novelty. ... Edwards had to defend the revival against these critics. But then there were men at the other extreme. ... These were the enthusiasts, the men who went to extremes, the men who were guilty of folly. Edwards had to deal with them also; so here he was, fighting on the two fronts. ... He was always warning on both sides, warning against quenching the Spirit, warning also against being carried away by the flesh and being deluded by Satan through the flesh.[33]

For these reasons, Lloyd-Jones does not hesitate to exhort others to read Edwards's works for anyone who wants to know anything about revival.[34] The following section will examine the similarity between Lloyd-Jones's doctrine of Spirit baptism and Edwards's doctrine of revival based on the general characteristics of Spirit baptism Lloyd-Jones proposes. The similarity will confirm that Lloyd-Jones's doctrine of Spirit baptism was substantially influenced by Edwards's theology of revival.

As surveyed in chapter 1 concerning the overwhelming character of Spirit baptism, Lloyd-Jones uses the terms "poured out" or "shed abroad" to describe the great profusion of the Holy Spirit. Edwards especially liked the term "pouring out" when he illustrated the tremendous profusion of the Spirit that took place in revivals. He uses the expression for the first time in a letter in 1716, when he was twelve years old, to describe an awakening in his father's church: "Through the wonderful mercy and goodness of God there hath in this place been a very remarkable stirring and pouring out of the Spirit of God."[35] Michael McClymond and Gerald McDermott maintain that the words "pouring out of the Spirit" in the letter were the most "prophetic of Edwards's future destiny as America's leading author on, and interpreter of, religious revivals."[36]

It is worthwhile to note that "the outpouring of the Spirit" was a favorite term used by many of Edwards's Puritan forerunners in both Old and New England.[37] For instance, Solomon Stoddard (1643–1729), Edwards's mater-

33. Lloyd-Jones, *Puritans*, 362–64.
34. Lloyd-Jones, *Puritans*, 361.
35. Edwards, *Letters and Personal Writings*, in *Works* 16:29.
36. McClymond and McDermott, *Theology of Jonathan Edwards*, 429.
37. Haykin, *Jonathan Edwards*, 52.

nal grandfather, was one of the spiritual leaders of New England deeply influenced by the England Puritans such as Robert Fleming (1630–1694), John Howe (1630–1705), and John Owen, who emphasized "the eschatological hope of successive outpourings."[38] In this regard, Edwards expresses strong conviction in *Faithful Narrative of a Surprising Work of God* that the remarkable outpourings of the Spirit at Northampton in 1734 and 1735 were the realization of what his Puritan predecessors had long prayed for.[39]

From their similar positions on this matter, we can assume that Edwards's theology of revival exerted much influence on Lloyd-Jones so that he was convinced that revival or baptism with the Spirit was an exceptional work of the Spirit, characterized by its overwhelming experience. However, when it comes to immediate work of the Spirit in relation to the word, there is a considerable difference between Lloyd-Jones's position and that of Edwards. This issue of the different opinions between the two regarding the immediate work of the Spirit in revival will be dealt with in the next chapter.

Lloyd-Jones's second conviction concerning baptism with the Spirit is that it is the Spirit's sovereign action and not the result of human actions or effort. As stated earlier, for Lloyd-Jones, there is little difference in essence between baptism with the Spirit and revival. He understands revival as a large number of people being baptized with the Holy Spirit simultaneously.[40] Thus, he strongly opposes the assertion that humans can produce revival or baptism with the Spirit if they only complete certain requirements.

Lloyd-Jones's conviction on this issue is not different from Edwards's. Edwards was convinced that an outpouring of the Spirit was absolutely dependent on the sovereignty of God. His position becomes very obvious when compared to that of Charles Finney (1792–1875). Edwards's view represents revival as God coming down, while Finney's view represents "revivalism," understood as humans working it up. McLoughlin describes the substantial difference between the two as follows: "The difference between Edwards and Finney is essentially the difference between the medieval and the modern temper. One saw God at the center of the Universe, the other

38. Smart, *Jonathan Edwards's Apologetic*, 15.

39. Haykin, *Jonathan Edwards*, 53.

40. Lloyd-Jones, *Joy Unspeakable*, 51.

saw man. One believed that revivals were "prayed down" and the other that they were 'worked up.'"[41]

Edwards's position on revival belongs to the Calvinistic Pneumatic School that believes that "these outpourings of the Spirit in awakenings are given seasonably according to the counsel of God's own will whenever and wherever Christ chooses."[42] In this regard, it can be argued that Lloyd-Jones also belongs to the Calvinistic Pneumatic School since he faithfully follows the Calvinistic interpretation of revival. The root of Lloyd-Jones's theology of revival will be discussed in more detail in the following chapter.

Lastly, Lloyd-Jones argues that just as Spirit baptism can be repeated many times; so revival is a kind of repetition of what occurred on the day of Pentecost. To Lloyd-Jones, what happened on Pentecost in Acts 2 is not a "once and for all" event that cannot be repeated. On the contrary, he believed that whenever revival takes place, the church has come back to its origin described in Acts 2.[43] Furthermore, he argues that the progress of the church has been made largely by these extraordinary outpourings of the Spirit. He states: "Surely the history of the progress and development of the church is largely a history of revival, of these mighty exceptional effusions of the Spirit of God. There is no question that God has really kept His work alive and has advanced it most of all by these unusual, exceptional, signal manifestations of His glory and of His power."[44] It is noteworthy that Edwards was similarly convinced that "remarkable pourings out of the Spirit" have been repeated in the history of the church so as to advance the work of redemption. This conviction is most clearly reflected in *A History of the Work of Redemption*:

> It may here be observed that from the fall of man to this day wherein we live the Work of Redemption in its effect has mainly been carried on by remarkable pourings out of the Spirit of God. ... The way in which the greatest things have been done towards carrying on this work always has been by remarkable pourings out of the Spirit at special seasons of mercy.[45]

41. Murray, *Pentecost Today?*, 33.
42. Smart, *Jonathan Edwards's Apologetic*, 67.
43. Lloyd-Jones, *Revival*, 199.
44. Lloyd-Jones, *Puritans*, 17.
45. Edwards, *Works* 9:143.

Accordingly, Lloyd-Jones's conviction that baptism with the Spirit can be repeated appears to have been influenced by Edwards's conviction that God was pleased to provide outpourings of the Spirit occasionally to promote His work of redemption. However, it should be noted that Edwards's theology of revival was firmly based on his post-millennial eschatology. He regarded outpourings of the Spirit as "harbingers of Christ's second coming and the end of the age."[46] Lloyd-Jones, though accepting Edwards's understanding of revival as God's occasional sovereign interventions, disagreed with post-millennial eschatology.[47]

So far, we have reviewed Edwards's influence on Lloyd-Jones's doctrine of Spirit baptism by examining the substantial similarity between the two figures' positions on revival. To sum up, Lloyd-Jones's doctrine of Spirit baptism is basically the same as and likely derives from Edwards's theology of revival in three aspects: (1) an exceptional work of the Spirit, (2) the sovereignty of God, and (3) the repetition of outpouring of the Spirit. This suggests that Lloyd-Jones's doctrine on the subject of Spirit baptism was greatly influenced by Edwards's writings concerning revival. However, regarding another general character of Spirit baptism—that it gives the Christian a full assurance of salvation—there exists a definite difference between the two. Lloyd-Jones regards the direct witness of the Spirit to the heart of a Christian as the highest degree of assurance of salvation, while Edwards depreciated it as too unreliable to be taken as evidence of salvation. The substantial difference between the doctrine of assurance and an immediate work of the Spirit will be discussed in the following chapter.

---

46. McClymond and McDermott, *Theology of Jonathan Edwards*, 444.

47. Lloyd-Jones cites Luke 18:8 to prove that the postmillennial view is biblically unacceptable since Jesus prophesies in this verse that there will be little faith left on the earth when he comes again. Lloyd-Jones says, "Indeed, there is one verse, one statement, which, as far as I am concerned, is enough to put the post-millennial view right out. It is Luke 18:8 where our Lord says, 'When the Son of man cometh, shall he find faith on the earth?' And faith there means the faith. He seems to prophesy there that when He comes, there will appear to be no faith at all left in the world. Now I find it very difficult to believe that there could ever be such a condition as that immediately after a tremendous golden period. ... It is straining the imagination too much to ask us to believe that, after such a period, men and women could so quickly and almost overwhelmingly suddenly turn against the gospel. I feel, therefore, that on those grounds I cannot accept the post-millennial interpretation of Revelation 20" (Lloyd-Jones, *Church and the Last Things*, 218).

THE HISTORY OF THE GREAT AWAKENING IN THE EIGHTEENTH CENTURY

In addition to his dependence on Edwards, Lloyd-Jones found consistent inspiration, encouragement, and guidance from reading about other great eighteenth-century revivals.[48] In *Preaching and Preachers*, he says, "When I get discouraged and over-tired and weary I also invariably go to the eighteenth century. I have never found George Whitefield to fail me." Without hesitation, he exhorts preachers: "Go to the eighteenth century! In other words, read the stories of the great tides and movements of the Spirit experienced in that century."[49] When he refers to the eighteenth century, he is pointing to the history of the Great Awakening in Britain and New England at that time. In particular, he has in mind the extraordinary preaching ministries of George Whitefield, John Wesley, and Howell Harris, which played a key role in the awakening. While reading their journals, he found that their stories demonstrate the general features of Spirit baptism in the ministry of preaching: a full assurance of salvation, authority, the enormous power of the Spirit, the sovereignty of God, and repetition.

Full Assurance of Salvation

According to Lloyd-Jones, these three prominent eighteenth-century preachers shared in common the experience of receiving full assurance of salvation after an extended period of agonizing uncertainty. He is convinced that the vital spiritual experience of Spirit baptism was a turning point to lead them to become powerful evangelists. For instance, John Wesley, as is well known, went through a long process of coming to full assurance that Jesus Christ had taken away his sins and saved him from the law of sin and death. For him, the first step was to come to the realization that he himself was a poor soul who needed the gospel, which happened after a complete failure of his ministry in Georgia. As he wrote in February 1738: "It is now two years and almost four months since I left my native country, in order to teach the Georgian Indians the nature of Christianity: But what I learned myself in the meantime? Why (what I the least of all suspected), that I who went to

48. Sargent, *Sacred Anointing*, 33.

49. Lloyd-Jones, *Preaching and Preachers*, 119.

America to convert others, was never myself converted to God."[50] A famous conversation between John Wesley and August Spangenberg (1704–1792), a leader of the Moravians, demonstrated that Wesley had not had any assurance in his heart that Jesus had died to save him, even though he had known it intellectually. He wrote about this conversation on February 7, 1736:

> [August Spangenberg] said, "My brother, I must first ask you one or two questions. Have you the witness within yourself? Does the Spirit of God bear witness with your spirit that you are a child of God?" I was surprised, and knew not what to answer. He observed it and asked, "Do you know Jesus Christ?" I paused and said, "I know He is the Saviour of the world." "True," replied he; "but do you know He has saved you?" I answered, "I hope He has died to save me." He only added, "Do you know yourself?" I said, "I do." But I fear they were vain words.[51]

When Wesley came back to England with deep disappointment, it was Peter Böhler (1712–1775), a Moravian missionary, who helped him to gain an understanding of justification by faith. On March 5, 1738, he wrote, "I was, on Sunday, the 5th, clearly convinced of unbelief, of the want of that faith whereby alone we are saved."[52] Stephen Tomkins, a biographer of Wesley, argues that this was "Wesley's real evangelical conversion—the acceptance that God can only be appeased by putting faith in his grace, not by attempts at holiness."[53]

A series of conversations with Böhler led Wesley to be convinced that faith is not just "a rational assent to propositional truths"; it requires "a personal experience of divine forgiveness, confirmed by the witness of the Spirit." Through these conversations, Wesley accepted "the validity of their theological presuppositions."[54] Finally, on May 24, 1738, Wesley had a pivotal spiritual experience, which is called the "Aldersgate experience," through which a full

50. Wesley, *Journal of John Wesley*, 54.

51. Wesley, *Journal of John Wesley*, 36–37.

52. Wesley, *Journal of John Wesley*, 58.

53. Tomkins, *John Wesley*, 58. On the other hand, Yates regards it as Wesley's *intellectual* conversion. He says, "There are comparatively few entries in Wesley's Journal between 7th March and 24th May 1738, but examination of these supports the view that the period from 5th to 7th March is almost as important as 24th May. They are the days of his intellectual conversion" (Yates, *Doctrine of Assurance*, 10).

54. Heitzenrater, *Mirror and Memory*, 122.

assurance of salvation was given to his heart.[55] Lloyd-Jones evaluates Wesley's Aldersgate experience as Spirit baptism; he asserts that it was the turning point of Wesley's preaching ministry from which time "this man began to preach with a new power and was greatly used by God."[56]

George Whitefield also went through a lengthy and painful process of conversion. He entered Pembroke College, Oxford, in the fall of 1732; one year later, he joined the Holy Club, a group of religiously earnest students whose moderator was John Wesley. With the members of the club, Whitefield committed himself to prayers, fasting, and visiting prisons, following their strict regimen, while assuming that performing good works would lead him to salvation. Meanwhile, he read *The Life of God in the Soul of Man* (1677) by Henry Scougal (1650–1678), which unexpectedly changed his entire perspective regarding salvation. This book shocked him as he came to realize that he was not a Christian but a man who needed to be born again. His assumption that doing good works would lead him to heaven was shattered. He recorded that moment as follows:

> God showed me that I must be born again, or be damned! I learned that a man may go to church, say prayers, receive the sacrament, and yet not be a Christian. ... God soon showed me ... that "a true Christianity is a union of the soul with God, and Christ formed within us," a ray of divine light was instantaneously darted into my soul, and from that moment, and not till then, did I know I must become a new creature.[57]

After that, he pushed himself to extreme self-denial to seek for salvation, spending many days groaning deeply with pain and despair: "God only knows how many nights I have laid upon my bed groaning under the weight I felt. ... Whole days and weeks have I spent in lying prostrate on the ground."[58]

Eventually, in 1735, three years earlier than John Wesley, Whitefield experienced "an evangelical conversion."[59] In his journal, Whitefield writes about the life-transforming moment when he was assured of his forgiveness and God's love through Jesus Christ:

---

55. See Wesley, *Journal of John Wesley*, 64.
56. Lloyd-Jones, *Preaching and Preachers*, 319.
57. Dallimore, *George Whitefield*, 73.
58. Dallimore, *George Whitefield*, 74.
59. Jones, Schlenther, and White, *Elect Methodists*, 6.

> God was pleased to remove the heavy load, to enable me to lay hold of his dear Son by a living faith, and by giving me *the Spirit of adoption*, to seal me, even to the day of everlasting redemption. O! with what joy—*joy unspeakable*—even joy that was full of and big with glory, was my soul filled when the weight of sin went off, and an abiding sense of the love of God broke in upon my disconsolate soul! Surely it was a day to be had in everlasting remembrance. My joys were like a spring-tide and overflowed the banks.[60]

According to Lloyd-Jones, it was at this time that Whitefield received baptism of the Spirit, which explains the unusual character of his preaching that was accompanied by great power and authority.[61] As was the case with Wesley, he argues, his Spirit baptism transformed Whitefield into one of the most powerful preachers who ignited the fire of the Great Awakening in the eighteenth century.

Authority and Power

As indicated in chapter 1, Lloyd-Jones was convinced that Spirit baptism leads both preacher and congregation to sense the power and presence of God coming upon the preacher; it endows a preacher with an unusual authority and power. Lloyd-Jones, as discussed in the first chapter, draws attention to an expression commonly found in the journals of Wesley, Whitefield, and Harris: "The Lord (God) came down among us." He interprets the expression as their sharing in the experience of God's powerful presence and unction of the Spirit in their preaching ministry, which always clothed them with divine power and authority.

In *John Wesley: A Biography*, Tompkins states that Wesley was pleased to say, "simply the power of God fell mightily among us." Indeed, Wesley often testified in his journal that the mighty power of God descended on him and the congregation while he was preaching. As an example, he recorded what happened while he was preaching on April 26, 1739: "Immediately *the power of* God *fell upon us*. One, another, and another, sunk to the earth. You might see them, dropping on all sides as thunderstruck. One cried out aloud. I went and prayed over her, and she received joy in the Holy Ghost. A second falling

60. Whitefield, *George Whitefield's Journals*, 58; emphasis added.
61. Lloyd-Jones, *Puritans*, 118.

into the same agony, we turned to her, and received for her also the promise of the Father."[62] With respect to Whitefield, Lloyd-Jones notes, his journals and various biographies about him include "endless accounts of his awareness of the Spirit of God coming upon him while he preached."[63] His journal entry on November 2, 1740, is one such example:

> After I had begun, however, *the Spirit of the Lord* gave me freedom, and at length *came down like a mighty rushing wind*, and carried all before it. Immediately, the whole congregation was alarmed. Crying, weeping, and wailing were to be heard in every corner; men's hearts failing them for fear, and many were to be seen falling into the arms of their friends. My soul was carried out till I could scarce speak any more. A sense of God's goodness overwhelmed me. A little boy was much concerned, on the pulpit stairs. One of my friends asked him why he cried. "Who can help it?" he said, "Mr. Whitefield's words cut me to the heart."[64]

As for Harris, Lloyd-Jones notes how Harris often used the term "authority" that, according to Lloyd-Jones, is equivalent to the expression, "The Lord came down among us."[65] To Harris, authority came from the presence and power of the Holy Spirit. He said, "I had authority, through the Spirit of God, to declare against the tares growing in the Lord's Garden; and at the same time to call sinners to the great atonement in the blood of Emmanuel."[66] Lloyd-Jones emphasizes how much Harris relied on "authority" in his preaching ministry. Harris' description of what happened when he preached on February 5, 1737, is a good example of his reliance on this authority.

> At first, I was strongest; but at length, while discoursing on the conversion of Zaccheus, and endeavoring to draw them by love, I lost my *authority*; it was dead and dry, until, near the end, the Lord lift up my voice like a trumpet, and enabled me to declare home about the Lord's enemies. I never tasted more power. I believe some were cut

62. Tomkins, *John Wesley*, 73; emphasis added.
63. Lloyd-Jones, *Preaching and Preachers*, 320.
64. Whitefield, *George Whitefield's Journals*, 487.
65. Lloyd-Jones, *Authority*, 86–87.
66. Hughes, *Life of Howell Harris*, 357.

> through; many wept, and one fainted; others felt a great trembling, and all were filled with awe.[67]

As all the records in the three preachers' journals quoted above indicate, their sense of the Spirit of God coming down on them and their listeners was closely connected to their powerful preaching, which invariably brought about many dramatic changes in the listeners. In this manner, the writings of the great evangelists in the eighteenth century furnished Lloyd-Jones with abundant historical evidence to firmly establish that Spirit baptism leads preachers to be equipped with divine power and authority from on high.

The Sovereignty of God and the Repetition of Baptism with the Spirit

In his lecture "Howell Harris and Revival," Lloyd-Jones emphasizes that neither Howell Harris nor George Whitefield nor Jonathan Edwards actually initiated the Great Awakening in the eighteenth century. He points out that the essential message of the movement was the sovereignty of God:

> We must not think of [Howell Harris] in terms of a man who starts a crusade or a movement. That is really to deny the essential message of this wonderful story. No, no! It is the sovereignty of God; and we see this not only in the story of Howell Harris, but also in the fact that at almost exactly the same time as God did this to Howell Harris, He was doing the same to Daniel Rowland. They had never heard of each other—long distance separated them from one another—but it happened at the same time; and we know that things were happening to George Whitefield at the same time. We know also that much the same was happening to Jonathan Edwards in America and others at the same time. What is this? The sovereignty of God! The sovereignty of God as regards time, place, persons![68]

Lloyd-Jones was strongly convinced that God chose Harris, Whitefield, Wesley, and Edwards according to his sovereign will. Baptizing them with the Holy Spirit, He used them to initiate the Great Revival in the eighteenth century.

---

67. Hughes, *Life of Howell Harris*, 69; emphasis added.
68. Lloyd-Jones, *Puritans*, 289.

Furthermore, the experiences of these leading figures demonstrate that Spirit baptism had been repeated several times. For instance, Howell Harris had several recurrences of Spirit baptism. Lloyd-Jones argues that it happened in 1736, 1747, and 1749.[69] He says, "[Howell Harris] would lose this at times for a while, and he would grieve; then it would come back again. He went on like that until he died in 1773."[70] In the case of John Wesley, Lloyd-Jones again asserts that Spirit baptism was repeated. The baptism that had happened to him at Aldersgate on May 24, 1738, recurred on January 1, 1739.[71] The same was true of George Whitefield, about whom Lloyd-Jones says: "If you read the Journals of Whitefield, you will find that this happened to him many times. He always lived on a high level but there were moments when he was transported into the heavens. He did not remain there, he came back again. Then he would be taken up again."[72]

To sum up, Lloyd-Jones was convinced that the general characteristics of Spirit baptism can be found in the journals of the great preachers of the eighteenth century. It seems plausible that the historical evidence that he found in the journals strengthened his conviction regarding Spirit baptism. However, it should be noted that his argument regarding these preachers' experience of Spirit baptism leaves room for debate. For instance, he interprets Whitefield's spiritual experience in 1735, as reviewed above, in terms of receiving full assurance of salvation. Ironically, Whitefield himself interpreted the life-changing experience as being born again, not as receiving Spirit baptism subsequent to regeneration. Later, when looking back on the unforgettable event, Whitefield said, "Jesus Christ first revealed himself to me [at that moment] and gave me the *new birth*."[73] As will be discussed in more detail later, there are also cases where Lloyd-Jones's interpretation of someone's experience differs from their own understanding. To a certain degree, this shows that Lloyd-Jones had a tendency to impose his subjective interpretation on others' writings to support his own doctrine, sometimes regardless of the others' own perspective.

---

69. Lloyd-Jones, *Puritans*, 291–92.
70. Lloyd-Jones, *Preaching and Preachers*, 321.
71. Lloyd-Jones, *Joy Unspeakable*, 62–63.
72. Lloyd-Jones, *Joy Unspeakable*, 245–46.
73. Whitefield, *Sermons on Important Subjects*, 755.

Thus far, I have examined the probable key factors that contributed to Lloyd-Jones's doctrine of Spirit baptism, while considering the general characteristics of Spirit baptism that Lloyd-Jones suggests. As noted, all the various factors considered here played significant roles in forming Lloyd-Jones's doctrine of Spirit baptism, providing him with biblical, historical, theological, and experiential evidence to validate his argument concerning the general characteristics of Spirit baptism. However, it can be argued that the most significant factors among them are Lloyd-Jones's background growing up as a Welsh Calvinistic Methodist and his appreciation of eighteenth-century revival. The basis for this argument is that, even though Lloyd-Jones began to preach in earnest about baptism with the Spirit as a well-developed doctrine after 1954 when the Ephesian series commenced at Westminster Chapel, he had already held his view on the need of Spirit baptism (or revival) since the 1920s,[74] which demonstrably originated from his upbringing and his interest in Welsh Calvinistic Methodism. His convictions regarding the need for Spirit baptism can even be found in his address on "The Problem of Modern Wales," which was presented to the Union of Welsh Societies at Pontypridd in April 1925. In the first sermon he ever delivered, he attributed the decline of Wales to the declension of the church, in particular, the absence of powerful preaching as the Methodist fathers showed:[75]

> Preaching has very largely become a profession. Instead of real Christian sermons we are given second-hand expositions of psychology. The preachers say that they give the congregations what they ask for! What a terrible condemnation both of the preachers themselves and their congregations! Daniel Rowland, Llangeitho used to preach hell. Has there been preaching which has had anything like the effect of his preaching since those days? We know quite well that there has not been. I am one of those who believe that until such men rise again in our midst, our condition—far from improving—will continue to

74. Eaton also argues, "His [Lloyd-Jones's] major emphasis on the Spirit's baptism seemed to commence in the 1950s although he had held his view from the earliest days of his theological thinking" (*Baptism with the Spirit*, 130).

75. Murray, *Life of Martyn Lloyd-Jones*, 59.

> deteriorate. Our pulpit today is effete and ineffective. It is the final touch in the tragedy of Modern Wales![76]

Before closing the sermon, he maintained that Wales needed another great spiritual awakening such as that which had taken place in the eighteenth century, rather than any social action or politics:

> Let us get rid of all injustices by all means, let us fight for the right to manage our own local affairs in our way, but do not let us delude ourselves into believing that we shall be better Christian men and women merely because we speak Welsh and have a parliament of our own. No, what Wales needs above everything today is not a republic but a revival, a revolution in the sense that we turn back to the things, to the one thing that has made us great. By a revival I do not mean a wave of emotionalism, but a great spiritual awakening such as took place in the eighteenth century under the influence and guidance of the Methodist Fathers.[77]

Thus, on the basis of his first sermon, we may conclude that even before beginning his church ministry, he was already convinced of the great need for another revival such as that which had occurred in the eighteenth century.

John Piper points out that what Lloyd-Jones addressed in his first sermon was the recurrent theme of his life: the need for the power of the Spirit and revival.[78] Eryl Davies also says that for Lloyd-Jones, revival was his life-long burden as a man "who was single-minded in taking Bible teaching and church history seriously with the supreme motive of seeing God glorified again in revival in his day."[79] Lloyd-Jones's life-long conviction regarding the necessity of revival, as his first sermon above reveals, traces back to the great influence in his youth by the history of eighteenth-century revival in Wales, and especially by the stories of Welsh Calvinistic fathers such as those

76. Murray, *Life of Martyn Lloyd-Jones*, 59.

77. Murray, *Life of Martyn Lloyd-Jones*, 60.

78. Piper, "Passion for Christ-Exalting Power." He maintains: "His [Lloyd-Jones's] first sermon there was in April 1925 and the note he sounded was the recurrent theme of his life: Wales did not need more talk about social action; it needed 'a great spiritual awakening.' The theme of revival and power and real vitality remained his lifelong passion."

79. Davies, *Dr. Martyn Lloyd-Jones: A Bite-Size Biography*. Chapter 14, paragraph 4, location 1348.

of Harris, Rowland, and Williams. The Welsh revival in the eighteenth century cannot be separated from the great awakenings that took place during the same period in Britain and New England. Therefore, as reviewed in this chapter, the revival theology of Edwards as well as the history of the great awakenings around Britain and New England—in particular, the stories of such great preachers as George Whitefield and John Wesley—have provided Lloyd-Jones with another valuable source for his convictions on revival. To sum up, Lloyd-Jones's upbringing in Welsh Calvinistic Methodism led him to the life-long aspiration and interest in revival; his personal reading and subsequent understanding of the Great Awakening, including the Welsh revival, in the eighteenth century became the most important factor to form his doctrine of baptism with the Spirit.

It should be noted that all general characteristics of Spirit baptism—an exceptional work of the Spirit, assurance, the sovereignty of God, repeatability, authority, and power—suggested by Lloyd-Jones are in essence the same characteristics of revival that he appreciates. Accordingly, one can argue that not only his aspiration for but also his understanding of revival was the matrix through which he developed and preached his view of the doctrine of Spirit baptism. As will be discussed in the next chapter, this matrix—Lloyd-Jones's aspiration for and appreciation of revival—is an important key to the question of why his doctrine of Spirit baptism is different from mainstream Reformed theology in some ways, even if it stands on the old Reformed tradition. The following chapters (6 and 7) will argue that the matrix can be found in Lloyd-Jones's definition of true preaching as "logic on fire" as well as in his exegetical works on the core verses related to Spirit baptism.

6

ASSURANCE AND REVIVAL

Reformed Influences on Lloyd-Jones's Theological Foundations for Spirit Baptism

Although Lloyd-Jones's critics accused him of adopting the Pentecostal doctrine of Spirit baptism, as we have seen in chapter 2, the present chapter will show that his understanding of Spirit baptism, emphasizing assurance of salvation and personal/collective revival, in fact, originates with Reformed theologians of the seventeenth to mid-nineteenth centuries. To make this case, I will examine Lloyd-Jones's sermons and lectures on baptism with the Spirit to ascertain the origin of his doctrine, exploring quotations from his published writings. This exploration into the quotations he uses will clarify that the theological foundation for his doctrine of Spirit baptism—assurance of salvation and revival—originates from the old Reformed tradition from the seventeenth to mid-nineteenth centuries.[1] However, we will also find a deviation from the old Reformed theology in reintroducing the doctrine of assurance in that Lloyd-Jones acknowledges the possibility of the immediate work of the Spirit without means of the written Word. His distinctive position confirms that his doctrine of Spirit baptism is a reflective re-appropriation of the older Reformed doctrines within the circumstances of the twentieth century in which he lived, rather than a simple repetition of their original substance.

---

1. According to an intellectual-history approach that focuses on "the published writings of key intellectuals or authors and their ideas," quotations from personal letters not intended for publication, hymns, indirect citations, and citations that are too short are excluded from the research.

ASSURANCE

Lloyd-Jones argues that his doctrine of baptism with the Spirit is related to "the older experimental view of full assurance,"[2] rebutting a contention that it is similar to two-stage Pentecostalism. In his sermons on Rom 8:16, which were preached at Westminster Chapel in 1961 and appear in *The Sons of God*, he attempts to show that his doctrine of Spirit baptism is not "something new and strange" but is the old doctrine of assurance that had been generally taught from the seventeenth to the nineteenth centuries.[3] To prove this, he provides many quotations related to the traditional experimental view of assurance arranged in chronological order from the seventeenth to the nineteenth century. Of note among the quotations are the earliest ones from the seventeenth century since they unveil the source from which the older experimental doctrine of assurance originated.

In his twenty-fifth and twenty-seventh sermons in *The Sons of God*, Lloyd-Jones quotes the writings and sermons on Rom 8:16 and Eph 1:13 of seventeenth-century figures such as John Owen, Thomas Brooks (1608–1680), John Preston (1587–1628), Thomas Horton (?–1673), William Guthrie,[4] Richard Sibbes, Edward Elton (1569–1624), and Thomas Goodwin, all of whom were Puritans. As will be discussed in more detail in the next section, Puritans were battling on a theological/pastoral front against nominalism and intellectualism in the Church of England. Their emphasis on a profound religious experience as well as their vision for restoring a true religion brought about the development of the doctrine of assurance (the witness of the Spirit), which exhorted believers to seek after further experiential assurance of their salvation as well as of God's love.

Importantly, at the time Lloyd-Jones preached these sermons (1961), he was convinced that the most significant problem of the church to be dealt with was believism: "the false doctrine which would have us 'take it by faith' and not to be concerned at all about our feelings." For Lloyd-Jones, the assertion that baptism with the Spirit is identical with regeneration and

2. Murray, David Martyn Lloyd-Jones: The *Fight of Faith*, 691.

3. Lloyd-Jones, *Romans: The Sons of God*, 338.

4. Even though Guthrie was a Scottish Presbyterian, he was one of several who were united with England's Puritans in terms of "the closest spiritual bonds of doctrine, worship, and church order" (Beeke and Pederson, *Meet the Puritans*, 647). In this respect, he can be considered a Puritan.

therefore not experiential is another form of believism.[5] He was persuaded that Puritans' doctrine of assurance, which had been neglected for a long time and which emphasized the experiential work of the Holy Spirit in general and the immediate work of the Spirit to the believer in particular, would be the effective remedy for the cold believism that was pervasive in his days. Eight partial excerpts of Lloyd-Jones's quotations from these Puritans' writings exemplify his stance.

The first three quotations come from Lloyd-Jones's twenty-fifth sermon in *The Sons of God*. In this sermon, Lloyd-Jones quotes three seventeenth-century Puritans—John Preston, John Owen, and Thomas Brooks—in succession to refute the assertion that none of the Puritans held the view that "believing must precede the testimony of the Holy Spirit."[6] In other words, Lloyd-Jones provides these quotations to support his argument that Puritans did not understand the sealing of the Spirit (or the witness of the Spirit) as identical with regeneration. After giving a brief introduction regarding each Puritan or his work, Lloyd-Jones cites each Puritan's statement related to the sealing (or witness) of the Spirit without explaining its original context in detail.

First, Lloyd-Jones quotes from John Preston's *The New Covenant or The Saints' Portion:*

> Now followes the testimony of God's Spirit; I named to you, Eph 1:13: Wherein after you believed, you were sealed with the Spirit of promise. When a man hath believed, and took Jesus Christ; secondly when he hath washed and purified himself, that is, he hath gone about his work, and so his own spirit gathers a testimony hence, That he is in a good estate; after he hath thus believed, then (saith he) comes the Holy Ghost, and seals the same things unto you, that is, the Lord leaves a man alone a while, as it were, to champ upon the bridle, (as I may say) he lets a man alone to some doubts and feares, that so he may purge himself the more carefully; but after a time, when a man hath put to his seal that God is true, then the Lord seals him again with the Spirit of promise; that is, the Lord sends the Spirit into his heart, and that Spirit gives witnesse to him, and when he hath put to

5. Lloyd-Jones, *Romans: The Sons of God*, 338.
6. Lloyd-Jones, *Romans: The Sons of God*, 318.

> his seal, that God is true, then the Lord puts to his seal, and assures him that he hath received him to mercy.[7]

This quotation is an excerpt from the twelfth sermon in *The New Covenant or The Saints' Portion*, dealing with the issue of how to find out whether one has the Spirit of the Son or not. In the sermon, Preston explains the differing effects of how the Spirit of bondage that Paul identifies in Rom 8:15 and the three testimonies articulated in 1 John 5:8—the blood, the water, and our own spirit—factor into a believer's assurance that he/she is a child of God.[8] Then, in this quotation, Preston describes the testimony of the Holy Spirit as the provision of an exceptional assurance of sonship that he identifies with the sealing of the Spirit in Eph 1:13.[9]

Then, Lloyd-Jones quotes John Owen's Of Communion with God the Father, Son, and Holy Ghost:

> When our spirits are pleading their right and title, He [the Holy Spirit] comes in and bears witness on our side, at the same time enabling us to put forth acts of filial obedience, kind and childlike, which is called "crying, Abba, Father." ... He doth it effectually, voluntarily, and freely. Hence sometimes the dispute hangs long, the case is pleading many years. The law seems sometimes to prevail, sin and Satan to rejoice, and the poor soul is filled with dread about its inheritance. Perhaps its own witness, from its faith, sanctification, former experience, keeps up the plea with some life and comfort; but the work is not done, the conquest is not fully obtained, until the Spirit who worketh freely and effectually, when and how He will, comes in with His testimony also. Clothing His power with a word of promise He makes all parties concerned to attend unto Him and puts an end to the controversy.[10]

This excerpt is from the third chapter of Part 3 ("Of Communion with God the Holy Ghost") in *Of Communion with God the Father, Son, and Holy Ghost*.

---

7. Preston, *New Covenant*, 340; Lloyd-Jones, *Romans: The Sons of God*, 318–19.

8. Preston, *New Covenant*, 334–49.

9. In the twenty-seventh sermon in *Romans: The Sons of God*, Lloyd-Jones quotes another two sections from the same work (Preston, *New Covenant*, 398–400, 354–55) that are related to sealing (witness) of the Spirit (Lloyd-Jones, *Romans: The Sons of God*, 340–41). I omit these quotations since I dealt with Preston's work here.

10. Owen, *Of Communion with God*, 164–65; Lloyd-Jones, *Romans: The Sons of God*, 320.

In the chapter, Owen explains nine effects of the Holy Spirit as a comforter in the believer.[11] As one of the effects, Owen presents the effectual witness of the Spirit to provide a Christian with an immediate assurance of his/her salvation, as the quotation describes.

Then, Lloyd-Jones quotes Thomas Brooks' *The Unsearchable Riches of Christ*:

> Christians, the high way to comfort is to mind comfort less and duty more. It is to mind more what thou shouldest do than what thou wouldest have, as you may see in Ephesians 1:13, "In whom ye also trusted, after that ye heard the word of truth, the gospel of your salvation: in whom also after that ye believed, ye were called with that Holy Spirit of promise." The original runs thus, "In whom believing, ye were sealed." While faith is busied and exercised about Christ and those varieties and excellences that are in Him, the Lord comes and by His Spirit seals up the life and love and glory of them.[12]

This quotation comes from Brooks' exposition of the second doctrine in this work: "all saints are not of an equal size and growth in grace and holiness." In this section, Brooks attempts to explain twelve features of weak Christians ("souls weak in grace"); the quotation belongs to the twelfth characteristic that he suggests: "weak saints mind their wages and veils more than their work." For Brooks, Christians' wages are "joy, peace, comfort, and assurance"; their work is "waiting on God, believing in God, walking with God, acting for God." He argues that "there is no such way to joy, peace, and assurance, as this, to mind your work more than your wages."[13] Presenting Eph 1:13 as biblical evidence for this assertion, he emphasizes that Christians hardly enjoy assurance without exercising their faith.

Lloyd-Jones argues that all three quotations from these seventeenth century Puritans show their agreement to teach that "believing first, faith engaged about Christ, and the Spirit comes and seals it up to us."[14] However, we should note that there was an obvious disagreement among these Puritans regarding defining the sealing of the Spirit. For instance, both John Preston

---

11. Owen, *Of Communion with God*, 161–70.
12. Brooks, *Works* 3:60; Lloyd-Jones, *Romans: The Sons of God*, 321.
13. Brooks, *Works* 3:48, 59–60.
14. Lloyd-Jones, *Romans: The Sons of God*, 321.

and Thomas Brooks considered the sealing of the Spirit (Eph 1:13) and the witness of the Spirit (Rom 8:16) as the same spiritual blessing to give an immediate assurance of salvation.[15] On the other hand, John Owen, while acknowledging the extraordinary effect of the testimony of the Holy Spirit to the heart of a believer as his quotation above showed, disagreed, understanding the sealing of the Spirit in Eph 1:13 as a post-conversion work of the Spirit to give assurance. He argued that the sealing should be understood as "the effectual communication of the image of God to us" or "the communication of the Spirit unto us."[16] Nonetheless, overlooking (or without disclosing) this disagreement among them, Lloyd-Jones presents their statements in harmony to support his assertion that these seventeenth century Puritans understood the sealing of the Spirit as a post-conversion event to furnish a Christian with an immediate assurance.

The other five quotations come from Lloyd-Jones's twenty-seventh sermon in *The Sons of God*. In the sermon, Lloyd-Jones attempts to provide further historical evidence in a chronological order from the seventeenth to the nineteenth century that his understanding of the witness of the Spirit in Rom 8:16 as an experiential event of the Spirit to give an immediate assurance "has been taught regularly throughout the centuries," rather than representing "something new and strange."[17] In the same manner in which Lloyd-Jones lists the previous three quotations in the twenty-fifth sermon, he enumerates five quotations from other seventeenth-century Puritans—Thomas Horton, William Guthrie, Richard Sibbes, Edward Elton, and Thomas Goodwin—one by one without providing their original contexts in detail.

The first quotation is from Thomas Horton's Forty-six Sermons upon the Whole Eighth Chapter of the Epistle to the Romans:

> Wherever it [the witness of the Spirit] comes in the reality and the fulness of it, and so long as it remains upon the soul, it silences all objections, scatters all temptations, removes all scruples, and doubts whatsoever to the contrary, and sets the heart at perfect rest.[18]

---

15. See Preston, *New Covenant*, 340; Brooks, *Works* 3:81.

16. Owen, *Of Communion with God*, 165; Owen, *Works* 4:400. On this matter, Packer states: "Owen affirmed the reality of this witness by God's sovereign gift of supernatural joy, though he would not identify it with the 'seal'" (Packer, *Quest for Godliness*, 189).

17. Lloyd-Jones, *Romans: The Sons of God*, 338.

18. Horton, *Forty-six Sermons*, 246; Lloyd-Jones, *Romans: The Sons of God*, 341.

This quotation comes from the eighteenth sermon in the work, in which Horton deals with the witness of the Spirit in Rom 8:16. Horton divides the witness of the Spirit into "the witness of the Spirit to our spirits" ("distinctive and immediate testimony") and "the witness of the Spirit with our spirits" ("conjunctive and concurrent testimony"). For the former witness, Horton suggests its threefold property: "secret and inexpressible, certain and infallible, and inconstant and various."[19] The quotation that Lloyd-Jones uses is from the section in which Horton explains the second ("certain and infallible") qualification regarding the witness of the Spirit.

Then, Lloyd-Jones quotes William Guthrie's *The Christian's Great Interest*:

> It is a glorious divine manifestation of God unto the soul, shedding abroad God's love in the heart. It is a thing better felt than spoke of. It is no audible voice, but it is a ray of glory filling the soul with God, as He is life, light, love and liberty, corresponding to that audible voice, "O man, greatly beloved"; putting a man in a transport with this on his heart, "It is good to be here." ... O how glorious is this manifestation of the Spirit! Faith here rises to so full an assurance, that it resolves wholly into sensible presence of God. This is the thing which best deserves the title of *sensible presence*, and, it is probable, is not given to all believers, some whereof are all their days under bondage, and in fear; but here, love, almost perfect, casts our fear. This is so absolutely let out upon the Master's pleasure, and so transient or passing, or quickly gone, when it is, that no man may bring his gracious state into debate for want of it.[20]

This quotation is an excerpt from the sixth chapter of the work that addresses "the special communications of God, and the singular gracious operations of His Spirit." In the chapter, Guthrie suggests twelve kinds of special work of the Spirit; the quotation belongs to the tenth ("a glorious divine manifestation of the Spirit," or "sensible presence of God"). Although Lloyd-Jones presents the quotation as another Puritan work to support his understanding of the witness of the Spirit, it should be noted that Guthrie obviously held

---

19. Horton, *Forty-six Sermons*, 245.

20. Guthrie, *Christian's Great Interest*, 173–74; emphasis original; Lloyd-Jones, *Romans: The Sons of God*, 341–42.

a different position on the subject. Guthrie deals with "the witness of God's Spirit" in Rom 8:16 as the ninth kind of special work of the Spirit in the same chapter. In the section, he explains the witness of the Spirit as co-witness of the Spirit with the believer's spirit (or conscience), not as the Spirit's immediate witness to the believer's spirit.[21] At this point, contrary to Lloyd-Jones's assertion, we can assume that some Puritans, including Guthrie, understood the witness of the Spirit as the co-witness of the Spirit with the believer's spirit. The different positions among Puritans regarding the witness of the Spirit in Rom 8:16 will be discussed later.

Then, Lloyd-Jones moves on to the next quotation from Richard Sibbes's *A Fountain Sealed*:

> But oft it falls out, that our own spirits, though sanctified, cannot stand against a subtle temptation strongly enforced. God superadds His own Spirit. Guilt often prevails over the testimony of blood; that of water, by reason of stirring corruptions, runneth troubled. Therefore the third, the immediate testimony of the Spirit, is necessary to witness the Father's love to us, to us in particular, saying "I am thy salvation," Psalm 35:3, "thy sins are pardoned," Matthew 9:2. And this testimony the word echoeth unto, and the heart is stirred up and comforted with joy inexpressible. So that both our spirits and consciences, and the Spirit of Christ joining in one, strongly witness our condition in grace, that we are the sons of God.[22]

This quotation comes from Sibbes' expository work on Eph 4:30 ("And grieve not the Holy Spirit of God, whereby you are sealed unto the day of redemption" [KJV]). Expounding "whereby you are sealed," Sibbes introduces three witnesses concerning a Christian's joy and comfort based on 1 John 5:8 ("And there are three that bear witness in earth, the Spirit, and the water, and the blood" [KJV]): the blood (justification), the water (sanctification), and the Holy Spirit (the immediate testimony of the Spirit). He argues that these three witnesses are all appropriated to the Holy Spirit; the witness of the

21. Guthrie, *Christian's Great Interest*, 160, 172–73.
22. Sibbes, *Fountain Sealed*, 440; Lloyd-Jones, *Romans: The Sons of God*, 343.

Spirit, as the quotation shows, is a "superadded seal of the Spirit"[23] to fully assure Christians of their state in God's grace and love.

Then, Lloyd-Jones quotes Edward Elton's The Triumph of a True Christian Described, Or an Explanation of the Eighth Chapter of the Epistle to the Romans:

> I take it therefore that the witness and testimony of the Spirit here spoken of is an inward secret and unspeakable inspiration of the Spirit; the Holy Spirit of God inwardly, secretly, and in an unspeakable manner, informing our hearts and inwardly persuading us that God is our Father and pouring into our heart a secret, wonderful and unspeakable sweet sense and feeling of God's love to us. Not of God's ordinary or common love, but of His special and Fatherly love, that God loves us with such love as He bears to His only begotten Son Christ Jesus in whom we are adopted to be His children. As the Lord Jesus Himself speaks in that excellent prayer of His (John 17:23) that God loves us, we believing in Christ, as He hath loved Him, and to this purpose the Apostle speaks plainly (Rom 5:5); the Holy Spirit of God given to us doth infuse and pour into our hearts a sense and feeling of God's love to us in Christ.[24]

This quotation is from Elton's sermon expounding Rom 16:8. In the sermon, Elton explains the witness of the Spirit, even though it is given in an indescribable manner, as "common to all true believers in their measure," rather than as "any extraordinary and special revelation, appropriated and belonging to some excellent and special men."[25]

The final quotation consists of several excerpts from Thomas Goodwin's fifteenth sermon on the first chapter of Ephesians in which Goodwin expounds the thirteenth and the fourteenth verses:

> There is light that cometh and over-powereth a man's soul and assureth him that God is his, and he is God's, and that God loveth him from everlasting. ... It is a light beyond the light of ordinary faith ... the next thing to heaven; you have no more, you can have no more, till you come

23. Sibbes, *Fountain Sealed*, 439–40.
24. Elton, *Triumph of a True Christian Described*, 386; Lloyd-Jones, *Romans: The Sons of God*, 344.
25. Elton, *Triumph of a True Christian Described*, 385.

> thither. ... It is faith elevated and raised up above its ordinary rate. ... It is electing love of God brought home to the soul.[26]

As all the eight quotations above show, the seventeenth-century Puritans whom Lloyd-Jones quotes understood the sealing of the Spirit (Eph 1:13) or the witness of the Spirit (Rom 8:16) as giving a Christian full assurance of God's everlasting love for him/her in an extraordinary way. Likewise, Lloyd-Jones wants to show that the doctrine of assurance was actively propagated by Puritans in the seventeenth century. However, it should be noted that there was a significant difference of views concerning the witness of the Spirit and its role in assurance among the Puritans at the time. Some Puritans understood the witness of the Spirit as the co-witness of the Spirit with the believer's conscience. Other Puritans distinguished between the co-witness of the Spirit with the believer's spirit that "leaves in its wake the self-conscious conviction 'I am a child of God'" and the immediate witness of the Spirit to the believer's spirit that "speaks of the Spirit's pronouncement on behalf of the Father, 'You are a child of God.'"[27] A few of the latter group such as Sibbes and Goodwin believed that the direct testimony of the Spirit gives much higher assurance to the believer. As will be dealt with in more detail later, Lloyd-Jones's view on assurance stands in line with Sibbes and Goodwin. Despite this clear disagreement among the Puritans, Lloyd-Jones simply quotes a series of excerpts from their works referring to the doctrine of assurance in his sermon, making it appear as if all Puritans agree in considering the direct witness of the Spirit as the highest degree of assurance. To confront the dead orthodoxy and the cold believism of the mid-twentieth century, Lloyd-Jones demonstrates that his articulation of the doctrine of Spirit baptism stems from the seventeenth-century Puritans who sought assurance of salvation through the exceptional work of the Holy Spirit. However, as we will discuss later, many Puritans were wary of pursuing full assurance as provided through the direct testimony of the Spirit—the view Lloyd-Jones espouses—since they thought it could fall into the fallacies of mysticism or enthusiasm as exemplified by other groups, such as the Quakers.

---

26. Goodwin, *Exposition on Ephesians*, in 233, 236, 237; Lloyd-Jones, *Romans: The Sons of God*, 344.

27. Beeke, *Quest for Full Assurance*, 143.

In the twenty-seventh sermon, going a step further, Lloyd-Jones attempts to prove that the experiential view of assurance was commonly shared among Methodists and New England Puritans in the eighteenth century, also. Lloyd-Jones quotes partial excerpts from these figures' journals, sermons, or biographies to support this view. First, from the journal of George Whitefield, Lloyd-Jones quotes the following excerpt:

> After a long night of desertion and temptation, the star which I had seen at a distance before began to appear again, and the day star arose in my heart. Now did the Spirit of God take possession of my soul and, as I humbly hope, seal me unto the day of redemption. … Having now obtained mercy from God and received the Spirit of adoption in my heart, my friends were surprised to see me look and behave so cheerfully after the many reports they had had concerning me.[28]

Second, Lloyd-Jones quotes the recorded words of Jonathan Edwards:

> Once, as I rode out into the woods for my health, in 1737, having alighted from my horse in a retired place as my manner commonly has been, to walk for divine contemplation and prayer, I had a view that for me was extraordinary, of the glory of the Son of God as Mediator between God and man, and His wonderful, great, full pure and sweet grace and love, and meek and gentle condescension. This grace that appeared so calm and sweet appeared also great above the heavens. The Person of Christ appeared ineffably excellent, with an excellency great enough to swallow up all thought and conception, which continued, as near as I can judge, about an hour; which kept me the greater part of the time in a flood of tears, and weeping aloud. I felt an ardency of soul to be, what I know not otherwise how to express, emptied and annihilated; to lie in the dust and be full of Christ alone; to love Him with a holy and pure love; to trust Him; to live upon Him; and to serve and follow Him; and to be perfectly sanctified and made pure with a divine and heavenly purity.[29]

---

28. Whitefield, *George Whitefield's Journals*, 58–59; Lloyd-Jones, *Romans: The Sons of God*, 345.
29. Edwards, *Letters and Personal Writings*, 801; Lloyd-Jones, *Romans: The Sons of God*, 346.

Third, from John Wesley's sermon "The Witness of the Spirit," Lloyd-Jones quotes:

> Is not [the witness of the Spirit] something immediate and direct, not the result of reflection or argumentation? ... There may be foretastes of joy, of peace, of love, and those not delusive, but really from God, long before we have the witness in ourselves, before the Spirit of God witnesses with our spirits that we have redemption in the blood of Jesus, even the forgiveness of sins.[30]

Fourth, Lloyd-Jones quotes from Richard Bennett's biography of Howell Harris:

> [Howell Harris] piles the richest biblical phrases one on top of the other in an attempt to give adequate expression to what he felt and experienced that day. That was when his heart was cleansed from all idols and the love of God was shed abroad in his heart. Christ had entered in before, but now to sup. Now he had received the Spirit of adoption, whereby we cry, Abba, Father, and he began to desire to depart and to be with Christ. All fears were cast out for months and perfect love took their place.[31]

Before commenting further on this second set of excerpts from eighteenth-century Methodists and New England Puritans, a contrast needs to be made with the first set of excerpts from the seventeenth-century figures. In the case of the seventeenth century, as we saw earlier, Lloyd-Jones quotes the sermons or writings of the Puritans to prove the point that the Spirit witnesses directly to the spirit of the believer to provide full assurance, whereas in the case of the eighteenth century writers he mainly presents records regarding individual spiritual experiences of figures such as George Whitefield, Jonathan Edwards, and Howell Harris, all of whom Lloyd-Jones believes experienced Spirit baptism. In other words, most evidence regarding the doctrine of assurance of the eighteenth century presented by Lloyd-Jones is not in the form of doctrine. Rather, it can be regarded as his subjective interpretation concerning the eighteenth-century figures'

---

30. Wesley, *Sermons on Several Occasions*, 102, 108; Lloyd-Jones, *Romans: The Sons of God*, 347.
31. Bennett, *Early Life of Howell Harris*, 27; Lloyd-Jones, *Romans: The Sons of God*, 348–49.

spiritual experiences within the framework of his doctrine of Spirit baptism. Therefore, it is not clear whether those who are quoted by Lloyd-Jones also understood their personal experiences as an experience of receiving full assurance as did Lloyd-Jones. A case in point can be made with Edwards's understanding of full assurance, which differs significantly from Lloyd-Jones's in terms of an immediate work of the Spirit. Such issues will be discussed later.

What should be noted here is that most of the figures in the eighteenth century that Lloyd-Jones quotes were Calvinistic or Arminian Methodists, except Jonathan Edwards, who was a New England Puritan. As reviewed in Chapter Three, both Methodist groups, despite holding different opinions concerning the issue of predestination, substantially agreed upon the doctrine of assurance. Jonathan Edwards, also, is regarded as one of the successors of the English Puritans' doctrine of assurance.[32]

According to Lloyd-Jones, all quotations from these seventeenth- and eighteenth-century figures show "a strange and curious unanimity with regard to the character of the experience of knowing the witness of the Holy Spirit with our spirits that we are children of God."[33] Nonetheless, as noted earlier, there existed an obvious difference of a view regarding the witness of the Spirit among the seventeenth-century Puritans. Moreover, in the case of the evidence from the eighteenth-century that Lloyd-Jones presents, most of them represent his own interpretation regarding the eighteenth-century preachers' individual experiences rather than their own teachings on the witness of the Spirit. Therefore, his logical foundation for arguing the existence of unanimity concerning the doctrine in the eighteenth century is inevitably tenuous.

To sum up, one can demonstrate that the doctrine of assurance propagated in the seventeenth century among Puritans lasted into the eighteenth century among Welsh and English Methodists, along with New England Puritans as Lloyd-Jones argues. According to him, his doctrine of baptism with the Spirit also originated from the old Reformed doctrine of assurance, rather than being a novel doctrine or one originating from the Pentecostal teaching on the Spirit. However, when we look deeper into the doctrine of assurance, we find that there is a clear difference of positions in the matter

---

32. Haykin, *Jonathan Edwards*, 48–49.

33. Lloyd-Jones, *Romans: The Sons of God*, 356.

of the direct testimony of the Holy Spirit. Most of all, as we will see, Lloyd-Jones's position on the immediate witness of the Spirit seems to deviate from the traditional Reformed doctrine. I will argue that this deviation is attributable to his personal understanding and aspiration of revival that influenced his doctrine of assurance.

THE DOCTRINE OF ASSURANCE IN THE PURITAN TRADITION

What, then, is the doctrine of assurance in Puritan tradition? What was the historical background that prompted Puritans to bring about this distinctive doctrine? Answering these questions is important for an in-depth understanding of Lloyd-Jones's doctrine of Spirit baptism. As we will see, a theological concern arising from a particular understanding of salvation, in combination with a pastoral concern for personal assurance and in contrast to widespread nominalism in the English church, led Puritan divines to conceive of normative Christian experience as a series of experiential steps or stages toward full assurance and maturity of faith.

Assurance of salvation has two aspects: objective and subjective.[34] The former amounts to or consists of objective certitude based on God's eternal election and the certainty of salvation in Christ. The latter concerns a believer's inward consciousness of his/her salvation in Christ. Calvin and the early Reformers, who had fought against Semi-Pelagian Roman Catholic teaching that rejected the doctrine of an absolute predestination and the certainty of complete justification in Christ,[35] concentrated on the objective aspect of assurance of salvation that could not be lost in the middle of a believer's life. On the other hand, the Puritans, the successors of the Reformation, focused more on the subjective aspect of assurance due to their pastoral concern for how the believer could be assured of his/her own election and salvation.[36]

By the late sixteenth century, in the Puritans' eyes, dead orthodoxy as well as spiritual apathy were prevalent in the Church of England. They were deeply concerned that many people who had grown up in the church tended to regard God's saving grace as normal; there was, as the Puritans perceived it, a growing tendency among such people to consider a superficial

34. Dever, *Affectionate Theology of Richard Sibbes*, 193.
35. Berkhof, *Assurance of Faith*, 12–14.
36. Beeke, *Quest for Full Assurance*, 129.

acknowledgement of some doctrines sufficient to obtain their salvation.[37] For English Puritans, in the absence of a deep religious experience, which led one to "encounter in an existential way God's wrath and God's redemptive love,"[38] such nominal faith could not be regarded as "a true religion." English Puritanism was a movement intended to awaken spiritually apathetic Christians, lukewarm churches, and even the nation, prompting profound religious experience through preaching of the Word of God. The vision of Puritan preachers of that time can be summed up as "the revival of a true religion."[39]

The Puritans' aspiration for the revival of true religion, and their emphasis on a profound religious experience, resulted in significant development of the doctrine of assurance of salvation, or the witness of the Spirit. In particular, the English Puritans of the Spiritual Brotherhood,[40] such as Richard Greenham, William Perkins, Richard Sibbes, and Thomas Goodwin, contributed to the advancement of the doctrine. All four of them represent "traditional Puritan experimental spirituality,"[41] emphasizing the heartfelt element as the essence of true piety. Richard Greenham (1535–1594), remembered as the first great teacher of the Spiritual Brotherhood, has been called "the patriarch of Puritan divines" and "the fountainhead of the affectionate strain in Puritanism."[42] He was convinced that a preacher should set his/her mind to "edify the heart and conscience [of the listeners] ... to quicken affections to embrace true godliness." He recognized the "heart" as "the root of religion,"

37. Beeke, "William Perkins," 264.

38. Brauer, "Nature of English Puritanism," 101.

39. Pettit, *Heart Prepared*, 56.

40. The Spiritual Brotherhood refers to "a group of men for whom the Cambridge of the late sixteenth and early seventeenth centuries became a center of reforming activity, teaching, and training that eventually sent many of them throughout the rest of England and even to the Netherlands and to the New World" (Schaefer, *Spiritual Brotherhood*, locs. 51–67). In *The Rise of Puritanism*, Haller explains its origin as follows: "English Puritanism, denied opportunity to reform the established church, wreaked its energy during a half century and more upon preaching and, under the impetus of the pulpit, upon unchecked experiment in religious expression and social behavior. ... [These Puritans] preached the word of God in the same spirit and felt themselves to be members of a brotherhood" (*Rise of Puritanism*, 15, 53).

41. Haykin, *Jonathan Edwards*, 122.

42. Pettit, *Heart Prepared*, 48; Walton, *Jonathan Edwards*, 66.

where "the foundation of our faith must be laid."[43] Accordingly, his focus was not on "externals, but the inward, affective disposition."[44]

Such emotional and experiential insights on the part of Greenham and the earlier generations of the Spiritual Brotherhood, Walton argues, were organized into "a lucid, systemic presentation"[45] by William Perkins (1558–1602). Perkins is now considered "one of the predominant pastoral theologians in the second generation of the Spiritual Brotherhood"; his main interests were "pastoral and pneumatological."[46] In his introduction of *The Work of William Perkins*, Breward maintains that "Perkins believed assurance to be more important than justification in day to day Christian experience."[47] Against the dead orthodoxy that he perceived as prevalent in the Church of England, which "regarded mere assent to the truths of Scripture as sufficient for salvation," he felt the burden of teaching the congregation to "distinguish between assurance of personal grace and certainty based on mere assent to Bible truth." Perkins expended great effort to convince other pastors and preachers to "lead their flocks into a well-grounded assurance of their election and salvation."[48]

On the topic of assurance, Perkins made "a distinction between weak faith and strong faith." Weak faith shows a tendency toward "low levels of illuminating knowledge and of applying to the promises but shows itself by a serious desire to believe and an endeavor to obtain God's favor." By contrast, strong faith, namely full assurance, "claims God's promises as a personal possession."[49] For those with strong faith, Perkins said, "to believe in Christ, is not confusedly to believe that he is a Redeemer of mankind, but

43. Greenham, *Works*, 26, 271.

44. Walton, *Jonathan Edwards*, 67.

45. Walton, *Jonathan Edwards*, 75.

46. Walton, *Jonathan Edwards*, 74–75. Walton later argues, "A tradition of puritan theological discussion was focused not on the process of conversion, but on the nature and signs of regeneration, and on the distinction between genuine piety and pretense. ... Since questions concerning regeneration refer to the work of the Holy Spirit, the discussion of the signs of true piety, and the difference between the regenerate and the hypocrite, belongs properly to pneumatology" (134).

47. Perkins, *Work of William Perkins*, 85.

48. Beeke, "William Perkins," 264.

49. Beeke, "William Perkins," 268–69.

withal to believe that he is *my* Savior, and *I* am elected, justified, sanctified, and shall be glorified."[50]

According to Perkins, there are three grounds for assurance: (1) the promise of the gospel, (2) syllogistic reasoning, and (3) the testimony of the Holy Spirit. This three-fold division regarding the grounds of assurance came to be expressed later in *The Westminster Confession of Faith*[51] by the Westminster Assembly.[52] For Perkins, based on Rom 8:16, there are two witnesses regarding the assurance of salvation: "our spirit" and "the Holy Spirit." According to him, the former is so weak that God leads the Holy Spirit to testify together with a believer's spirit that he/she is a child of God.[53] As such, the witness (or testimony) of the Spirit is one of the significant grounds for believers to attain their full assurance, enjoying God's promises as their personal possession. Though weak faith is authentic faith, Perkins argued, Christians should continue to seek after strong faith (full assurance), "a fruit of faith ascertained by a personal, Spirit-worked appropriation of the benefits of faith."[54]

Richard Sibbes upheld, as Greenham and Perkins also had, "both a strongly theocentric doctrine of redemption and this deeply experiential, spiritual, and affectionate piety in which the human responds to grace." Like other members in the Spiritual Brotherhood, he argued that true religion should be "wholehearted, with the believer being intimately involved in growing in grace." Furthermore, as Perkins, his predecessor, did, he also devoted himself to preaching and teaching the doctrine of assurance. Dever asserts that Sibbes's understanding of assurance is the core characteristic of his preaching;[55] he emphasized the necessity of assurance as well as its spiritual benefits and comforts in most of his sermons.[56] For Sibbes, as Perkins also

50. Perkins, *Discourse of Conscience*, in *Works* 1:523; emphasis added.

51. Macpherson, *Westminster Confession of Faith*, 113–14. Chapter XVIII, "Of the Assurance of Grace and Salvation," says: "This certainty is not a bare conjectural and probable persuasion, grounded upon a fallible hope; but an infallible assurance of faith, founded upon the divine truth of the promises of salvation, the inward evidence of those graces unto which these promises are made, the testimony of the Spirit of adoption witness with our spirits that we are the children of God: which Spirit is the earnest of our inheritance, whereby we are sealed to the day of redemption" (§ii).

52. Beeke, *Quest for Full Assurance*, 87.

53. Keddie, "Unfallible Certenty," 242.

54. Beeke, "William Perkins," 269.

55. Dever, *Richard Sibbes*, 162.

56. Dever, *Richard Sibbes*, 162, 182.

maintained, assurance is not intrinsic to saving faith. To explain this, he used the notion of a "double act of faith." Dever summarizes this idea as follows:

> First there was "an act whereby the soul relies upon God as reconciled in Christ, and relies upon Christ as given of God, and relies upon the promise." This was the gift of saving faith every Christian had. Also, "there is a reflect act, whereby (by which), knowing we do thus, we have assurance." Yet this second act was not always done by all Christians. "We first by faith apply ourselves to God, and then apply God to us, to be ours; the first is the conflicting exercise of faith, the last is the triumph of faith; therefore faith properly is not assurance." Saving faith and assurance were not to be confused.[57]

For Sibbes, there are three kinds of Christians: (1) those who have saving faith but still live under a spirit of bondage, (2) those who are under the Spirit of adoption but still suffer from fears, and (3) those who have full assurance as a result of an immediate "sealing" of the Spirit.[58] He regards this sealing of the Spirit as the direct witness of the Spirit to the heart of a believer. For him, this immediate testimony is for the Spirit "to witness the Father's love to us, to us in particular, saying, 'I am thy salvation (Ps 35:3),' 'thy sins are pardoned (Matt 9:2).'"[59]

It should be noted that Sibbes used the expression "immediate" when he talked about full assurance. According to Nuttall, Sibbes led the way to see reason as having "an intuitive aspect as well as a discursive."[60] Whereas "discursive" knowledge represents little more than the application of reason in response to the testimony of Scripture, Sibbes explains an intuitive knowledge as follows: "It is a knowledge with a taste. ... God giveth knowledge *per modum gustus* [by the method of taste]. When things are to us as in themselves, then things have a sweet relish."[61] Sibbes believed that the highest degree of assurance was given by the immediate witness of the Spirit to the believer's spirit by direct application of the Word of God (intuitive), rather than

57. Dever, *Richard Sibbes*, 175–76.
58. Beeke and Jones, *Puritan Theology*, loc. 21949.
59. Sibbes, *Fountain Sealed*, 440.
60. Nuttall, *Holy Spirit in Puritan Faith*, 38.
61. Sibbes, *Yea and Amen*, in *Works* 4:334–35.

by the co-witness of the Spirit with his/her spirit by syllogistic reasoning (discursive).

Both the distinction between saving faith and full assurance and the teachings on the witness of the Spirit come from his pastoral concerns rather than academic ones. From Sibbes' pastoral experience, he found that many Christians were "content with the measure of faith and assurance they received upon their conversion and did not labor for further growth." He wanted to encourage them to strive for the advancement of their faith and assurance. Moreover, he was convinced that genuine assurance does not only result in "an increased desire for holiness and for more intimate communion with God," but also furnishes a Christian with "spiritual invulnerability."[62] His concern for the sealing of the Spirit—the direct witness of the Spirit—was to prompt "an experiential, behavioral, and character-modifying realization of the depth of the love of God"[63] in Christian living.

Thomas Goodwin, of a later generation of the Spiritual Brotherhood, continued this discussion about the witness of the Spirit. Regarding the subject of assurance, Packer argues that there is "an evident genealogical connection"[64] between Sibbes and Goodwin. As Sibbes had maintained, Goodwin also regarded assurance as "the triumph of faith," and therefore different from initial saving faith. He argued:

> Assurance comes in as a reward of faith. ... A man's faith must fight first, and have a conquest, and then assurance is the crown, the triumph of faith. ... And what tries faith more than temptation, and fears, and doubts, and reasonings against a man's own estate? That triumphing assurance, Romans 8:37–38 ... comes after a trial, as none are crowned till they have striven.[65]

For Goodwin, full assurance transforms a believer's entire life: "[Assurance] will make a man differ from himself in what he was before in that manner almost as conversion doth before he was converted. There is a new edition of all a man's graces."[66]Assurance, he believed, leads a Christian (1) to deepen

62. Beeke and Jones, *Puritan Theology*, locs. 21947, 21977, 21993; Dever, *Richard Sibbes*, 182.
63. Beeke and Jones, *Puritan Theology*, loc. 21993.
64. Packer, "Witness of the Spirit," loc. 351.
65. Goodwin, *Object and Acts of Justifying Faith*, in *Works* 8:346.
66. Goodwin, *Exposition on Ephesians*, 251.

his/her communion with God, (2) to promote his/her spiritual understanding, (3) to become bold and powerful in prayer, (4) to encourage holiness, (5) to become tireless in Christian service, and (6) to enjoy the "joy unspeakable and full[ness] of glory" mentioned in 1 Pet 1:8. Following Sibbes's teaching, Goodwin also believed that full assurance comes from the direct witness of the Spirit. He insisted that "Christians do not enjoy the full riches of assurance till they know, not merely the Spirit's indirect witness through conscience, but His direct witness also; those who lack it, therefore, should stir themselves up to seek it from God."[67]

However, it should be noted that even though Goodwin and Sibbes preferred intuitive or immediate assurance, they never attempted to disconnect the direct witness of the Spirit from the Word of God as did certain radical Puritans such as the Quakers.[68] For Goodwin, like Sibbes, the extraordinary experience of the direct testimony of the Spirit is given to a Christian's heart in an immediate way, but always through applying the Word to his/her heart:

> [W]e heard that Jesus Christ was sealed when he was baptized; but he was sealed by a promise, it was not by an immediate revelation only, but by bringing home a truth to his heart. What was it? "This is my beloved Son, in whom I am well pleased." This is a Scripture promise, you shall find it in Isa 42:1 "This is my servant, in whom I delight; my elect, in whom my soul is well pleased." That which had been spoken before of the Messiah is brought home to his heart. He sealeth not up his Son when he speaks from heaven immediately, but he doth it by a promise; therefore much more, my brethren, doth he seal up you. The Word and the Spirit are joined; they are joined in the new Jerusalem,

67. Packer, "Witness of the Spirit," locs. 417–30, 468–81.

68. In *The Holy Spirit in Puritan Faith and Experience*, Nuttall considers George Fox and the Quakers radical Puritans, asserting that they "repeat, extend, and fuse so much of what is held by the radical, Separatist party within Puritanism, that they cannot be denied the name or excluded from consideration" (13). Lloyd-Jones also regards them as a radical school of Puritanism. In his lecture "Further Reflections on the Baptism of the Spirit," he argues: "Puritanism, which started as one school of thought, divided up into two schools. On the one hand, you had George Fox and the Quakers, and on the other hand you had some of those great Puritan teachers such as John Owen, and Dr Thomas Goodwin in London. ... George Fox was most certainly calling attention to something vital but he went too far. He almost went to the point of saying that the Scriptures did not matter, that it was only this 'inner light' and the Spirit within that mattered, and the result of that has been that modern Quakerism—the Society of Friends—is almost entirely non-doctrinal and, indeed, at times almost reaches the point at which you would query whether it is even Christian" (*God the Holy Spirit*, 245).

> much more now. Isa 59:21, the promise there, that "my Word and my Spirit shall not depart out of thy mouth," is spoken of the calling of the Jews plainly, for the Apostle quoteth it in Rom 11:26. ... Therefore when we say, it is an immediate testimony, the meaning is not that it is without the Word; no, it is by a promise; but the meaning is, it is immediate in respect of using your own graces as an evidence and witness. ... We do not speak for enthusiasm; it is the Spirit applying to the Word to the heart that we speak of. ... He fasteneth the Word upon your hearts, sealeth you by a promise; therefore he is called a Spirit of promise.[69]

To summarize thus far, the doctrine of assurance in the Puritan tradition, which had developed among the pietistic Puritans in the Spiritual Brotherhood, can be stated as follows. First, they agreed that all believers do not necessarily enjoy full assurance since it is not intrinsic to saving faith but is rather a fruit or triumph of faith. Second, they recognized that there are degrees of faith as well as degrees of assurance among Christians. Third, therefore, they encouraged all believers to continue to seek this personal experience of full assurance. Lastly, the seventeenth-century pietistic Puritans such as Sibbes and Goodwin placed more emphasis on the intuitive aspect of assurance (an immediate witness of the Spirit to the believer's spirit) than on a discursive one (a co-witness of the Spirit with the believer's conscience by syllogistic reasoning), but without any disconnection between the Word and the Spirit.

Nonetheless, it should be noted that there existed an obvious disagreement regarding the witness of the Spirit among the Puritans in the seventeenth century, in particular, among the writers of the Westminster Confession. Some writers understood the witness of the Spirit as "the co-witness of the Spirit with the believer's spirit." They argued that "the Spirit's witness referred exclusively to His activity in connection with the syllogisms, whereby He brings conscience to unite with His witness that the Christian is a child of God." These Puritans held this position in order to stand against mysticism and antinomianism that focused on the direct witness of the Spirit, while disregarding any fruit of faith.[70]

---

69. Goodwin, *Exposition on Ephesians*, in *Works* 1:249–50.

70. Beeke, *Quest for Full Assurance*, 142–43.

Other writers of the Westminster Confession, including Thomas Goodwin, distinguished between "the co-witness of the Spirit with the believer's spirit" and "the immediate witness of the Spirit to the believer's spirit." According to Beeke, Puritans can be divided into two groups depending on their regard for which witness of the Spirit is more powerful and higher. The most accepted approach among them, Beeke argues, was to regard the co-witness of the Spirit as more spiritual and helpful than the direct witness of the Spirit.[71] However, as noted above, Goodwin regarded the direct witness of the Spirit as much more powerful than the co-witness of the Spirit. Accordingly, we should consider that even though the doctrine of assurance was one of the prevalent old Reformed doctrines propagated by the Puritans in the seventeenth century, there existed a significant difference of opinion over the witness of the Spirit and its role in assurance.

When we look at Lloyd-Jones's general understanding of assurance, it is not significantly different from Puritan tradition in that Lloyd-Jones also argued that there is an apparent distinction between saving faith and an assurance of faith; Christians should earnestly seek full assurance since it is the blessing that the children of God are offered to enjoy without limit of time and place. However, specifically with respect to the witness of the Spirit, his understanding of assurance should be considered as belonging to the pietistic Puritans of the seventeenth century in the Spiritual Brotherhood, such as Richard Sibbes and Thomas Goodwin, who placed more emphasis on the direct witness of the Spirit rather than on the co-witness of the Spirit, arguing that full assurance was given as a result of the former.[72] Lloyd-Jones also believed that the affective or experiential testimony of the Spirit, and not simply intellectual conviction inspired by the Spirit, was what gives a Christian full assurance of salvation without fear and doubt. As both Sibbes and Goodwin asserted, he also regarded the immediate witness of the Spirit as the highest assurance, while assurance given by deduction from Scripture or by evidence of change in a Christian's life he considered less important than the direct testimony of the Spirit. Thus, it can be argued that Lloyd-Jones's doctrine of assurance was inherited from a Puritan view of assurance;

---

71. Beeke, *Quest for Full Assurance*, 143–44.

72. In this regard, Randall argues, "One leading Puritan influence on Lloyd-Jones was Thomas Goodwin" ("Martyn Lloyd-Jones and Methodist Spirituality," 108).

with respect to the witness of the Spirit, in particular, his understanding follows the Puritans who emphasized the direct witness of the Spirit in giving full assurance to a Christian.

Nonetheless, there are two significant concerns that should be dealt with before we can accept Lloyd-Jones's argument that his doctrine of Spirit baptism was fully in line with the Puritans' experiential understanding of full assurance. First, as suggested in the previous chapter in discussion of Lloyd-Jones's interpretation regarding Daniel Rowland's, Howell Harris', and George Whitefield's experience of assurance, we should consider that there may exist an element of Lloyd-Jones's subjective interpretation of these men's experiences, even though he presents numerous quotations from historical materials as objective evidence. Second, the Puritan tradition regarding assurance never attempted to separate the work of the Spirit from the Word of God, even when it came to emphasizing the immediate testimony of the Spirit to the heart of a believer, standing firmly against enthusiasm or mysticism. By contrast, Lloyd-Jones's doctrine of Spirit baptism opens the possibility of the direct work of the Spirit apart from the Word of God.

LLOYD-JONES'S INTERPRETATION OF GREAT PREACHERS' CRUCIAL EXPERIENCES

When Lloyd-Jones's lectures and sermons regarding Spirit baptism are examined, it is apparent that he frequently quotes the records of preachers' spiritual experiences to provide historical evidence for his argument. With respect to assurance of salvation, he quotes the cases of John Flavel, Jonathan Edwards, John Wesley, George Whitefield, Howell Harris, D. L. Moody (1837–1899), and Christmas Evans. The question, however, is whether or not they themselves thought of their experiences as full assurance of salvation (or the witness of the Spirit), as Lloyd-Jones claims. Furthermore, apart from their experiences, their opinions on the witness of the Spirit may have been different from Lloyd-Jones's view. For these matters, I will review the experiences of John Flavel, Jonathan Edwards, and George Whitefield, all of whom were Reformed preachers from whom Lloyd-Jones frequently quotes.

John Flavel

Lloyd-Jones often referred to John Flavel's personal experience that he had on a particular journey, describing what the experience of the sealing of the Spirit (the immediate work of the Spirit) would be like. The concise excerpt from Flavel's *Treatise of the Soul of Man* that Lloyd-Jones used four times in his sermons or lectures is as follows:

> Thus going on his way his thoughts began to swell and rise higher and higher like the waters in Ezekiel's vision till at last they became an overflowing flood. Such was the intention of his mind, such the ravishing tastes of heavenly joys, and such the full assurance of his interest therein, that he utterly lost a sight and sense of this world and all the concerns thereof, and for some hours he knew no more where he was than if he had been in a deep sleep upon his bed. Arriving in great exhaustion at a certain spring he sat down and washed, earnestly desiring that if it were God's pleasure, that it might be his parting place from this world. Death had the most amiable face in his eyes that ever he beheld, except the face of Jesus Christ which made it so, and he could not remember, though he believed himself dying, that he had one thought of his dear wife or children or any other earthly concernment. On reaching his Inn the influence still continued, banishing sleep. Still, still the joy of the Lord overflowed him, and he seemed to be an inhabitant of the other world. He many years after called that day one of the days of heaven, and said that he understood more of the light of heaven by it than by all the books he ever read or discoveries he ever had entertained about it.[73]

However, Flavel himself understood his experience as an example of a mediate testimony of the Spirit to lead a believer to sense "foretastes of heaven" given as a result of exercising his/her faith and examining his/her heart with blessing of the Spirit. According to Flavel, the unusual experience came to him as he was seeking "a close examination of the state of his soul, and then of the life to come, and the manner of its being, and living in

73. Flavel, *Treatise of the Soul of Man*, 210–12. Lloyd-Jones quotes this excerpt in *God's Ultimate Purpose* (276), *God the Holy Spirit* (248–49), and *Joy Unspeakable* (79, 111). Although Flavel introduces the story in third person ("this account of a Minister"), it is known that he wrote about his experience. Lloyd-Jones, too, grasps the minister in the narration as Flavel himself.

heaven, in the views of all those things which are now pure objects of faith and hope."[74] Flavel, in his other work, argued, "I will not deny but there may be an immediate testimony of the Spirit; but sure I am his mediate testimony by his graces in us, is his usual way of sealing believers."[75] Therefore, after offering his experience as an example, he concluded, "This was, indeed, an extraordinary foretaste of heaven for degree, but it came in the ordinary way and method of faith and meditation."[76]

More importantly, Flavel did not understand the sealing of the Spirit only as an immediate work of the Spirit to the soul of a believer as Lloyd-Jones asserts.[77] Rather, Flavel argued that the sealing of the Spirit is usually given in a mediated manner (for example, "subjecting his understanding to the Scriptures, and comparing his own heart with them") rather than in an immediate manner, while being wary of being too dependent on the direct work of the Spirit to attain assurance of salvation.[78]

George Whitefield

Another quotation that Lloyd-Jones used twice to describe the sealing of the Spirit is George Whitefield's personal testimony regarding his new birth experience that took place in the spring of 1735:

> Soon after this, I found and felt in myself that I was delivered from the burden that had so heavily oppressed me. The spirit of mourning was taken from me, and I knew what it was truly to rejoice in God my Saviour: and, for some time, could not avoid singing psalms wherever I was; but my joy gradually became more settled, and, blessed be God, has abode and increased in my soul, saving a few casual intermissions, ever since. Thus were the days of my mourning ended. After a long night of desertion and temptation, the Star, which I had seen at a distance before, began to appear again, and the Day Star arose in my

74. Flavel, *Treatise of the Soul of Man*, 210.
75. Flavel, *Reply to Mr. Cary's Solemn Call*, in *Whole Works* 6:354.
76. Flavel, *Treatise of the Soul of Man*, 212.
77. Lloyd-Jones, *God's Ultimate Purpose*, 274.
78. Flavel, *Saint Indeed*, in *Whole Works* 5:434; Flavel, *Reply to Mr. Cary's Solemn Call*, 354.

> heart. Now did the Spirit of God take possession of my soul, and, as I humbly hope, seal me unto the day of redemption.[79]

This excerpt from Whitefield's journal indicated to Lloyd-Jones that Whitefield had already been regenerated some time before the experience; he received the sealing of the Spirit in this post-conversion experience.[80]

Nonetheless, as indicated in the previous chapter, Whitefield himself regarded this experience as his new birth experience. He understood conversion as a gradual process rather than a singular event. In his sermon "Repentance and Conversion," Whitefield stated: "At first it [conversion] begins with terror and legal sorrow, afterwards it leads to joyfulness; first we work for spiritual life, afterwards from it: first we are in bondage, afterwards we receive the Spirit of adoption to long and thirst for God, because he has been pleased to let us know that he will take us to heaven."[81] His appreciation of conversion as a process is reflected in the account in his journal regarding the process of his dramatic new birth. According to his journal, being handed a copy of Henry Scougal's *The Life of God in the Soul of Man* by Charles Wesley, a member of the Holy Club, shocked him into realizing that he was not a Christian but a man who needed to be born again. Whitefield wrote about the life-changing moment that took place in 1734, when he was 19 years old:

> At my first reading it, I wondered what the author meant by saying, "That some falsely placed religion in going to church, doing hurt to no one, being constant in the duties of the closet, and now and then reaching out their hands to give alms to their poor neighbours," "Alas!" thought I, "if this be not true religion, what is?" God soon showed me; for in reading a few lines further, that "true religion was union of the soul with God, and Christ formed within us," a ray of Divine light was instantaneously darted in upon my soul, and from that moment, but not till then, did I know that I must be a new creature.[82]

---

79. Whitefield, *George Whitefield's Journals*, 58. Lloyd-Jones quotes this excerpt in *God's Ultimate Purpose* (277) and *Romans: The Sons of God* (345).

80. Lloyd-Jones, *God's Ultimate Purpose*, 278. Introducing the experience of Whitefield, Lloyd-Jones states, "He [Whitefield] had been a believer for some time before this (experience)" (278).

81. Whitefield, *Sermons on Important Subjects*, 664.

82. Whitefield, *George Whitefield's Journals*, 47.

Since he was convinced that his soul "must totally be renewed ere it could see God," having spent many days groaning deeply with pain and despair, he wrote, "God only knows how many nights I have lain upon my bed groaning under the weight I felt. ... Whole days and weeks I spent in lying prostrate on the ground."[83]

However, after undergoing such appalling days of agonies, Whitefield eventually had a dramatic experience of new birth—the event Lloyd-Jones interprets as Whitefield's sealing of the Spirit—which happened in the spring of 1735. It should be noted that the excerpt regarding the experience that Lloyd-Jones uses comes from *A Short Account*, one of the early editions of Whitefield's journal, published in 1740, which dealt with the days from his early life to his ordination in 1735.[84] In the revised edition of his journal, published in 1756, he rewrote the experience with more mature reflection:

> After having undergone innumerable buffetings of Satan, and many months inexpressible trials by night and day under the spirit of bondage, God was pleased at length to remove the heavy load, to enable me to lay hold on His dear Son by a living faith, and, by giving me the spirit of adoption, to seal me, as I humbly hope, even to the day of everlasting redemption. But oh! with what joy—joy unspeakable—even joy that was full of, and big with glory, was my soul filled, when the weight of sin went off, and an abiding sense of the pardoning love of God, and a full assurance of faith broke in upon my disconsolate soul! Surely it was the day of my espousals, —a day to be had in everlasting remembrance. At first my joys were like a spring tide, and, as it were, overflowed the banks. Go where I would, I could not avoid singing of psalms aloud; afterwards it became more settled—and, blessed be God, saving a few casual intervals, had abode and increased in my soul ever since.[85]

According to his account in this revised edition, Whitefield describes the period from the day of realizing the necessity of the new birth to the day of the dramatic experience as living "under the spirit of bondage." Although

83. Whitefield, *George Whitefield's Journals*, 50, 52.

84. Whitefield, *George Whitefield's Journals*, 13. Whitefield wrote this account in 1739, when he was twenty-four years old.

85. Whitefield, *George Whitefield's Journals*, 58.

Lloyd-Jones argues that Whitefield went through the new birth at some point, there is no evidence in Whitefield's records during this period. In other words, for Whitefield, the unforgettable experience recorded above was the new birth experience. He illustrated the moment as receiving "the spirit of adoption" as well as "the sealing of the Spirit" ("God was pleased ... to seal me ... even to the day of everlasting redemption"). Therefore, it appears that Whitefield understood "the Spirit of adoption," or "the sealing of the Spirit," as taking place at the moment of regeneration, rather than as a post-conversion experience. More importantly, Whitefield believed that the new birth is identical with being baptized with the Spirit. In his sermon "Repentance and Conversion," Whitefield, emphasizing the necessity of true conversion to come into heaven, while warning against the notion of water baptism as the new birth, argues: "For to be baptized when young, or, as some, to come out of the water at age, and turn out as bad as ever, is a plain proof of the necessity of being baptized by the Holy Ghost."[86] From this evidence, we can confirm that Lloyd-Jones's interpretation of Whitefield's experience is significantly different from Whitefield's own; Whitefield understood the sealing of the Spirit (or baptism with the Spirit) as given at the moment of the new birth, whereas Lloyd-Jones understood it as a post-conversion event.

Furthermore, Whitefield opposed the view that the witness of the Spirit entails the immediate communication from the Spirit in the mode of an impression on the imagination. In *Jonathan Edwards: A New Biography*, Murray introduces a personal conversation between George Whitefield and Samuel Hopkins (1721–1803) regarding the witness of the Spirit that they had in 1770. Hopkins asked about Whitefield's position concerning the witness of the Spirit by posing two different definitions: (1) "an impression on the imagination, by some immediate communication from the Spirit, that your sins are forgiven, and that you are a child of God," or (2) "an influence of the Spirit of God, exciting such a love for God and Jesus Christ, such clear views of their character, as that the subject of it knows from experience and from Scripture, that he is a child of God and an heir of salvation."[87] Whitefield said that the latter was more in accord with his view, while rejecting the former,

86. Whitefield, *Sermons on Important Subjects*, 665.

87. Murray, *Jonathan Edwards*, 490, quoted in Hopkins, *Works of Samuel Hopkins* 1:87.

more enthusiastic position.[88] Likewise, Whitefield, as an heir of the theology of the Puritans,[89] was convinced that a believer could attain assurance as a child of God by self-examination with the Scriptures, confirming his/her bearing the fruit of sanctification, and the witness of the Spirit with his/her conscience, while opposing the enthusiasm that relied upon the immediate revelation of the Spirit for assurance.

Jonathan Edwards

The excerpt below from Edwards's record regarding his personal experience in 1737 is quoted six times in Lloyd-Jones's sermons and lectures on Spirit baptism:

> Once, as I rode out into the woods for my health, in 1737, having alighted from my horse in a retired place as my manner commonly has been, to walk for divine contemplation and prayer, I had a view that for me was extraordinary, of the glory of the Son of God as Mediator between God and man, and His wonderful, great, full pure and sweet grace and love, and meek and gentle condescension. This grace that appeared so calm and sweet appeared also great above the heavens. The Person of Christ appeared ineffably excellent, with an excellency great enough to swallow up all thought and conception, which continued, as near as I can judge, about an hour; which kept me the greater part of the time in a flood of tears, and weeping aloud. I felt an ardency of soul to be, what I know not otherwise how to express, emptied and annihilated; to lie in the dust and be full of Christ alone; to love Him with a holy and pure love; to trust Him; to live upon Him; and to serve and follow Him; and to be perfectly sanctified and made pure with

88. Murray, *Jonathan Edwards*, 490.

89. Haykin, *Revived Puritan*, 71. Haykin describes Whitefield's lifelong commitment to reading the Puritan works as follows: "And despite the busyness of his life, he found time to read and digest not only Bunyan's writings, but also such Puritan works as *Human Nature in Its Four-fold State* by Thomas Boston (1677–1732), Thomas Goodwin's commentary on various passages from Paul's letter to the Ephesians, *The Christian in Complete Armour* by William Gurnall (1617–1679), the annotations on the Scriptures by Samuel Clarke (1626–1701), and some of the works of John Owen (1616–1683). He also read and warmly recommended other Puritan divines, men like John Flavel (*c.*1630–1691), John Howe (1630–1706), Solomon Stoddard (1643–1729), Thomas Halyburton (1674–1712), and was familiar with the life of Philip Henry (1631–1696)" (73–74).

> a divine and heavenly purity. I have several other times had views very much of the same nature, and which have had the same effects.[90]

There is, however, some doubt that Edwards accepted his experience as the sealing of the Spirit, or the witness of the Spirit, as Lloyd-Jones suggests.[91] As Donald Macleod points out in *The Spirit of Promise*, the experience did not bring about full assurance of God's love for him as Lloyd-Jones defines the sealing of the Spirit, but rather "an ardency of soul to be emptied and annihilated; to lie in the dust, and to be full of Christ alone."[92] Furthermore, for Edwards, the sealing of the Spirit was intimately related to the sanctifying influence of the Spirit. In *The Religious Affections*, he argues:

> And when the Scripture speaks of the seal of the Spirit, it is an expression which properly denotes, not an immediate voice or suggestion, but some work or effect of the Spirit, that is left as a divine mark upon the soul, to be an evidence, by which God's children might be known. ... When God sets his seal on a man's heart by his Spirit, there is some holy stamp, some image impressed and left upon the heart by the Spirit, as by the seal upon the wax. And this holy stamp, or impressed image, exhibiting clear evidence to the conscience, that the subject of it is the child of God, is the very thing which in Scripture is called the seal of the Spirit, and the witness, or evidence of the Spirit. And this image enstamped by the Spirit on God's children's hearts, is his own image: that is the evidence by which they are known to be God's children, that they have the image of their Father stamped upon their hearts by the spirit of adoption.[93]

Edwards's understanding of the sealing of the Spirit (or the witness of the Spirit) as "the sanctifying communication and influence of the Spirit"[94] shows a demonstrable difference from Lloyd-Jones's view of sealing as the immediate work of the Spirit. More importantly, expounding Rom 8:15–16,

---

90. Edwards, *Letters and Personal Writings*, 801. Lloyd-Jones quotes it in *Puritans* (357–58), *God the Holy Spirit* (249–50), *Revival* (411), *Joy Unspeakable* (79), *God's Ultimate Purpose* (276), and *Romans: The Sons of God* (346).

91. Lloyd-Jones, *God's Ultimate Purpose*, 276; *Romans: The Sons of God*, 346.

92. Macleod, *Spirit of Promise*, 53.

93. Edwards, *Religious Affections*, in *Works* 2:232.

94. Edwards, *Religious Affections*, 237.

Edwards offers the syllogistic reasoning that when a Christian realizes that he/she loves God, he/she can be assured of his/her salvation. This serves as the fundamental means of attaining assurance, a position distinct from the one that emphasizes the direct testimony of the Spirit to the believer's spirit, such as with an immediate impression or revelation for full assurance. Edwards explains this as follows:

> The Apostle says, we haven't received the spirit of bondage, or of slaves, which is a spirit of fear; but we have received the more ingenuous noble spirit of children, a spirit of love, which naturally disposes us to go to God, as children to a father, and behave towards God as children. And this is the evidence or witness which the Spirit of God gives us that we are children ... it disposes us to go to God, and behave ourselves towards God as children; and it gives us clear evidence of our union to God as his children, and so casts out fear. So that it appears that the witness of the Spirit the Apostle speaks of, is far from being any whisper, or immediate suggestion or revelation; but that gracious holy effect of the Spirit of God in the hearts of the saints, the disposition and temper of children, appearing in sweet childlike love to God, which casts out fear, or a spirit of a slave.[95]

Based on the quotes given above, it is clear that the three preachers' understandings of their personal experiences are actually quite different from the interpretation presented by Lloyd-Jones to support his argument on the sealing of the Spirit. Their opinions on the sealing of the Spirit are also different from Lloyd-Jones'. What is common among these old Reformed preachers is that all of them were very wary of the attitude of relying too much on the direct testimony of the Spirit, especially when disconnected from the Word of Scripture and evidence of a sanctified life, to obtain full assurance of salvation, since they believed such assurance could be "too ephemeral and too often deluding."[96] It can be hardly denied that each of them reported profound personal experiences of the Spirit, even though they argued that such experiences should not be trusted too much. This position needs to be considered in its historical context, since the Puritans

95. Edwards, *Religious Affections*, 238.

96. Cherry, *Theology of Jonathan Edwards*, 144.

and the Methodists were fighting against the Anglican and the Old Lights' accusation that they were "enthusiasts." So, they all had profoundly "enthusiastic" experiences, but were very careful to call them something else. As surveyed earlier, even the minority opinion among Puritans (Richard Sibbes and Thomas Goodwin) who placed more emphasis on the immediate witness of the Spirit, regarded claiming the direct work of the Spirit apart from the Word as falling into the fallacy of enthusiasm. Importantly, Lloyd-Jones, even though he argues that his doctrine of assurance was inherited from the Puritan tradition, opens the possibility of the immediate witness of the Spirit apart from the Word of God, unlike the Puritans he quotes.

THE IMMEDIATE WITNESS OF THE SPIRIT APART FROM THE WORD OF GOD

In *Prove All Things*, Lloyd-Jones provides some general principles for testing whether a particular experience is a genuine work of the Spirit or not. He first suggests that believers should "always be suspicious of anything that claims to be a fresh revelation of truth." Second, "if what someone claims is a message from the Spirit, contradicts quite patently a teaching of the Scripture, again you reject it." Third, "anything that is merely spectacular should always be regarded with suspicion, or anything that we perceive with our minds and reasons to be foolish should always be under suspicion."[97] From these general principles and in agreement with the Puritans, Lloyd-Jones rejects any possibility that the direct work of the Spirit could be in conflict with the teachings of the Scripture or that a new revelation of truth could be given apart from the Word of God.

However, Lloyd-Jones opens the possibility that the immediate work of the Spirit can take place without being directly connected to the preaching of the Word. He does not emphasize the absolute necessity of the Word as the precondition for the direct work of the Spirit. For him, this does not cause any theological problems as long as the message delivered by the direct work of the Spirit does not contradict the teaching of the Scripture, as his general principles above suggest. In his sermon "Doctrinal Impurity," he argues:

97. Lloyd-Jones, *Prove All Things*, 79, 82, 85.

> What so many are disputing and denying and ignoring, is what I would call the immediate and direct action of the Holy Spirit. They say that the Spirit only works through the Word, and that we must not expect anything from the Spirit apart from that which comes immediately through the Word. And so, it seems to me, they are quenching the Spirit, because I read in Acts 13 that the Holy Ghost said unto the church at Antioch, "Separate me Barnabas and Saul ..." And I read in chapter 15 that the council in Jerusalem said, "It seemed good to the Holy Ghost, and to us ..." I read in chapter 16 that Paul was anxious to preach the gospel in Asia but the Spirit "suffered him not." He wanted to preach in Bithynia, and the Holy Spirit restrained him and stopped him. The living, powerful, activity of the Spirit; the Spirit coming directly, as it were, and controlling, and leading, and guiding, and giving orders, and indicating what was to be done; the Spirit descending upon them; that is what you always have in revival. But that is the thing that seems to have gone entirely out of the minds of men and women.[98]

In The Sons of God, he makes the same argument:

> [T]he assurance does not always come through the Scripture. It has happened to many without any words at all; it is just an inner consciousness in the spirit given by the Spirit of God Himself apart from Scripture. I am much concerned to emphasize this, and for this reason, that there are some who have disputed it. Some of the Puritans did so. They were so afraid of the Quakers who arose at the same time, that they went so far as to say that you can never have this experience of assurance apart from the Word. In my view that is quite mistaken. The Quakers were undoubtedly wrong in much of their teaching. Some of them said that the Word did not matter at all, and that what counted was the "inner light," and the work of the Spirit directly and immediately. That is clearly unscriptural, because the Scripture has been given by the Spirit. But we must not go to the extreme of saying that He can never deal with us immediately and directly, and without the Word, for He has often done so. ... We must be careful lest, in our fear

98. Lloyd-Jones, *Revival*, 53.

> of a certain emphasis on the part of people who talk much about the Holy Spirit, we may become guilty of "quenching the Spirit." Normally, this testimony is given through the Word, but it can be given without the Word.[99]

As has been discussed so far, the traditional Puritan view on the witness of the Spirit, including the most progressive Puritans, never acknowledged any attempt to separate the testimony of the Spirit, whether indirect or direct, from the Word of God. In this regard, it should be noted that Lloyd-Jones's position on the possibility of the immediate witness of the Spirit apart from Scripture can be regarded as a notable deviation from the old Puritan doctrine of assurance. In addition, with respect to understanding of the "immediate" operation of the Spirit, there is a significant chasm between Edwards and Lloyd-Jones. For Edwards, the immediacy of the Spirit does not mean the severance of the Spirit from the Word.[100] The meaning of "immediacy" is that God works on souls by using the Word (Scripture or preaching) as a means, but God's works are not restricted to this means, nor accomplished by the power of this means. It is an expression to indicate that all these things are ultimately done by the power of God. In his sermon "A Divine and Supernatural Light," Edwards clearly states:

> When it is said that this light [a divine and supernatural light] is given immediately by God, and not obtained by natural means, hereby is intended, that 'tis given by God without making use of any means that operate by their own power, or a natural force. God makes use of means; but 'tis not as mediate causes to produce this effect. There are not truly any second causes of it; but it is produced by God immediately. The Word of God is no proper cause of this effect: it don't operate by any natural force in it. The Word of God is only made use of to convey to the mind the subject matter of this saving instruction: and this indeed it doth convey to us by natural force or influence. It conveys to our minds these and those doctrines; it is the cause of the notion of them in our heads, but not of the sense of the divine excellency of them in our hearts. Indeed a person can't have spiritual light

99. Lloyd-Jones, *Romans: The Sons of God*, 307.
100. Cherry, *Theology of Jonathan Edwards*, 44.

> without the Word. But that don't argue, that the Word properly causes that light. The mind can't see the excellency of any doctrine, unless that doctrine be first in the mind; but the seeing the excellency of the doctrine may be immediately from the Spirit of God; though the conveying of the doctrine or proposition itself may be by the Word. So that the notions that are the subject matter of this light, are conveyed to the mind by the Word of God; but that due sense of the heart, wherein this light formally consists, is immediately by the Spirit of God. As for instance, that notion that there is a Christ, and that Christ is holy and gracious, is conveyed to the mind by the Word of God: but the sense of the excellency of Christ by reason of that holiness and grace, is nevertheless immediately the work of the Holy Spirit.[101]

On the contrary, Lloyd-Jones's understanding of the immediate operation of the Spirit, as we saw, opens the possibility for the Spirit to work immediately on souls apart from the Word unless an inner consciousness or impression attributed to by His direct work contradicts the truths in Scripture.

Such deviation, as briefly discussed in Chapter 4, is attributable to the fact that Lloyd-Jones's personal research and his understanding of revival was the matrix to form his doctrine of Spirit baptism. Lloyd-Jones emphasizes that "the nerve of this whole doctrine of the baptism with the Spirit" is that "the Spirit also works and operates in a direct manner (without means)."[102] His conviction of the immediate work of the Spirit, sometimes apart from the Scriptures, can be said to be the result of his personal research on revival, aroused by his interest and desire for it. Lloyd-Jones, through his personal study of the history of revival, believes that in ordinary times the Holy Spirit usually works in indirect ways through the Word, but in the exceptional days of revival, extraordinary works of the Holy Spirit not only in their intensity but in their immediacy (possibly apart from the Word) are commonly found. Such belief, consolidated from his study on revival, is reflected in his understanding of Spirit baptism as "the immediate work of the Spirit." His conviction and aspiration regarding the direct work of the Spirit witnessed in the period of revival predisposed him to accept the traditional doctrine of

101. Edwards, *Sermons and Discourses, 1730–1733*, in *Works* 17:416–17.

102. Lloyd-Jones, *Joy Unspeakable*, 67.

assurance selectively and to interpret the Reformed preachers' experiences of the Spirit subjectively within the framework of his doctrine of Spirit baptism.

Murray explains that Lloyd-Jones's deviation from the old Reformed tradition in this matter was due to his belief that it was a remedy for "cold, intellectual believism."[103] Lloyd-Jones believed that the greatest danger that evangelical churches and Christians were confronting at that time was "a dead orthodoxy."[104] For him, a dead orthodoxy, which leads churches and Christians to be satisfied with themselves for mere intellectual assent to their creed or to maintain their orthodoxy against modernists without any vitality, experience, and emotion,[105] is a more serious problem to the church than enthusiasm or fanaticism. His diagnosis of the contemporary church led him to be more open to the possibility of the immediate work of the Spirit apart from the Word, exhorting Christians to seek a more direct and experiential certainty of their salvation and sonship. In this regard, it can be argued that Lloyd-Jones's doctrine of Spirit baptism—more open to the possibility of the immediate work of the Spirit without the means of the Word—should be regarded as a reflective re-appropriation of the older doctrines within the circumstances of the twentieth century in which he had lived, rather than as simple repetition of their original substance.

REVIVAL

For Lloyd-Jones, there is little difference between baptism with the Spirit and revival since he understands revival as a large number of people being baptized with the Holy Spirit simultaneously: "The difference between the baptism of the Holy Spirit and a revival is simply one of the number of people affected. I would define a revival as a large number, a group of people, being baptized by the Holy Spirit at the same time; or the Holy Spirit falling upon, coming upon a number of people assembled together."[106] Accordingly, baptism with the Spirit is an experience of the great outpouring of the Spirit individually; revival is an experience of the same collectively. The essence of both is that believers experientially enjoy full assurance of their salvation,

103. Murray, *Lloyd Jones: Messenger of Grace*, 158.

104. Lloyd-Jones, *Revival*, 68.

105. Lloyd-Jones refers to such phenomena as "smug contentment" (*Revival*, 68).

106. Lloyd-Jones, *Joy Unspeakable*, 51.

their sonship, and God's overflowing love toward them. As Lloyd-Jones suggests the doctrine of assurance is a Reformed view that the contemporary church has disregarded, he further suggests the theology of revival, the other significant axis of his doctrine of Spirit baptism, is another Reformed doctrine that once prevailed but had almost entirely disappeared or else had been seriously distorted since the nineteenth century.

On January 11, 1959, Lloyd-Jones commenced twenty-six Sunday sermons on the subject of revival at Westminster Chapel, commemorating the centenary of revival in 1859 that took place in the British Isles. Then on December 16 of the same year, he gave a lecture on the same theme to pastors and seminarians, titled "Revival: An Historical and Theological Survey," at the Puritan Conference. In this way, facing the one hundredth anniversary of the revival, he desired to remind evangelicals that revival was what the church needed most in his days. Above all, he mourned that since the 1880s "this whole notion of a visitation, a baptism of God's Spirit upon the Church," that is, revival, had disappeared.[107] In the aforementioned series sermons (in particular, "Expecting Revival" and "The Glory of God Revealed") and lecture on revival, and in his lecture of Edwards ("Jonathan Edwards and the Crucial Importance of Revival") at the Westminster Conference in 1976, Lloyd-Jones quotes excerpts from the old Reformed tradition to explain and support his argument regarding revival, all of which show clearly that his theology of revival also originated from that tradition. The multiplicity of these excerpts can be divided into two groups: (1) the New England Puritans in the eighteenth century and (2) the Free Church of Scotland Presbyterians in the nineteenth century.

THE NEW ENGLAND PURITANS IN THE EIGHTEENTH CENTURY

As surveyed in the previous chapter, Lloyd-Jones's understanding of revival is much indebted to Jonathan Edwards's writings on the subject. Lloyd-Jones often quotes Edwards's works to describe what revival looks like or to advocate for the necessity of revival. William Cooper (1694–1743) was another New England Puritan whom Lloyd-Jones quotes in his lectures on revival.

107. Lloyd-Jones, *Revival*, 54.

Jonathan Edwards

In his sermon "Expecting Revival," delivered at Westminster Chapel in 1959, commemorating the revival in 1859, Lloyd-Jones defines revival as follows: "This is God visiting his people. Days of heaven on earth, the presidency of the Holy Spirit in the Church, life abundant given to God's people without measure."[108] For a perfect example of revival as "days of heaven upon earth" and "a visitation of the Spirit of God," he presented in his sermon Edwards's writings about the revival that took place at Northampton in 1735:

> This work soon made a glorious alteration in the town. So that in the Spring and Summer following it seemed, that is to say the town, seemed to be full of the presence of God. It never was so full of love nor so full of joy and yet so full of distress as it was then. There were remarkable tokens of God's presence in almost every house. It was a time of joy in families on account of salvation being brought to them. Parents rejoicing over their children as newborn, husbands over their wives and wives over their husbands. The doings of God were then seen in his sanctuary. God's day was a delight and His tabernacles were amiable. Our public assemblies were then beautiful. The congregation was alive in God's service. Everyone earnestly intent on the public worship. Every hearer eager to drink in the words of the minister as they came from his mouth. The assembly in general were from time to time in tears while the Word was preached. Some weeping with sorrow and distress, others with joy and love, others with pity and concern for the souls of their neighbours.[109]

Then, Lloyd-Jones argues that the revival one hundred years previously was little different from the revival in 1735 that Edwards described above in terms of a powerful visitation of the Holy Spirit. If this kind of revival were to happen today, he asserted, "it would solve our problems." He concludes the sermon as follows: "we might feel it to such an extent that we begin to plead with God to have pity and to have mercy and to visit us in that way with his great visitation."[110]

---

108. Lloyd-Jones, *Revival*, 104.
109. Edwards, *The Great Awakening*, in *Works* 4:151; Lloyd-Jones, *Revival*, 103–4.
110. Lloyd-Jones, *Revival*, 104.

In the same year, Lloyd-Jones presented the final address of the Puritan Conference, titled "Revival: An Historical and Theological Survey," whose participants were mostly ministers and ministerial students. The purpose of the address was to "attempt to face some of the problems and difficulties which seem to surround this whole subject [revival]." One of the problems that he deals with in the lecture is regarding two extreme groups: a group of people who "always talk about revival and only about revival" and a group of people who "distrust the whole notion of the unusual and exceptional." While guarding against both extremes, he emphasizes the fact that when looking at church history, "the history of the progress and development of the church is largely a history of revivals, of these mighty exceptional effusions of the Spirit of God."[111] To support his view, Lloyd-Jones quotes another of Edwards's works:

> It may be observed that from the fall of man to our day, the work of Redemption in its effect has mainly been carried on by remarkable communications of the Spirit of God. ... Though there be a more constant influence of God's Spirit always in some degree attending His ordinances, yet the way in which the greatest things have been done towards carrying on this work always has been by remarkable effusions at special seasons of mercy.[112]

Then, Lloyd-Jones concludes: "There is no question that God has really kept His work alive and has advanced it most of all by these unusual, exceptional, signal manifestations of His glory and of His power."[113]

William Cooper

Lloyd-Jones gave another lecture regarding revival titled "Jonathan Edwards and the Crucial Importance of Revival" at the Westminster Conference held in 1976 on the general theme of "The Puritan Experiment in the New World." In the lecture, Lloyd-Jones suggests that "the element of the Holy Spirit is more prominent in Edwards than in any other of the Puritans." In particular, he places an emphasis on Edwards's belief in "a direct and immediate

---

111. Lloyd-Jones, *Puritans*, 1, 15–17.
112. Edwards, *History of the Work of Redemption*, in *Works* 9:143; Lloyd-Jones, *Puritans*, 17.
113. Lloyd-Jones, *Puritans*, 17.

influence of the Spirit, and in sudden and dramatic conversion,"[114] keeping Edwards's theology of revival in mind. Lloyd-Jones uses the following excerpt from William Cooper's preface to Edwards's *Distinguishing Marks of a Work of the Spirit of God*, which describes the lasting period of spiritual barrenness in New England right before the Great Awakening:

> But what a dead and barren time has it now been, for a great while, with all the churches of the Reformation. The golden showers have been restrained; the influences of the Spirit suspended; and the consequence has been, that the gospel has not had any eminent success. Conversions have been rare and dubious; few sons and daughters have been born to God and the hearts of Christians not so quickened, warmed and refreshed under the ordinances, as they have been. That this has been the sad state of religion among us in this land, for many years (except one or two distinguished places which have at times been visited with a shower of mercy while other towns and churches have not been rained upon) will be acknowledged by all who have spiritual senses exercised, as it has been lamented by faithful ministers and serious Christians.[115]

In support of his cyclical view of revival, Lloyd-Jones notes this quotation as historical evidence that revivals follow after "a period of considerable lifelessness in the churches." He suggests that his own day was a time when revival could be expected, because the spiritual condition of the church was very similar to that of the day right before the Great Awakening in the New England.[116]

THE FREE CHURCH OF SCOTLAND PRESBYTERIANS IN THE NINETEENTH CENTURY

According to Lloyd-Jones, the gradual disappearance of Reformed revival theology beginning in the 1860s was a result of the decline of Calvinism.[117] In his lecture "Revival: An Historical and Theological Survey," Lloyd-Jones

114. Lloyd-Jones, *Puritans*, 350.
115. Edwards, *Great Awakening*, 216–17; Lloyd-Jones, *Puritans*, 351.
116. Lloyd-Jones, *Puritans*, 351.
117. Lloyd-Jones, *Puritans*, 4–5.

refers to the pneumatology in the works of two Free Church of Scotland Presbyterian scholars—James Buchanan's (1804–1870) *The Office and Work of the Holy Spirit* (1842) and George Smeaton's (1814–1889) *The Doctrine of the Holy Spirit* (1882)—as the last scholars of Calvinistic revival theology.

James Buchanan

In this lecture, Lloyd-Jones argues that the churches of Lloyd-Jones's day seemed to be split into two main groups: one group that was only interested in the exceptional work of the Spirit, while disregarding the regular work of the Spirit, and the other group that focused only on the ordinary work of the Spirit, while distrusting the unusual work of the Spirit.[118] Disagreeing with either extreme, Lloyd-Jones quotes at considerable length from James Buchanan's *The Office and Work of the Holy Spirit* to argue that both the ordinary and the extraordinary work of the Spirit should be regarded as God's work employed in His sovereignty and wisdom:

> The Holy Spirit is not limited to any one mode of operation in the execution of His glorious work; and His sovereignty ought ever to be remembered when we are considering a subject of this nature. It has, unfortunately, been too much overlooked, when, on the one hand, some have insisted, as we think, with undue partiality and confidence, on a general and remarkable revival, as being in itself the best manifestation of the Spirit's grace, and as being, in all cases, a matter of promise to believing prayer; and when, on the other hand, not a few have looked to the quiet and gradual success of the Gospel ministry, to the exclusion, or at least disparagement, of any more sudden and remarkable work of grace. The former have given a too exclusive preference to what is extraordinary and striking; while the latter have fallen into the opposite error, of preferring what is more usual and quiet. We think it were better to admit of both methods of conversion, and to leave the choice to the sovereign wisdom and grace of the Spirit. It is equally possible for Him to convert souls successively or simultaneously; and in adopting either course doubtless He has wise ends in view. We have no sympathy with those who, overlooking the

118. Lloyd-Jones, *Puritans*, 15–16.

> steady progress of the great work of conversion under a stated ministry, make no account of the multitudes who are added, one by one, to the church of the living God, merely because their conversion has not been attended with the outward manifestations of a great religious revival; nor can we agree with them in thinking, that the church has any sure warrant to expect that the Spirit will be bestowed, in every instance, in that particular way. But as little have we any sympathy with those who, rejecting all revivals as unscriptural delusions, profess to look exclusively to the gradual progress of divine truth, and the slow advance of individual conversion under a stated ministry. Both methods—the simultaneous and the successive conversion of souls, are equally within the power of the Spirit; and there may exist wise reasons why, in certain cases, the first should be chosen, while, in other cases, the second is preferred.[119]

In full agreement with Buchanan on these matters, Lloyd-Jones states: "There, I believe, you have a remarkable statement synthesizing the characteristic experiences of the seventeenth and eighteenth centuries, and God forbid that we should ever pit the one way of Divine working against the other. Both happen, in the providence and wisdom of God."[120]

Then, Lloyd-Jones continues to quote from the same work to persuade pastors and seminary students who attended the conference that God has often manifested his power and grace in an extraordinary manner to awaken the lifeless church and to convert many souls. It is this extraordinary work that Lloyd-Jones and others call revival:

> We have been so much accustomed to look to the more slow, and quiet, and gradual method of maintaining and extending the kingdom of Christ, that we are apt to be startled, and even to listen with some degree of incredulous surprise, when we hear of any sudden and general work of the Spirit of God; nay, we cease even to expect and to pray for any more remarkable or more rapid change in the state of the church and world, than what is usually observed under her regular ministry. But God's "ways are not as our ways, neither are His

119. Buchanan, *Office and Work of the Holy Spirit*, 420–21; Lloyd-Jones, *Puritans*, 16.

120. Lloyd-Jones, *Puritans*, 16.

> thoughts as our thoughts"; and often, in the history of His church, He has been pleased, for wise reasons, to manifest His grace and power in a very extraordinary and remarkable manner; partly to awaken and arouse a slumbering church; partly also, to alarm and convince gainsayers; and most of all, to teach them at once the sovereignty and the power of that grace which they are too prone to despise.[121]

Quoting Buchanan's statement, Lloyd-Jones wants to urge the attendees to seek the extraordinary works of the Spirit that have taken place periodically in the history of the church according to His sovereign will, rather than just being content with the regular work of the Spirit in the manner of the present day's trend.

George Smeaton

In the same lecture, Lloyd-Jones persuaded his audience to come to the conclusion that revival is absolutely needed for "the age in which we are living and the condition of the church, not to mention the world."[122] As ministers, he claimed to the attendees, they should go on with their regular work of preaching and use "every biblical and legitimate means to propagate and to defend the faith." Nonetheless, he argued, they are not enough; nothing less than revival "will avail us in the fight in which we are engaged."[123] He then quoted another Scottish Reformed theologian from the nineteenth century, George Smeaton, with his own annotations,[124] calling for the incessant prayers of the church for a great outpouring of the Spirit:

> As to the peculiar mode of praying, we may say that in every season of general awakening the Christian community waits just as they

121. Buchanan, *Office and Work of the Holy Spirit*, 402–3; Lloyd-Jones, *Puritans*, 17.

122. Lloyd-Jones, *Puritans*, 20. In the first sermon ("The Urgent Need for Revival Today") of his sermon series on revival in 1959, Lloyd-Jones diagnoses the condition of the world in his days as the absence of "the whole notion of the spiritual" (i.e., the belief about God, religion, salvation, and authority of the Bible) and "an amoral or a non-moral society" (Lloyd-Jones, *Revival*, 13, 14). In the situation, he argues, any human effort such as apologetics, new translations of the Bible, using mass media, and popular evangelism cannot change the spiritual and religious condition of the world, even though it may bring about individual conversions. He argues, "We need a power that can enter into the souls of men and break them and smash them and humble them and then make them anew. And that is the power of the living God" (Lloyd-Jones, *Revival*, 19).

123. Lloyd-Jones, *Puritans*, 20.

124. Lloyd-Jones's annotations are marked as italics in the quotation.

waited for the effusion of the Spirit, with one accord in prayer and supplication in the interval between the Ascension and Pentecost. No other course has been prescribed; and the church of the present has all the warrant she ever had to wait, expect, and pray. The first disciples waited in the youthfulness of simple hope, not for a spirit which they had not, but for more of the Spirit which they had; and Christianity has not outlived itself. *Ten days they waited with one accord in prayer, when of a sudden the Spirit came to give them spiritual eyes to apprehend divine things as they never knew them before, and to impart a joy which no man could take from them. It was prayer in the Spirit (Eph 6:18) and prayer for the Spirit, the great "promise of the Father." But the prayer which brought down the Holy Ghost was not that style of petition which ceases if it is not heard at once, or if the heart is out of tune. The prayer which prevails with Him who gives the Spirit is that which will not let Him go without the blessing. When the spirit of extraordinary supplication is poured out from on high—when an urgent desire is cherished for the Holy Ghost—when the church asks according to God's riches in glory, and expects such great things as God's promises warrant and Christ's merits can procure—the time to favour Zion, the set time, is come (Ps 102:16–18). When we look at the prayers in Scripture, we find that God's glory, the church's growth and welfare, her holiness and progress, were ever higher in the thoughts and breathings of the saints than personal considerations. And if we are animated with any other frame of mind, it is not prayer taught by the Spirit, nor offered up in the Name of Christ*. The attitude of the church in the first days after the Ascension, when the disciples waited for the Spirit, should be the church's attitude still. *I need not refer to the copious references of the Apostles to the urgent duty of praying "in the Spirit" and praying "for the Spirit," or shall I refer at large to the habits of all true labourers, such as Luther, Welsh, Whitefield, and others, in proof of the great truth that prayer is the main work of the ministry*. And no more mischievous and misleading theory could be propounded, nor any one more dishonouring to the Holy Spirit, than the principle *adopted by the Plymouth Brethren,* that because the Spirit was poured out at Pentecost, the church has no need, and no warrant, to pray any more for the effusion of the Spirit of God. On the contrary, the more the church asks the Spirit and waits for His communication, the more she receives. *The prayer of faith in one incessant cry comes up from the earth in support of the efforts put forth for the conversion of a people ready to perish. This prayer goes before and follows after all the calls to repentance.*[125]

THE DOCTRINE OF REVIVAL IN THE REFORMED TRADITION

As reviewed above, all the sources on which Lloyd-Jones relied to support his assertion about the necessity of revival came from the old Reformed tradition—the New England Puritans and the Scottish Reformed theologians—from the eighteenth and nineteenth centuries. According to Lloyd-Jones, the theology of revival is rarely found in the seventeenth-century's Puritans' works. This is because, he argues, the Puritans' main concern at that time was "pastoral and experiential in a personal sense"; they were so afraid of the pneumatological excesses demonstrated by such groups as the Quakers that their writings on the Holy Spirit were mainly polemical in nature.[126] He implies, therefore, that the theology of revival came to the fore in the eighteenth century when the Great Awakening took place in England, Wales, and New England, in particular, as reflected in the theological works of Jonathan Edwards on the subject. Murray also argues that the theological term "revival" in the conventional sense—"sudden and remarkable success for the gospel in the world"—became popularized in the 1740s when Edwards used the word "revival" with the same meaning as older terms such as "effusion" or "outpouring of the Spirit."[127]

However, Michael Crawford finds the origin of revival theology of the Reformed tradition in the English Nonconformists of the seventeenth century who lived through the restoration of the monarchy in 1660, such as Robert Fleming the Elder, John Howe, and John Owen.[128] Crawford describes the era when the Puritans suffered severe persecution during the Restoration, which also included the decline of religion in general. Fleming, in *Fulfilling of the Scripture*, lamented the spiritual darkness of his days:

> It is a dark time now with the church of Christ, which we see everywhere almost suffering and afflicted, whilst the whole earth besides

125. Smeaton, *Doctrine of the Holy Spirit*, 254–55; Lloyd-Jones, *Puritans*, 21–22.
126. Lloyd-Jones, *Puritans*, 10–11.
127. Murray, *Pentecost Today?*, 3–4.
128. Crawford, *Seasons of Grace*, 23–28.

> seemeth to be at ease. ... Atheism doth now appear on so formidable a growth, and hath a more threatening aspect, than the rage or violence of men. We see a sad decay likewise on the churches abroad; religion everywhere under a great consumption, and wearing out, that seemeth to have reached it in its vital parts, Men search after an unusual way of sinning, as if they scorned to be wicked, at a common and ordinary rate; prejudice easily taken up, and entertained against the way of God, whilst the good man doth, alas! perish, without any affecting observation; the choice and excellent of the earth pluckt away, and none to fill their room; Christian burials now frequent, but the birth and in-bringing of such to the church rare.[129]

These Puritans commonly preached about the millennial promises in the Scriptures, which they believed would be realized through a great outpouring of the Spirit. They hoped for "not only greater personal holiness and more numerous conversions, but also moral reformation in the nation and the purification of the national church."[130] For instance, in his sermon "The Use of Faith in a Time of General Declension in Religion" (1680), John Owen exhorted hearers who lived in the days of religious decay to put their faith in God's promises that God would send forth His Spirit to renew the church and the nation:

> Faith will also mind the soul that God hath yet *the fulness and residue of the Spirit*, and can pour it out when he pleases, to recover us from this woeful state and condition, and to renew us to holy obedience unto himself. There are more promises of God's giving supplies of his Spirit to deliver us from inward decays, than there are for the putting forth the acts of his power to deliver us from our outward enemies. ... there is deadness upon all churches and professors, in some measure, at this time;—but God, who hath the fulness of the Spirit, can send him forth and renew the face of the soul,—can give professors and profession another face ... humble, meek, holy, broken-hearted, and self-denying. God can send forth his Spirit when he pleases, and give all our churches and professors a new face, in the

129. Fleming, *Fulfilling of the Scripture*, vi.
130. Crawford, *Seasons of Grace*, 28.

> verdure and flourishing of his grace in them. When God will do this I know not: but I believe God can do this; he is able to do it,—able to renew all his churches, by sending out supplies of the Spirit, whose fulness is with him, to recover them in the due and appointed time. And more; I believe truly, that when God hath accomplished some ends upon us, and hath stained the glory of all flesh, he will renew the power and glory of religion among us again, even in this nation.[131]

From the end of the seventeenth century to the beginning of the eighteenth century, both sides of the Atlantic fell into a period of spiritual decline accelerated by "the decay of ministerial authority, the growth of rationalism, the spread of material wealth and luxury, and the frivolity and spiritual indifference of the young."[132] After seeing all their efforts for a moral reformation and a revival of religion come to nothing, New England Puritans such as Increase (1639–1723) and Cotton Mather (1663–1728), Samuel Danforth (1626–1674), and Solomon Stoddard began to shift their emphasis from reformation as human effort to revival as God's sovereign work.[133] By the 1720s, they came to a consensus that without the outpouring of the Spirit neither a moral reformation nor a revival of piety could be accomplished; pious Christians were therefore urged to pray incessantly for a great effusion of the Holy Spirit.[134] Stoddard's sermon "The Benefit of Gospel," published in 1713, shows well the prevailing conviction regarding the necessity of the outpouring of the Spirit for reformation:

> If religion don't revive, the country will become more wicked. Pride and wantonness, and worldliness, and prophaness do abound in the land. There be many bad examples; there is a great deal of the breaking out of sin. In many places they have a very ill name on the account of their iniquities. Many people do declare their sin as Sodom, and hide it not. And how shall a stop be put to it, unless religion do revive?

131. Owen, "Use of Faith," in *Works* 9:514. While Lloyd-Jones claims that Owen, like other Puritans, did not deal with the subject of revival, Crawford's study of Owen's volumes on the work of the Holy Spirit (vols. 3–4) finds several of Owen's sermons published in other volumes (8–9) that show the Puritans' conviction and yearning for revival (Lloyd-Jones, *Puritans*, 10; Crawford, *Seasons of Grace*, 27–28).

132. Haykin, *Jonathan Edwards*, 51.

133. Crawford, *Seasons of Grace*, 42.

134. Haykin, *Jonathan Edwards*, 52.

> Unless men be awakened and convinced? … Some think family government may put a stop to sin. Some think the zeal of rulers, and faithfulness of officers may put a stop to sin. But how shall these things be come at, if the Spirit of religion do not revive among us?[135]

Likewise, it can be argued that since the 1660s Puritan preachers on both sides of the Atlantic had preached about the outpouring of the Spirit in order to call on their audience to pray for that blessing, hoping that the great effusion of the Spirit would reform their churches and nations through the revival of religion. Therefore, it is reasonable to view Jonathan Edwards's revival theology as being in continuity with preceding Puritans' understanding of the subject. For the New Light Puritans, including Edwards, who supported revival as God's genuine work, the 1734–1735 revival in Northampton was interpreted as the great effusion of the Spirit that their predecessors had preached, prayed, and waited for since the 1660s. In this regard, Haykin argues that Edwards was "boldly declaring that what English Dissenters and New England Puritans had long been praying for had finally come" when he spoke of the "remarkable pouring out of the Spirit of God" at Northampton in *A Faithful Narrative*.[136]

The prefaces to Edwards's works on the Northampton revival—*A Faithful Narrative* (the third edition, Boston, 1738)[137] and *The Distinguishing Marks of a Work of the Spirit of God* (1741)—reflected well how the New Lights viewed the spiritual awakening that occurred in Northampton and the Connecticut River Valley. In the case of *A Faithful Narrative*, the preface was jointly written by Edwards's fellow ministers: Joseph Sewall (1688–1769), Thomas Prince (1687–1758), John Webb (1667–1712), and William Cooper. The preface reveals the revival proponents' interpretation regarding the Awakening in Northampton as one of the great outpourings of the Spirit that had been given seasonally upon the church according to God's "sovereign liberty and irresistible power"[138] since the great effusion of the Spirit at Pentecost.

---

135. Stoddard, *Efficacy of the Fear of Hell*, 53–54.

136. Haykin, *Jonathan Edwards*, 53.

137. Its first (1737) and second (1738) edition were published in London, with the preface written by Isaac Watts (1644–1748) and John Guyse (1680–1761), both of whom were English dissenting ministers.

138. Edwards, *Great Awakening*, 139.

The preface to *The Distinguishing Marks*, written by William Cooper, discusses another of the New Lights' important convictions on revival, namely, that it always comes "in the context of the preaching of His gospel."[139] In the preface, Cooper quoted his predecessor John Howe's work, *The Prosperous State of the Christian Church Before the End of Time by a Plentiful Effusion of the Holy Spirit*:[140]

> In such a time (says he), when the Spirit shall be poured forth plentifully, sure ministers shall have their proportionable share. And when such a time as that shall [once] come, I believe you will hear much other kind of sermons, or they will who shall live to such a time, than you are wont to do nowadays: souls will surely be dealt withal at another kind of rate. It is plain (says he), too sadly plain, there is a great retraction of the Spirit of God even from us: we know not how to speak living sense unto souls, how to get within you: our words die in our mouths, or drop and die between you and us. We even faint when we speak; long experienced unsuccessfulness makes us despond: we speak not as persons that hope to prevail, that expect to make you serious, heavenly, mindful of God, and to walk more like Christians. The methods of alluring and convincing souls, even that some of us have known, are lost from amongst us in a great part. There have been other ways taken, than we can tell now how to fall upon, for the mollifying of the obdurate and the awakening of the secure, and the convincing and persuading of the obstinate, and the winning of the disaffected. Sure there will be a large share, that will come even to the part of ministers, when such an effusion of the Spirit shall be, as is [here] expected [*sic*, signified]: that they shall know how to speak to better purpose, with more compassion, [and some] with more seriousness, with more authority and allurement, than we now find we can.[141]

Cooper went on to claim that the Great Awakening he was witnessing was a season when the Holy Spirit was poured out plentifully on preachers, just as Howe had anticipated almost sixty years before:

---

139. Smart, *Jonathan Edwards's Apologetic*, 67.
140. This work is composed of fifteen sermons on Ezek 39:29 that were preached in 1678.
141. Howe, *Outpouring of the Holy Spirit*, 77.

> Agreeable to the just expectation of this great and excellent man [John Howe], we have found it in this remarkable day. A number of preachers have appeared among us, to whom God has given such a large measure of his Spirit, that we are ready sometimes to apply to them the character given of Barnabas, that "he was a good man, and full of the Holy Ghost, and of faith" (Acts 11:24). They preach the Gospel of the grace of God from place to place with uncommon zeal and assiduity.[142]

Cooper emphasized that what the preachers proclaimed was the essential Reformed doctrine: "man's guilt, corruption, impotence, supernatural regeneration by the Spirit of God, free justification by faith in the righteousness of Christ, and the marks of the new birth." Their preaching manner was "not with enticing words of man's wisdom" (1 Cor 2:4); rather their hearts were warmed by "an ardent love to Christ and souls," he argued.[143] Most of all, he testified that their preaching ministry was accompanied by God's presence and power, resulting in dynamic reformation that human efforts had failed to produce:

> God has made these his ministers active spirits, a flame of fire in his service: and his word in their mouths has been as a fire; and as a hammer that breaketh the rock in pieces [Ps 104:4 and Heb 1:7; Jer 23:29]. In most places where they have labored, God has evidently wrought with them, and confirmed the Word by signs following [Mark 16:20]. Such a power and presence of God in religious assemblies, has not been known since God set up his sanctuary amongst us: he has indeed glorified the house of his glory [Ezek 37:26; Isa 60:7].[144]

As these prefaces show clearly, the proponents of revival among Puritans believed that "these outpourings of the Spirit in awakenings are given seasonally according to the counsel of God's own will whenever and wherever Christ chooses; yet always in the context of the preaching of His gospel." Robert Smart has named the group of ministers and theologians who have held this theological position from the seventeenth century until today the Calvinistic Pneumatic School. This school, Smart argues, is a close reflection

142. Edwards, *Great Awakening*, 218.
143. Edwards, *Great Awakening*, 218.
144. Edwards, *Great Awakening*, 218–19.

of Edwards's Calvinistic theological position on revival through his valuable work on the subject.[145]

Richard Lovelace argues that Edwards's major works are "consistent applications of Calvin's teaching on God's grace and sovereignty."[146] Edwards's revival theology, also, reflected well the characteristics of Calvinism as his theological roots in terms of his God-centered theology that places the most emphasis on God's glory. For Edwards, the object of revival is to manifest the glory of God. He argued that God's plan was designed to glorify each person in the Trinity more greatly through the work of redemption than through the work of creation.[147] He boldly argued, "the work of God in the conversion of one soul, considered together with the source, foundation and purchase of it, and also the benefit, end and eternal issue of it, is a more glorious work of God than the creation of the whole material universe: it is the most glorious of God's works, as it above all others manifests the glory of God."[148]

According to him, the work of redemption has "mainly been carried on by remarkable pourings out of the Spirit of God."[149] Therefore, revival is the most glorious of any work of God in its nature. In addition, revival is the most glorious work of God in its degree, circumstances, and extent because of the great number of conversions, the extraordinary events, and the high attainments of Christians such as spiritual joy and love.[150] Likewise, revival is the greatest means for manifesting the exceeding greatness of power and grace of God.

To view God's sovereignty as the only cause of revival as well as of conversion of a soul also reflects Edwards's God-centered theology as a Calvinist. It highlights humanity's complete dependence on God's sovereign grace and power in revival and conversion; when people entirely depend on God, Edwards believed, God is glorified the most. In this regard, Packer argues that "[t]he thought of man's complete dependence on a free omnipotent God controlled Edwards's whole religious outlook, and acted as the guiding principle

145. Smart, *Jonathan Edwards's Apologetic*, 67, 297, 308.
146. Lovelace, "Edwards' Theology," 22.
147. Edwards, *History of the Work of Redemption*, 125; Edwards, *Great Awakening*, 344.
148. Edwards, *Great Awakening*, 344.
149. Edwards, *History of the Work of Redemption*, 143.
150. Edwards, *Great Awakening*, 345–46.

of his entire theology."[151] For Edwards, who believed in total depravity and human impotence along with his Calvinistic predecessors, regeneration is the result of the supernatural work of the Holy Spirit, rather than of a person's decision with his/her free will. This thorough reliance on God's work for a person's salvation is closely connected with the glory of God since, Edwards believes, if salvation were left for human work as Arminianism claims, it would "compromise the glory of God and God's absolute sovereignty."[152] In this regard, Edwards's theology of revival, Robert Caldwell argues, preserves the standard Calvinist view of God's sovereignty in redemption, holding that "only God can transform the sinner's nature by granting the soul a new disposition that sees God as their greatest good."[153]

Such Calvinist convictions regarding humanity's complete dependence on God in the cause of revival and of conversion were later opposed by Charles Finney's revivalism in the nineteenth century. As William McLoughlin suggests, Finney discarded traditional theocentric Calvinism, rejecting "its exaltation of the sovereign and miraculous power of God in regard to conversions and the promotion of revivals." As for the cause of revival, Finney argues that revival is "as naturally a result of the use of the appropriate means as a crop is of the use of the appropriate means," even though he admits that "means will not produce a revival, we all know, without the blessing of God." For Edwards, revival is "a shower of divine blessing," which "came miraculously through the divine hand of Providence," while for Finney, it is "the result of cause and effect in which the revival preacher was the principal agent."[154] As for conversion, Finney strongly opposes the Calvinistic doctrines of original sin and total depravity. He denounces the fact that the Presbyterians held "the doctrine that moral depravity was constitutional, and belonged to the very nature; that the will, though free to do evil, was utterly impotent to all good."[155] Finney, on the contrary, regards depravity as a "voluntary condition" so that a human can also voluntarily decide to follow Christ if he/she wills to become a new creation.[156]

---

151. Packer, *Quest for Godliness*, 311.
152. Rast, "Jonathan Edwards on Justification," 354.
153. Caldwell, *Theologies of the American Revivalists*, 67.
154. Finney, *Lectures on Revivals of Religion*, ix–x, 13–14.
155. Finney, *Memoirs of Rev. Charles G. Finney*, 154.
156. Murray, *Pentecost Today?*, 39.

In short, Finney's revival theology largely supplanted the Calvinists' inviolable realm of God's sovereignty in revival and conversion with human effort and voluntary decision. Finney's anthropocentric theology against the old Calvinistic doctrines came to "dominate popular American thought until well into the twentieth century." William McLoughlin even says that the old Calvinistic tradition "was in its death throes when Finney wrote [*Lectures on Revivals of Religion*], and it is not too farfetched to say that through him it received its *coup de grâce*."[157] Most of all, Finney's belief that revival of religion could be worked out when appropriate means were employed replaced the old Calvinistic understanding of revival that believed that it was given to the church seasonally according to God's sovereign will. Murray says: "Seasons of revival became 'revival meetings.' Instead of being 'surprising' they might now be even announced in advance, and whereas no one in the previous century had known of ways to secure a revival, a system was popularized by 'revivalists' which came near to guaranteeing results."[158]

Nonetheless, Robert Smart argues, the Calvinistic pneumatic school's influence was "not completely overthrown in America or elsewhere." Edwards's Calvinistic interpretation of revival was passed on by professors at Princeton Theological Seminary such as Archibald Alexander (1772–1851), Samuel Miller (1769–1850), and Charles Hodge, along with Free Church of Scotland Presbyterians such as James Buchanan, George Smeaton, and Alexander Moody Stuart (1809–1898) as well as the Welsh Calvinistic Methodists.[159]

Lloyd-Jones, no doubt, should be considered as one of the significant figures of the Calvinistic pneumatic school in the twentieth century. As indicated in the previous chapter, he inherited Edwards's Calvinistic position on revival. Lloyd-Jones not only emphasizes God's sovereignty as the sole cause of revival but also emphasizes God's glory as the ultimate end of revival, which faithfully follows its cyclical (or declension) model of interpretation: "after periods of declension, new effusions of the Spirit of God are given to the life of the churches"[160] in the context of the preaching of the gospel.

157. Finney, *Lectures on Revivals of Religion*, x–xi.

158. Murray, *Revival and Revivalism*, xviii.

159. Smart, *Jonathan Edwards's Apologetic*, 68–69.

160. Smart, *Jonathan Edwards's Apologetic*, 70.

It should be noted, however, that Lloyd-Jones understands the revivals in England, Wales, and New England in the eighteenth century to be disconnected from Puritanism in the seventeenth century. As stated earlier, he affirms that revival theology did not exist for the seventeenth-century Puritans. He also argues that although the eighteenth-century Calvinistic Methodists were earnest readers of Puritan writings, Calvinistic Methodism was "not a mere continuation of Puritanism." Rather, he says, a new element—the emphasis on the revival aspect—was introduced into Calvinistic Methodism, which distinguished the movement in essence from Puritanism.[161] He even states:

> It seems to me that the societies that were started in England and Wales by the Methodist Fathers of both schools of thought in the eighteenth century were much nearer to the New Testament church than were the Puritan churches of the seventeenth century. There was more of the freedom of the spirit, more spontaneity, more taking part by the mass of the people.[162]

Likewise, Lloyd-Jones emphasizes not only the discontinuity between seventeenth-century Puritanism and eighteenth-century revivalism, but also the superiority of eighteenth-century Methodism to seventeenth-century Puritanism.[163] On account of Lloyd-Jones's position, we can confirm the centrality of revival in his interpretation of church history and his theology as well as the profound influence of eighteenth-century Methodism on his understanding of revival. He found in the history of revival of Calvinistic

161. Lloyd-Jones, *Puritans*, 205.

162. Lloyd-Jones, *Puritans*, 13.

163. David Bebbington also observes a discontinuity between seventeenth-century Puritanism and eighteenth-century evangelicalism, noting "the transition from Puritan introspection to evangelical activism" ("Revival and Enlightenment in Eighteenth-Century England," 22). He attributes this transition to a change in the doctrine of assurance: "Whereas the Puritans had held that assurance is rare, late and the fruit of struggle in the experience of believers, the Evangelicals believed it to be general, normally given at conversion and the result of simple acceptance of the gift of God. The consequence of the altered form of the doctrine was a metamorphosis in the nature of popular Protestantism. There was a change in patterns of piety, affecting devotional and practical life in all its departments. The shift, in fact, was responsible for creating in Evangelicalism a new movement and not merely a variation on themes heard since the Reformation" (*Evangelicalism in Modern Britain*, 42–43).

Methodism not only the vision of the revived church,[164] but also, as will be discussed in the next chapter, a good example of true preaching. And, as stated in the previous section, these facts explain why his stance on the immediate witness of the Spirit in assurance of salvation departs from the general understanding of the seventeenth-century Puritans, even though his doctrine of Spirit baptism has its root in their doctrine of assurance. In other words, Lloyd-Jones's doctrine of Spirit baptism can be seen as adding elements of revivalism—the direct work of the Spirit that stands out during the period of revival, as he believes—to the Puritan doctrine of assurance. This reappropriation of the old doctrine comes from Lloyd-Jones's conviction that the outpouring of the Holy Spirit (or the immediate work of the Spirit in their hearts) as powerful as the eighteenth-century revival is absolutely needed, rather than any organization, human effort, or skill. He believed that only the outpouring of the Spirit could enable the churches of his day that existed in a state of dead orthodoxy and spiritual inertia to regain vitality, power, and authority, and to turn unbelievers to the gospel in the age of the absence of moral and spiritual notions.

So far, we have reviewed the citations Lloyd-Jones used in his lectures and sermons on baptism with the Spirit to trace the origin of the two axes of his doctrine of Spirit baptism: assurance and revival. Both doctrines originated from the Reformed tradition from the seventeenth to the mid-nineteenth centuries. Therefore, Lloyd-Jones's doctrine of Spirit baptism should be considered reappropriation within the context of his day of the older teachings on the assurance of salvation and revival that had been prevalent in the Reformed tradition rather than a mere repetition of their original content. His notable deviation from the Reformed tradition in reappropriating the doctrine of assurance—the possibility of the immediate work of the Spirit without means of the Word—was developed to be an efficient remedy for a dead orthodoxy and cold believism that he diagnosed as the greatest danger confronting contemporary churches. His understanding of eighteenth-century Methodism, in particular Calvinistic Methodism, as superior to Puritanism in the seventeenth century was due to the Methodists'

164. In this regard, Randall states: "[Lloyd-Jones's] model of church life was largely shaped by his appreciation of eighteenth-century Methodism, especially Welsh Calvinistic Methodism" ("Lloyd-Jones and Revival," 107).

emphasis on revival, which he believed was rarely found among Puritans. His continuing study of and aspiration for revival, and his conviction that what the church needed most was the outpouring of the Spirit as happened in the eighteenth century, led him to find his vision for the revived church and true preaching as appeared in the New Testament in the history of revival in Calvinistic Methodism.

7

TRUE PREACHING AND SPIRIT BAPTISM

Lloyd-Jones's understanding of genuine Christian preaching is inextricably related to his doctrine of baptism with the Spirit. Focusing on his homiletics, this chapter will investigate the intimate relationship between Lloyd-Jones's homiletics and Spirit baptism. For him, preaching should be expository in method, doctrinal in content, and experiential in goal, all of which he inherited from the old Reformed homiletical tradition, in particular the English Puritans and Jonathan Edwards. However, his emphasis on the necessity of Spirit baptism in preaching differentiates his homiletics from other forms of Reformed experiential preaching.

I will argue that the distinctiveness of his homiletics should be considered a result of being influenced by the old Calvinistic revival theology as well as the history of revival of Calvinistic Methodism in the eighteenth century, in which he found a vision for true preaching modeled according to preaching in the New Testament. First, I will survey Puritan preaching, including Jonathan Edwards, to demonstrate that Lloyd-Jones's homiletics—expository, doctrinal, and experiential preaching—has its root in the old Reformed homiletics tradition. Then I will explore Lloyd-Jones's distinctive understanding of true preaching—Spirit-baptized preaching—to argue that his unique understanding of preaching was the result of being influenced by the old Calvinistic revival theology as well as his interest and research into the history of revival.

PURITAN PREACHING

In his lecture "Puritanism and Its Origins," given at The Westminster Conference of 1971, Lloyd-Jones confessed to the audience, "My whole ministry has been governed by this," referring to the Puritans and their works.[1] To Lloyd-Jones, who described himself as "a great admirer of the Puritans," they were great examples of "a true ministry of the Word."[2] Not only does Lloyd-Jones's conviction regarding the primacy of preaching follow the tradition of Puritan preaching, but so also does his understanding of genuine preaching, defined according to the priorities of being expository in method, doctrinal in content, and experiential in goal. In this section, we will survey the main features of Puritan preaching, including the Puritans' conviction on the supremacy of preaching as well as the type, structure, and style of Puritan preaching.

It is indisputable that preaching is at the heart of Puritanism. William Haller defines Puritanism as "vital rage for utterance."[3] Additionally, John F. H. New argues, "Preaching, by mouth and by pen, was life for the Puritan."[4] For Puritans, preaching was God's ordained way to gather the elect from the world and to build up their faith as the body of Christ. William Ames (1576–1633) explains that "preaching is the ordinance of God, sanctified for the begetting of faith, for the opening of the understanding, for the drawing of the will and affections to Christ."[5] John Downame (1571–1652) also emphasizes the specific status of preaching as an ordinance of God for conversion and sanctification: "God's own ordinance which he hath instituted and ordained for the gathering of the saints, and building the body of his Church, as appeareth Eph 4:11, 12. Neither doth he use ordinarily, any other means (especially where this is to be had) for the true conversion of his children, and for the working of the sanctifying graces of his Spirit in them."[6] For Puritans, the preaching office itself was highly dignified. Richard Sibbes elevated the preaching office to be the highest gift, other than the Holy Spirit, that the ascended Christ had given to his church:

---

1. Lloyd-Jones, *Puritans*, 238.
2. Lloyd-Jones, *Knowing the Times*, 269; Lloyd-Jones, *Puritans*, 238.
3. Haller, *Rise of Puritanism*, 258.
4. New, *Anglican and Puritan*, 71.
5. Ames, *Marrow of Theology*, 194.
6. Downame, *Christian Warfare*, 158.

> "Christ, when he ascended on high and led captivity captive" (he would give no mean gift then, when he was to ascend triumphantly to heaven) the greatest gift he could give was "some to be prophets, some apostles, some teachers (and preachers) for the building up of the body of Christ till we all meet, a perfect man in Christ." "I will send them pastors according to my own heart" saith God (Jer 3:15). God esteems it so, Christ esteems it so, and so should we esteem it.[7]

Puritans believed that Christ himself preached as the chief preacher when a preacher delivered his sermon in the pulpit. Paul Baine's (1573–1617) exposition of Ephesians 2:17 ("He came and preached peace to you who were far away and peace to those who were near" [NIV]) provides one overt explanation of this conviction:

> He saith *Christ* preached to them. ... Now he was never a minister but of the circumcision (Rom 15:8), to the lost sheep of the house of Israel (Matt 15:24) in his own person. Therefore we see that Christ is present and hath a part in preaching even when *men* preach ... for this is the office of Christ our great Prophet, not only in his own Person to open to us the will of his Father ... but to be present and teach inwardly in the heart with that Word which is outwardly sounded unto the ear by men. ... Thus Paul preached to the ear, but Christ to the heart of Lydia. This must teach us to look upon Christ as the chief Prophet among us, and the chief Preacher whosoever speaketh.[8]

The Puritans' high view of preaching—that Christ himself preaches—was validated by audiences who experienced Christ personally through preaching. For instance, one who listened to John Cotton's (1584–1652) sermon wrote: "Mr. Cotton preaches with such authority, demonstration, and life that, methinks, when he preaches out of any Prophet or Apostle I hear not him; I hear that very Prophet and Apostle; yea, *I hear the Lord Jesus Christ speaking in my heart*."[9]

The Puritans' conviction of the dignity of preaching as God's ordinance led them to place preaching at the center of public worship. Their belief in the primacy of preaching stands in stark contrast with Anglican conviction

---

7. Sibbes, *Fountain Closed*, in *Works* 5:509.
8. Bayne, *Entire Commentary*, 246; emphasis added.
9. Mather, *Magnalia Christi Americana*, 275; emphasis added.

regarding the predominance of sacraments over preaching. In the speech of William Laud (1573–1645), this Anglican belief is clearly unveiled. He asserts that sacraments are more important than preaching as the body of Christ is more important than his word.

> And you, my honourable Lords of the Garter, in your great solemnities, you do your reverence, and to Almighty God, I doubt it not; but yet it is *versus altare*, "towards His altar," as the greatest place of God's residence upon earth. (I say the greatest, yea, greater than the pulpit; for there 'tis *Hoc est corpus meum*, "This is my body"; but in the pulpit 'tis at most but *Hoc est verbum meum*, "This is My Word." And a greater reverence, no doubt, is due to the body than to the word of our Lord.)[10]

Furthermore, Anglicans regarded the Puritan conviction regarding the primacy of preaching as an overemphasis. Besides preaching, Anglicans believed, there were many other means to be used for salvation, sanctification, and edification, such as "conversation in the bosom of the Church, religious education, the reading of the learned men's books, information received by conference, as well as the public and private reading of the Scriptures and of the Homilies." Reading the authorized sermons in the Anglican Books of Homilies, written by English Reformers such as Thomas Cranmer (1489–1556) and John Jewel (1522–1571) to teach a Reformed theology and practical application rather than preaching, they argue, is preferable since it "preserves the Word of God unadulterated," while sermons might be "the corrupt productions of men."[11]

However, Puritans argued that "any mediation of grace through the minister was not through any supposed priestly act of his, but through the Word of Christ spoken by him in the Spirit of Christ to the people of Christ." Distinct from the Anglican concept of public worship as a priestly act, Puritans regarded public worship as a prophetic act since they believed that "the priestly element in worship rests on the two great truths of Christ's perpetual High Priesthood and the consequent priesthood of all believers."[12] Puritans argued that a pulpit, not an altar, should be positioned at the center

10. Laud, *Works* 6:57.
11. Davies, *Worship of the English Puritans*, 185–86.
12. Lewis, *Genius of Puritanism*, 53.

of corporate worship. Regarding the Anglican position on the priority of homilies over extemporaneous preaching, Puritans responded that preaching, due to its applicability, was far superior in its effectiveness to the mere reading of homilies. A letter from Archbishop Grindal (1519–1583) to Queen Elizabeth, written when he was ordered to prohibit the practice of "prophesying"—the preaching conference—in England, is a good example of this conviction. Grindal writes:

> The Godly Preacher is termed in the Gospel, a Faithful Servant, who knoweth how to give his Lord's family their apportioned food in season; who can *apply* his speech according to the diversity of times, places, and hearers; which cannot be done in the Homilies: exhortations, reprehensions, and persuasions, are uttered with more affections, to the moving of the Hearers, in Sermons than in Homilies. Besides, Homilies were devised by the Godly Bishops in your Brother's time, only to supply necessity, for want of Preachers; and are by Statute not to be preferred, but to give place to Sermons, whensoever they may be had.[13]

Richard Baxter (1615–1691) also maintained that the reading of homilies prevented a pastor from delivering an adequate message to a congregation that had a specific situation of need: "If I know my hearers to be most addicted to drunkenness, must I be tyed up from preaching or reading against that sin, and tyed to Read and Preach only against Covetousness or the like, because it seemeth meet to Governours to tye me a constant course?"[14]

Puritans were convinced that the efficacy and power of preaching were far superior to the mere reading even of Scriptures. Thomas Cartwright (1535–1603) argues that it is only by preaching that the word of God pierces the hearts of the hearers. He illustrates this point as follows: "As the fire stirred giveth more heat, so the Word, as it were, blown by preaching, flameth more in the hearers than when it is read."[15] Along the same lines, Thomas Goodwin also emphasizes the necessity of preaching to lead the word to reach and transform the hearts of the congregation:

---

13. Strype, *History of the Life*, 79.
14. Baxter, *Five Disputations*, 440.
15. Quoted in Knott, *Sword of the Spirit*, 38.

> It is not the letter of the Word that ordinarily doth convert, but the spiritual meaning of it, as revealed and expounded. ... There is the letter, the husk; and there is the spirit, the kernel; and when we by expounding the word do open the husk, out drops the kernel. And so it is the spiritual meaning of the Word let into the heart which converts it and turns it unto God.[16]

To sum up, Puritans were convinced that the primacy of preaching as God's ordinance could be replaced by any other means, such as the reading of Scripture or authorized homilies, nor must it be subordinate to sacraments or any liturgy. Preaching, they believed, was "the means chosen by God for illuminating the minds, mollifying the hearts, sensitizing the consciences, strengthening the faith, quelling the doubts, and saving the souls of mankind."[17]

According to the Puritan perspective, proper preaching is "expository in its method" and "doctrinal in its content."[18] Both of these features warrant discussion. First, Puritan preaching followed an expository method. The reason Puritan preachers held fast to expository preaching can be found in John Preston's definition of preaching as "a public interpretation or dividing the Word, performed by an ambassador or minister who speaks to the people instead of God, in the name of Christ."[19] As this definition reveals, Puritan preachers were regarded as "the mouthpiece of God and the servant of His Word."[20] Accordingly, the primary task of preachers was not imposition but exposition, "extracting from his texts what God had encased within them."[21] Millar MacLure, who studied the sermons in the Paul's Cross pulpit from 1534 to 1642, summarizes well Puritan expository preaching:

> For the Puritans, the sermon is not just hinged to Scripture; it quite literally exists inside the Word of God; the text is not in the sermon, but the sermon is in the text. The physical opening of the Book on the pulpit symbolizes this, so does the opening of the text itself, so

16. Goodwin, *Government of the Churches of Christ*, in *Works* 11:364.
17. Davies, "Elizabethan Puritan Preaching," 101.
18. Packer, *Quest for Godliness*, 284.
19. Thomas, *Golden Treasury of Puritan Quotations*, 221.
20. Beeke and Jones, *Puritan Theology*, 683.
21. Packer, *Quest for Godliness*, 284.

> does the repetition of the words of the text throughout the sermon, supported by numbers of proof-texts, setting up a palisade of holy sounds around the exhortation. Denominations, doctrines, and uses do not move from the Word to the world, but lead the world into the Word; that is, the preacher, in every application of his text, actually rehearses the divine judgment. Put summarily, listening to a sermon is being in the Bible.[22]

Second, Puritan preaching is doctrinal in its content. For Puritans, to be a good expositor was to draw out doctrine from the texts of Scripture, which, they believed, God implanted in them.[23] For the Puritan minister, systematic theology—the grasp of the whole body of divinity, the Bible—was like the knowledge of anatomy to the physician. If it were not for this body of theological knowledge, they argued, pastors could not "provide a diagnosis of, prescribe for, and ultimately cure spiritual disease in those who were plagued by the body of sin and death."[24]

Puritan preaching was composed of three parts: opening (exposition), doctrine, and use (application). In *The Art of Prophesying*, William Perkins's summary shows clearly the three-part structure of Puritan preaching. His summary regarding how to prepare a sermon reads as follows:

> 1. To read the text distinctly out of the canonical scriptures.
> 2. To give the sense and understanding of it being read, by the scripture itself.
> 3. To collect a few and profitable points of doctrine out of the natural sense.
> 4. To apply, if he have the gift, the doctrines rightly collected to the life and manners of men in a simple and plain speech.[25]

Describing the typical Puritan sermon structure in a slightly different way, Horton Davies finds the three divisions to be doctrine (declaration), reason

22. MacLure, *Paul's Cross Sermons*, 165.
23. Packer, *Quest for Godliness*, 285.
24. Ferguson, "Evangelical Ministry," 266.
25. Perkins, *Work of William Perkins*, 349.

(explanation), and use (application).[26] This construal of Puritan preaching, particularly with its recognition of the place of reason in the structure of the sermon, which entails "a logical defense of the assumptions of the first section [doctrine]," unveils one of the significant characteristics of Puritan preaching: "belief in the primacy of intellect."[27] J. I. Packer explains this conviction as follows:

> It was a Puritan maxim that "all grace enters by the understanding." God does not move men to action by mere physical violence, but addresses their minds by his word, and calls for the response of deliberate consent and intelligent obedience. It follows that every man's first duty in relation to the word of God is to understand it; and every preacher's first duty is to explain it. The only way to the heart that he is authorized to take runs via the head.[28]

Puritan preachers first "seek to convince the reason" and then "aim at warming the affections into acceptance of the doctrine."[29] The statement of F. J. Powicke, a biographer of Richard Baxter, concurs:

> He [Baxter] tells us expressly indeed, that the preacher's aim should be first to convince the understanding and then to engage the heart. Light first, then heat. And such was his unvarying method. Beginning with a careful opening of the text, he proceeded to the clearance of possible difficulties or objections; next, to a statement of uses; and lastly to a fervent appeal for acceptance by conscience and heart.[30]

Jonathan Edwards, as representative of New England Puritan practice, emulated the three-part sermon structure of previous Puritans: text, doctrine, and application. Douglas Sweeney describes how Edwards organized his sermons:

---

26. Davies, *Worship of the English Puritans*, 191. In *Worship and Theology in England: From Cranmer to Hooker, 1534–1603*, however, he writes, "The structure took the form of the exposition of a passage of Scripture ... by collecting lessons (or doctrines) from each verse and adding the moral applications (or uses) of them" (304).

27. Davies, *Worship of the English Puritans*, 191; Packer, *Quest for Godliness*, 281.

28. Packer, *Quest for Godliness*, 281.

29. Davies, *Worship of the English Puritans*, 191.

30. Powicke, *Life of the Reverend Richard Baxter*, 50.

> (1) the text, a brief section in which he described the historical setting of his chosen Scripture passage; (2) the doctrine, a longer section in which he identified and developed a thesis statement for his sermon, one that he took from the text itself but supported with other Scriptures; (3) the application, or use, the longest section of the sermon, in which he applied his Scripture doctrine to his listeners' daily lives.[31]

Following the traditions of the Puritans, Edwards began with exegetical work on the text and then arrived at a specific doctrine contained within it. Importantly, before the application of the doctrine, he "reasons about this doctrine, shows how it is to be found elsewhere in Scripture, and its relationship to other doctrines, and then establishes its truth."[32] Accordingly, like John Calvin (1509–1564) and the Puritans before him, Edwards's method was based on the assumption of the unified message of Scripture, which led him to expend the effort to prove that the doctrine in the text was in harmony with other biblical doctrines.

For Edwards, the primary task of preaching was to give information to the minds of the listeners, for which he often used rational and deductive arguments. He attempted to evoke the deep emotions of his audience through sermons mainly composed of theological arguments and doctrinal "what" rather than practical "how to."[33] He believed that without delivering doctrine to the mind by the word of God, there would not be a sense of divine excellence given to the heart, which the doctrine was willing to reveal. This was important even though Edwards also believed that the sense of divine excellence was ultimately given to the heart by the immediate work of the Spirit. In his sermon "A Divine and Supernatural Light Immediately Imparted to the Soul by the Spirit of God, Shown to Be Both a Scriptural and Rational Doctrine," he argues:

> The mind can't see the excellency of any doctrine, unless that doctrine be first in the mind; but the seeing the excellency of the doctrine may be immediately from the Spirit of God; though the conveying of the

---

31. Sweeney, *Jonathan Edwards*, 74.

32. Lloyd-Jones, *Puritans*, 359.

33. Park, "Integration of Mind," 236.

> doctrine or proposition itself may be by the Word. So that the notions that are the subject matter of this light, are conveyed to the mind by the Word of God; but that due sense of the heart, wherein this light formally consists, is immediately by the Spirit of God. As for instance, that notion that there is a Christ, and that Christ is holy and gracious, is conveyed to the mind by the Word of God: but the sense of the excellency of Christ by reason of that holiness and grace, is nevertheless immediately the work of the Holy Spirit.[34]

Edwards believed that the ultimate goal of preaching was to have the listeners moved in their hearts, not just to have their minds instructed, so as to bring about "a warm, emotional type of religion, touched and vivifed by a sense of personal and immediate communion with God."[35] His conviction regarding the necessity of experiential preaching is reflected in *Some Thoughts Concerning the Revival*:

> Though as I said before, clearness of distinction and illustration, and strength of reason, and a good method, in the doctrinal handling of the truths of religion, is in many ways needful and profitable, and not to be neglected, yet an increase in speculative knowledge in divinity is not what is so much needed by our people, as something else. Men may abound in this sort of light and have no heat: how much has there been of this sort of knowledge, in the Christian world, in this age? Was there ever an age wherein strength and penetration of reason, extent of learning, exactness of distinction, correctness of style, and clearness of expression, did so abound? And yet was there ever an age wherein there has been so little sense of the evil of sin, so little love to God, heavenly-mindedness, and holiness of life, among the professors of the true religion? Our people don't so much need to have their heads stored, as to *have their hearts touched*; and they stand in the greatest need of that sort of preaching that has the greatest tendency to do this.[36]

---

34. Edwards, *Sermons and Discourses, 1730–1733*, in *Works* 17:416–17.
35. Turnbull, *Jonathan Edwards*, 97.
36. Edwards, *Great Awakening*, 387–88; emphasis added.

As a preacher, he states without hesitation, "I should think myself in the way of my duty to raise the affections of my hearers as high as possibly I can, provided that they are affected with nothing but truth, and with affections that are not disagreeable to the nature of what they are affected with."[37] Preaching as a tool of God, he believed, was supposed to "bring ideas and doctrine to life, to lead the congregation to see, feel, and be affected by what they hear."[38]

The great emphasis on application in a sermon is also noteworthy in the structure of Puritan preaching. As noted earlier, the main reason Puritans objected to reading homilies as a substitute for preaching was that there was little place left for application in reading scripted texts. For Puritans, preaching without practical application was lifeless. James Durham (1622–1658) maintains:

> Application is the life of preaching; and there is no less study, skill, wisdom, authority, and plainness necessary in the applying of a point to the conscience of hearers, and in the pressing of it home, than is required in the opening of some profound truth: and therefore ministers should study the one as well as the other. ... Hearers are often ready to shift by the most particular words, much more when they are more shortly and generally touched. Hence, preaching is called persuading, testifying, beseeching, entreating, or requesting, exhorting, etc. All which import some such dealing in application: which is not only a more particular breaking of the matter, but a directing it to the consciences of the present hearers. And in this especially, doth the faithfulness, wisdom and dexterity of the preacher, and the power and the efficacy of the gift appear.[39]

Why was the application section so important to Puritan preachers? For them, preaching was "a subversive activity."[40] The goal of preaching was not just to provide information to hearers but to "influence the will, to animate the emotions, and to reform the life."[41] Thus, William Ames asserts, "They sin ... who stick to the naked finding and explanation of the truth, neglecting the

37. Edwards, *Great Awakening*, 387.
38. Smith, *Jonathan Edwards*, 139.
39. Durham, *Learned and Complete Commentary*, 281.
40. Ryken, *Worldly Saints*, 101.
41. Lewis, *Genius of Puritanism*, 50.

use and practice in which religion and blessedness consist. Such preachers edify the conscience little or not at all."[42] Through their preaching ministry, Puritan ministers sought to "build bridges from biblical truth to everyday living." Their ultimate end of preaching was holy living on the part of the congregation.[43] In this regard, Thomas Manton (1620–1677) states, "That knowledge is best, which endeth in practice. ... The hearer's life is the preacher's best commendation."[44]

The seven categories of hearers that Perkins suggests in *The Art of Prophesying* is one of the best examples of how much Puritan preachers emphasized effective application in preaching ministry. The categories include (1) those who are unbelievers and are both ignorant and unteachable, (2) those who are teachable but ignorant, (3) those who have knowledge but have never been humbled, (4) those who have already been humbled, (5) those who already believe, (6) those who have fallen back, and (7) churches with both believers and unbelievers. As Perkins states: "There are basically seven ways in which application should be made, in keeping with seven different spiritual conditions."[45] This classifying work came from a deep concern about the matter of application in the ministry of preaching.

The list of types of application that *The Westminster Directory for Publick Worship* suggests is another good example on this matter.[46] Before enumerating the list, the directory emphasizes the necessity of application in preaching and preachers' effort on the application section. Its exhortation goes as follows:

> He is not to rest in general doctrine, although never so much cleared and confirmed, but to bring it home to special use, by application to his hearers: which albeit it prove a work of great difficulty to himself, requiring much prudence, zeal, and meditation, and to the natural and corrupt man will be very unpleasant; yet he is to endeavor to perform it in such a manner, that his auditors may feel the word

42. Ames, *Marrow of Theology*, 192.
43. Ryken, *Worldly Saints*, 101–2.
44. Manton, *Complete Works* 4:153.
45. Perkins, *Art of Prophesying*, locs. 685–774.
46. It was a manual of directions for ministers and congregations regarding public worship, produced by the Westminster Assembly of Divines in 1644.

> of God to be quick and powerful, and a discerner of the thoughts and intents of the heart; and that, if any unbeliever or ignorant person be present, he may have the secrets of his heart made manifest, and give glory to God.[47]

Then the directory suggests six types of application: (1) the use of instruction or information for knowledge, flowing out of the doctrine; (2) confutation of false doctrines; (3) exhorting to duties; (4) dehortation, reprehension, and public admonitions; (5) applying comfort; and (6) giving some notes of trial.[48] Likewise, the Puritans' detailed categories of hearers as well as the divisions of application types demonstrate how important they regarded application to be in preaching. For the Puritans, therefore, the effectiveness of a preacher relied on "the clarity, wisdom, authority, and searchingness that hearers find in his application."[49]

The style of Puritan preaching can be expressed as, in a word, "plainness." The plain style originated from the Puritans' belief that "the content of a sermon is more important than its form."[50] To the Puritans, Anglican sermons were not only "weighed down with classical and patristic quotations," but they also showed off their pedantic style and rhetorical ornaments.[51] Puritans, in contrast to the Anglican preaching style, declared "a crucified style" of preaching. John Flavel argues:

> A crucified style best suits the preachers of a crucified Christ. ... Prudence will choose words that are solid, rather than florid: as a merchant will [choose] a ship by a sound bottom, and capacious hold, rather than a gilded head and stern. Words are but servants to matter. An iron key, fitted to the wards of the lock, is more useful than a golden one that will not open the door to the treasures. ... Prudence will cast away a thousand fine words for one that is apt to penetrate the conscience and reach the heart.[52]

---

47. Macpherson, *Westminster Confession of Faith*, 536.
48. Macpherson, *Westminster Confession of Faith*, 536–37.
49. Packer, *Quest for Godliness*, 288.
50. Ryken, *Worldly Saints*, 106.
51. Davies, *Worship of the English Puritans*, 197; Lewis, *Genius of Puritanism*, 47.
52. Flavel, *Character of an Evangelical Pastor*, 15–16.

In *Worldly Saints*, Leland Ryken summarizes well why Puritans disliked the high style of Anglican sermons. First, they were concerned that this style could "divert attention from the content of sermon to the preacher." Second, through preaching, they aimed at "reaching the whole of society." Third, they believed the ultimate end of preaching was "not aesthetic excellence but spiritual edification."[53]

John Knott argues that the plain style of Puritan preaching was shaped according to 1 Corinthians 2:4 ("My message and my preaching were not with wise and persuasive words, but with a demonstration of the Spirit's power" [NIV]). For Puritans, he declares, effective and powerful preaching came from plainness rather than from eloquence.[54] Their plainness can be understood as "studied plainness" or "dignified simplicity." Packer explains the feature as follows: "The studied plainness of Puritan preaching often possesses a striking eloquence of its own—the natural eloquence that results when words are treated not at all as the orator's playthings, but entirely as the servants of a noble meaning."[55]

So far, we have surveyed the main features of Puritan preaching by examining Puritan convictions concerning preaching as well as the type, structure, and style of Puritan preaching. The main characteristics of Puritan preaching can be summarized as follows: (1) preaching should be primary in public worship, (2) preaching should be expository in method and doctrinal in content, (3) preaching should lean on the supremacy of intellect and emphasize application, and (4) preaching should rely on dignified simplicity rather than eloquence. It should be noted that the primary purpose of Puritan preaching, on which these various aspects converge, was seeking the experience of God through preaching. The main concern of Puritan preachers was to lead people to know God, not just to give information regarding him. Their preaching, Packer argues, was "avowedly practical and concerned with experience of God."[56] The Puritans' belief that only a deep religious experience could transform hearers' heart and life and that preaching was God's ordained

53. Ryken, *Worldly Saints*, 105.
54. Knott, *Sword of the Spirit*, 5.
55. Packer, *Quest for Godliness*, 286.
56. Packer, *Quest for Godliness*, 286.

way to bring them to know him shaped their conviction on the supremacy of preaching as well as the type, structure, and style of Puritan preaching.

LLOYD-JONES'S REFORMED-TRADITIONAL UNDERSTANDING OF TRUE PREACHING: EXPOSITORY, DOCTRINAL, AND EXPERIENTIAL

Lloyd-Jones's conviction as to the primacy of preaching and his understanding of true preaching—expository in method, doctrinal in content, and experiential in goal—were both inherited from the Puritan preaching tradition explored above. Jung Keun-Doo points out that Lloyd-Jones's conviction regarding the primacy of preaching originated from "the Puritans and the Reformers in general and with John Calvin in particular, who calls preaching 'the Church's chief sinew, indeed its very soul.'"[57] Lloyd-Jones argues that the fundamental task of the church and the minister is to preach the word of God. He substantiates this argument with evidence from the New Testament to reveal that Jesus and his disciples' primary ministry was to preach the word.[58] He asserts that the Reformers and Puritans believed in the supremacy of preaching based on the fact that in the New Testament Jesus, John the Baptist, and the apostles were all ultimately preachers:

> All these men [the Reformers] claimed, and the Puritans claimed, and all who believe in the supremacy of preaching have always claimed, that this [preaching] was our Lord's own method of teaching the Truth. Our Lord was a preacher. John the Baptist, the forerunner, was also a preacher primarily. In the Book of Acts we find the same: Peter on the day of Pentecost got up and preached, and he continued to do so. The Apostle Paul was pre-eminently a great preacher. We see him preaching in Athens, as he declares the Truth to the Athenians.[59]

The history of the church, he says, is another conspicuous proof that "preaching has always occupied a central and a predominating position in the life of the Church, particularly in Protestantism." Most of all, his ultimate reason for the primacy of preaching is theological. He claims that "man's real

57. Jung, "Evaluation of the Principles," 30.

58. Lloyd-Jones, *Preaching and Preachers*, 20–24, 26.

59. Lloyd-Jones, *Puritans*, 375.

trouble is that he is a rebel against God and consequently under the wrath of God."[60] Accordingly, the urgent task of the church and the minister is to make known to people their ultimate need of salvation as well as the only way to receive it:

> If [salvation] is the greatest need of man, if his ultimate need is something that arises out of this ignorance of his which, in turn, is the result of rebellion against God, well then, what he needs first and foremost is to be told the truth about himself, and to be told of the only way in which this can be dealt with. So I assert that it is the peculiar task of the Church, and of the preacher, to make all this known.[61]

Therefore, Lloyd-Jones insists that any other activities such as personal counseling and psychological treatment are "meant to supplement the preaching, not to supplant it." Preaching, he believes, is God's own method "by which churches have always come into being" and that "He has always honored it, and still honors it in this modern world."[62] He concludes, "The most urgent need in the Christian Church today is true preaching; and since it is the greatest and the most urgent need in the Church, it is obviously the greatest need of the world also."[63]

In the same way as the Puritans, Lloyd-Jones was convinced that in order for the content of the sermon's message to be considered true preaching, it had to be expository and doctrinal. He argues that "[a] sermon should always be expository"[64] since its message should come from the word of God. True expository preaching, for him, is doctrinal preaching, since to expound the word of God is "to set out the principles or doctrines which the words are

60. Lloyd-Jones, *Preaching and Preachers*, 11, 27.

61. Lloyd-Jones, *Preaching and Preachers*, 28–29.

62. Lloyd-Jones, *Preaching and Preachers*, 40, 51–62. He says, "[Preaching] may be slow work; it often is; it is a long-term policy. But my whole contention is that it works, that it pays, and that it is honored, and must be, because it is God's own method. This is the thing to which He calls us, it is the thing into which He thrusts us forth, and therefore He will honor it. He has always honored it, and still honors it in this modern world, and after you have tried these other methods and schemes, and found that they will come to nothing, you will be driven back to this ultimately. This is the method by which churches have always come into being. You see it in the New Testament, and you see it in the subsequent history of the Church, and you can see it in this modern world" (51–52).

63. Lloyd-Jones, *Preaching and Preachers*, 9.

64. Lloyd-Jones, *Preaching and Preachers*, 71.

intended to convey." The purpose of expository preaching is to "address specific truths from God to man."[65] The most important matter in expository preaching is for a preacher to discern the specific doctrine expressed in the biblical text, which is a special message that the preacher should convey. If preachers have understood one passage or section of the text, they will always perceive the particular proposition or significant doctrine that God placed in the text.[66]

In this regard, Lloyd-Jones emphasizes that "there is nothing more important in a preacher than that he should have a systematic theology, that he should know it and be well grounded in it."[67] He maintains:

> The systematic theology, this body of truth which is derived from the Scripture, should always be present as a background and as a controlling influence in his preaching. Each message, which arises out of a particular text or statement of the Scripture, must always be a part or an aspect of this total body of truth. It is never something in isolation, never something separate or apart. The doctrine in a particular text, we must always remember, is a part of this greater whole—the Truth or the Faith. ... All our preparation of a sermon should be controlled by this background of systematic theology.[68]

His argument, in short, is that expository preaching is ultimately doctrinal preaching in that to expound is to extract and deliver a particular doctrine from the text. It should always be controlled by systematic theology as the whole body of truth derived from Scripture. Lloyd-Jones describes preaching as "logic on fire," since doctrinal truth conveyed through preaching ignites the hearts of both the preacher and the listeners.[69] Therefore, according to Steven Lawson, Lloyd-Jones believed that "setting forth the theology of the passage is essential to achieving the desired effect of the sermon."[70] Were it not for clear understanding of doctrine in the mind, there would be little

65. Murray, *Life of Martyn Lloyd-Jones*, 307.

66. Park, "Integration of the Word," 530.

67. Lloyd-Jones, *Preaching and Preachers*, 66.

68. Lloyd-Jones, *Preaching and Preachers*, 66.

69. Lloyd-Jones views "fire" as coming not only from preacher's understanding of a truth but also as a result of the baptism with the Spirit on the preacher (*Puritans*, 368).

70. Lawson, *Passionate Preaching of Martyn Lloyd-Jones*, 128.

change in the hearts of listeners, and likely no transformation in their daily life. Lloyd-Jones follows Puritan belief in the primacy of intellect in the relation to emotion and will:

> The emotions and the will should always be influenced through the mind. Truth is intended to come to the mind. The normal course is for the emotions and the will to be affected by the truth after it has first entered and gripped the mind. It seems to me that this is a principle of Holy Scripture. The approach to the emotions and the will should be indirect. Still less should we ever bring any pressure to bear upon either the emotions or will. We are to plead with men but never to bring pressure. We are to beseech, but we are never to browbeat. This, it seems to me, is a vital distinction which every preacher and missioner must always bear in mind.[71]

For Lloyd-Jones, preaching doctrine encourages the congregation to think clearly so that eventually their new understanding of doctrine leads them to examine themselves, to pay attention to their sin, to respond to the preacher's call for a decision, and to experience the abundance of God's grace. In his sermon "Men as Trees, Walking," he declares:

> It is the doctrine that hurts, it is the doctrine that focuses things. It is one thing to look at pictures and to be interested in words and shades of meaning. That does not disturb, that does not focus attention on sin, nor call for decision. We can sit back and enjoy that; but doctrine speaks to us and insists upon a decision. This is truth, and it examines us and tries us and forces us to examine ourselves. So, if we start by objecting to doctrine as such, it is not surprising that we do not see clearly. The whole purpose of all the creeds drawn up by the Christian Church, together with every confession of faith on doctrine and dogma was to enable people to see and to think clearly. This is how they came to be formulated.[72]

---

71. Lloyd-Jones, *Knowing the Times*, 88.
72. Lloyd-Jones, *Spiritual Depression*, 45.

Lloyd-Jones emphasizes, as the Puritans also did, that the doctrinal message in the sermon should not end as a lecture, but should be applied to the lives of the audience:

> But as you have presented your message in this way it is important that you should have been applying what you have been saying as you go along. … This again shows that you are not just lecturing, that you are not dealing with an abstract or academic or theoretical matter; but that this is a living matter which is of real concern to the people in the whole of their life and being. So you must keep on applying what you are saying. Then to make absolutely certain of this, when you have ended the reason and the argument, and have arrived at the climax, you apply it all again. This can be done in the form of an exhortation which again may take the form of a series of questions, or a series of terse statements. But it is vital to the sermon that it should always end on this note of application or of exhortation.[73]

In this regard, it can be argued that Lloyd-Jones's sermon structure follows the Puritan three-part sermon structure: exposition, doctrine, and application.

To preach doctrine from Scripture, Lloyd-Jones argues, is not just to give information to listeners, nor to help them to build up knowledge alone. The ultimate purpose is to lead them to experience God. For him, preaching is "theology coming through a man who is on fire." He believes that a preacher should be, as the apostle Paul was, "on fire" when the preacher is greatly moved by realizing and speaking the great doctrines of the Bible. In this regard, "a true understanding and experience of the Truth"[74] must go together. For Lloyd-Jones, true preaching, in short, is to preach doctrines in the texts experientially. His conviction on this matter is evident in the preface of *Romans*: "My hope is that this volume and those that are to follow, God willing, will not only help Christian people to understand more clearly the great central doctrines of our Faith, but that they will also fill them with a joy 'unspeakable and full of glory' and bring them into a condition in which they will be 'Lost in wonder, love, and praise.'"[75] True preaching, Lloyd-Jones

73. Lloyd-Jones, *Puritans*, 77–78.

74. Lloyd-Jones, *Preaching and Preachers*, 97.

75. Lloyd-Jones, *Romans: Atonement and Justification*, xiii.

argues, gives listeners "a sense of God and His presence."[76] The primary purpose of preaching is not only to give information but also to make an impression on the hearts of listeners. The business of preaching is to make doctrine live, warm, and earnest.[77]

As covered so far, Lloyd-Jones's conviction regarding the supremacy of preaching and his view of true preaching—expository in method, doctrinal in content, and experiential in goal—was inherited from the Puritan preaching tradition. Lloyd-Jones, like the Puritans and Edwards, was convinced of the significant role of doctrine for applying Scripture to listeners' hearts and lives. All exegetical work and doctrines connected to the chosen text in preaching should be examined as particular aspects of a more comprehensive, systematic theology since an understanding of the whole body of Scripture is important to understand invidual texts. Most of all, like his Reformed forerunners, Lloyd-Jones was certain that without convincing the minds of his listeners, he could not reach their hearts through preaching. The final goal of the sermon, for Lloyd-Jones, was not to have listeners informed but to have their hearts touched by leading them to experience the presence of God through preaching.

LLOYD-JONES'S DISTINCTIVE UNDERSTANDING OF TRUE PREACHING: SPIRIT-BAPTIZED PREACHING

According to Lloyd-Jones, preaching consists of two elements: the sermon (the message) and the act of preaching (the delivery). In order to be true preaching, these elements must be combined in the right proportions.[78] With respect to the sermon, as we saw, it should be expository and doctrinal; as to the act of preaching, preachers themselves require baptism with the Spirit. Experience as the goal of preaching, discussed earlier, also belongs to the category of the act of preaching. Lloyd-Jones believed that preaching under the influence of Spirit baptism inevitably led the audience to experience the compelling presence of God.

---

76. Lloyd-Jones, *Preaching and Preachers*, 97.
77. Lloyd-Jones, *Puritans*, 360.
78. Lloyd-Jones, *Preaching and Preachers*, 56, 96.

In fact, at the heart of Lloyd-Jones's original understanding of true preaching is a distinction between the sermon itself and the act of preaching. To clarify the difference between the two, Lloyd-Jones introduces a conversation that George Whitefield had with someone who was trying to publish Whitefield's sermons:

> A man came—I think it was actually in Philadelphia—on one occasion to the great George Whitefield and asked if he might print his sermons. Whitefield gave this reply; he said, "Well, I have no inherent objection, if you like, but you will never be able to put on the printed page the lightning and the thunder." That is the distinction—the sermon, and "lightning and the thunder."[79]

For Lloyd-Jones, "the lightning and the thunder" to which Whitefield referred meant the power of the Spirit that took place in the act of preaching. Accordingly, in Lloyd-Jones's thought, the close connection between Spirit baptism and preaching was applied not to the sermon, but to the act of preaching. He paid much attention to how Spirit baptism on a preacher affected the act of preaching ("the way in which the message is presented and conveyed")[80] and, as a result, the effect on the listeners.

This uniqueness of Lloyd-Jones's understanding of preaching is the result of his interest in and research on the history of revival. He established his particular homiletics, which is closely related to the experience of Spirit baptism on a preacher and the listeners, on his study of the records of the extraordinary work of the Spirit and in particular of powerful preaching ministries during periods of revival. Above all, he discovered a vision of true preaching in the history of the eighteenth-century Calvinistic Methodists; he believed that what the Christian church as well as the world in his days most needed was this kind of preaching.

Now we will explore the act of preaching, the second element of true preaching, that is directly related to baptism with the Spirit in Lloyd-Jones's homiletics. Then we will discuss his apostolic method of preaching, intimately connected with the element of power in the act of preaching.

---

79. Lloyd-Jones, *Preaching and Preachers*, 58.

80. Lloyd-Jones, *Puritans*, 122.

THE ACT OF PREACHING

In the fifth chapter of *Preaching and Preachers*, "The Act of Preaching," Lloyd-Jones confesses that to define the act of preaching seems to be as baffling as for the apostle Paul to define love in 1 Corinthians 13. Therefore, the best way for Lloyd-Jones to define it is to identify certain elements that must be present in true preaching.[81] He suggests and discusses ten such essential elements of true preaching, summarized below.

The first element of true preaching is the whole personality of the preacher involved in preaching. Lloyd-Jones argues that the entire person of the preacher, including the preacher's body, gestures, and activities, should be involved in preaching. In particular, noting the Greek philosopher Demosthenes's stress on the importance of action in successful oratory, Lloyd-Jones emphasizes action in preaching since he believes a preacher's whole personality includes the preacher's body:

> You will remember that when Demosthenes was asked what is the first great essential in oratory, his reply was "Action." Then he was asked, "Well, what is the second greatest desideratum?" He replied again, "Action." "Well," they said, "what is the third most important point?" Still the reply was, action; and that is why I stress that the whole personality must be involved in preaching.[82]

For Lloyd-Jones, true preaching was "something to look at as well as to hear because the whole man is involved in the action."[83] To prove his definition, he introduces an illustration about the preaching of James Henry Thornwell (1812–1862) made by his biographer:

> What invented symbols could convey that kindling eyes, those trembling and varied tones, the expressive attitude, the foreshadowing and typical gesture, the whole quivering frame which made up in him the complement of the finished author! The lightning's flash, the fleecy clouds embroidered on the sky, and the white crest of the ocean wave, surpass the painter's skill. It was indescribable.[84]

81. Lloyd-Jones, *Preaching and Preachers*, 81.
82. Lloyd-Jones, *Preaching and Preachers*, 82.
83. Lloyd-Jones, *Preaching and Preachers*, 98.
84. Lloyd-Jones, *Preaching and Preachers*, 98.

Likewise, Lloyd-Jones claims that everything reflecting a preacher's personality, such as eyes, tone of voice, and gestures, should be considered part of the act of preaching.

The second element of true preaching is a sense of authority and control. Lloyd-Jones claims that a preacher should regard the preacher's self as an ambassador or a messenger sent by God to declare his messages "under commission and under authority." Therefore, he stresses, "Far from being controlled by the congregation the preacher is in charge and in control of the congregation." Restoring authority to the pulpit, he argues, is the greatest need in the church. According to him, in the nineteenth century the church attempted to restore this authority in the wrong way, by putting vestments on preachers or escalating preachers' scholarship. He regards these methods as wrong since the authory that the pulpit really needs to recover is spiritual authority. This authority, he believes, is given only when the preacher is filled (or baptized) with the Holy Spirit.[85]

The third element is freedom. Lloyd-Jones asserts that a preacher must be open to the inspiration given in the moment of preaching without being too tied to preparation. Also, the preacher should be open to something given by "the responsiveness and eagerness" of the congregation, while being aware of an aspect of exchange with them in preaching. For Lloyd-Jones, the quality of freedom is crucial in true preaching. He argues, "The preaching should be always under the Spirit—His power and control—and you do not know what is going to happen. So always be free."[86] This element of freedom shows that Lloyd-Jones's understanding of preaching differs from the Reformed tradition in its emphasis regarding the work of the Holy Spirit. In the Reformed tradition, emphasis is placed on the illuminating work of the Spirit that not only helps the preacher to understand Scripture properly in the preparation of the sermon, but also applies the words of the sermon to the specific situation of the listeners in the act of preaching.[87] Lloyd-Jones, while acknowledging these illuminating works of the Spirit in preaching,[88] focuses more

85. Lloyd-Jones, *Preaching and Preachers*, 83, 159, 160.

86. Lloyd-Jones, *Preaching and Preachers*, 84–85.

87. Barbee, "Allurer of the Soul," 111.

88. For instance, in "No Substitute," published in *Preaching and Preachers*, Lloyd-Jones states: "My contention is that if the Gospel is truly preached, in a most astonishing manner it can be so

on the possiblity of and openness to the unpredictable work of the Holy Spirit that takes place in the act of preaching itself. In this regard, he argues:

> It may sound contradictory to say "prepare, and prepare carefully," and yet "be free." But there is no contradiction, as there is no contradiction when Paul says, "Work out your own salvation with fear and trembling, for it is God that worketh in you both to will and to do of his good pleasure" (Phil 2:12–13). You will find that the Spirit who has helped you in your preparation may now help you, while you are speaking, in an entirely new way, and open things out to you which you had not seen while you were preparing your sermon.[89]

The fourth element is seriousness. Lloyd-Jones states, "The preacher must be a serious man; he must never give the impression that preaching is something light or superficial or trivial."[90] The impression of seriousness comes from the fact that the preacher deals with the most urgent matter:

> What is happening is that [the preacher] is speaking to them from God, he is speaking to them about God, he is speaking about their condition, the state of their souls. He is telling them that they are, by nature, under the wrath of God—"the children of wrath even as others"—that the character of the life they are living is offensive to God and under the judgement of God, and warning them of the dread eternal possibility that lies ahead of them.[91]

Lloyd-Jones quotes the well-known statements of Richard Baxter to describe the sense of seriousness in the act of preaching: "I preached as never sure to preach again. And as a dying man to dying men." Therefore, to Lloyd-Jones, it is important for a preacher to "create and convey the impression of the seriousness of what is happening the moment he even appears in the pulpit." Such seriousness, he argues, is given to the congregation when the sight of a

---

applied by the Spirit to these individual cases and problems that they are dealt with without the preacher knowing it at all" (38).

89. Lloyd-Jones, *Preaching and Preachers*, 85.

90. Lloyd-Jones, *Preaching and Preachers*, 85.

91. Lloyd-Jones, *Preaching and Preachers*, 86.

preacher gives the impression that the preacher has come from the presence of God to deliver his message to them.[92]

The fifth element is liveliness. For Lloyd-Jones, a dull preacher is "a contradiction in terms" since "with the grand theme and message of the Bible dullness is impossible." He determines that if a preacher presents a sermon in a dull manner, "the most interesting, the most thrilling, the most absorbing subject in the universe," the preacher has never really understood the doctrine delivered. "A true understanding and experience of the truth" must lead a preacher to be moved and caught on fire.[93]

The sixth element is zeal and a sense of concern. According to Lloyd-Jones, the two elements of zeal and concern are closely related. Preachers cannot be detached either from the message they convey or from the congregation to whom they preach. Regarding the element of zeal, Lloyd-Jones argues that "a preacher must always convey the impression that he himself has been gripped by what he is saying. If he has not been gripped nobody else will be. ... He is so moved and thrilled by it himself that he wants everybody else to share in this." As for a sense of concern, Lloyd-Jones states, "[The preacher] is concerned about [his congregation]; that is why he is preaching to them. He is anxious about them; anxious to help them, anxious to tell them the truth of God. So he does it with energy, with zeal, and with this obvious concern for people." Thus, Lloyd-Jones concludes that a genuine preacher is a witness, not an advocate, who is involved personally in the content of the sermon as well as being truly concerned for the congregants who listen.[94]

The seventh element is warmth. Zeal and concern for people in the preacher's heart inevitably leads to warmth. Lloyd-Jones believes that if a preacher really understands the great truths in the Bible in mind, the preacher's heart will be moved by them. He holds up the apostle Paul and Whitefield as good examples of those who were moved in their hearts by what they understood in their minds, even preaching with tears if necessary.[95] He deplores the absence of emotional warmth in modern preaching:

---

92. Lloyd-Jones, *Preaching and Preachers*, 86.
93. Lloyd-Jones, *Preaching and Preachers*, 87, 97.
94. Lloyd-Jones, *Preaching and Preachers*, 87–89.
95. Lloyd-Jones, *Preaching and Preachers*, 90.

> Where is the passion in preaching that has always characterized great preaching in the past? Why are not modern preachers moved and carried away as the great preachers of the past so often were? The Truth has not changed. Do we believe it, have we been gripped and humbled by it, and then exalted until we are "lost in wonder love and praise?"[96]

As a manifestation of this warmth coming from a preacher's understanding of the truth as well as the preacher's zeal to share it with the congregation, he also concludes that everything about a preacher—voice, manner, and emotional engagement with the sermon content and the congregation—should demonstrate an intimate rapport between the preacher and congregation so that there would be connection, rather than detachment, to the word of God being preached.[97]

The eighth element is urgency and persuasiveness. The task of preaching is not simply the act of conveying information but also involves dealing with "matters not only of life and death in this world, but with eternal destiny." Accordingly, Lloyd-Jones claims that "if the preacher does not suggest this sense of urgency, that he is there between God and men, speaking between time and eternity he has no business to be in a pulpit." The element of urgency naturally leads to persuasiveness in preaching since the preacher desires to persuade listeners to be reconciled with God and to lead them to the truth.[98]

The ninth element is pathos. In addition to warmth, urgency, and persuasiveness, Lloyd-Jones argues that "this element of pathos and of emotion is ... what has been so seriously lacking in the present century." Pathos comes from compassion for people and from an understanding of what God has done for humanity in Christ. If a preacher knows nothing of the compassion with which Jesus was filled when he interacted with people, the preacher should not be in a pulpit. And because this compassion should be grounded in the preacher's own experience of the greatness of Christ's work, Lloyd-Jones states emphatically that "if you contemplate these glorious truths that are committed to our charges as preachers without being moved by them there is something defective in your spiritual eyesight." He is convinced that the

96. Lloyd-Jones, *Preaching and Preachers*, 90.
97. Lloyd-Jones, *Preaching and Preachers*, 90.
98. Lloyd-Jones, *Preaching and Preachers*, 91–92.

gospel should so envelop the whole personality of a person, including the emotions, that "this element of pathos and emotion, this element of being moved, should always be very prominent in preaching."[99]

The last element of true preaching Lloyd-Jones discusses is power. He affirms that it is not genuine preaching if there exists no power since "true preaching, after all, is God acting." As the apostle Paul indicates in 1 Corinthians 2:4 ("And my speech and my preaching was not with enticing words of man's wisdom, but in demonstration of the Spirit and of power") and 1 Thessalonians 1:5 ("For our gospel came not unto you in word only, but also in power, and in the Holy Ghost, and in much assurance"), Lloyd-Jones argues that true preaching takes place when a preacher is "under the influence of the Holy Spirit." For Lloyd-Jones, the element of power is the central aspect of true preaching that is directly connected with his doctrine of Spirit baptism, a topic "so important that it deserves a whole section to itself."[100] Accordingly, he commits the whole last chapter of *Preaching and Preachers*, "Demonstration of the Spirit and of the Power," to the subject. The following section will consider this topic in detail.

APOSTOLIC METHOD OF PREACHING: SPIRIT-BAPTIZED PREACHING

The element of power in true preaching is intimately connected with Lloyd-Jones's understanding regarding the apostolic manner of preaching. Another way of describing true preaching for Lloyd-Jones was to call it "apostolic preaching," the content and method of which are illustrated in the New Testament, particularly in Paul's Epistles. It is noteworthy that Lloyd-Jones quotes Paul's letters most often to describe what true preaching should be like. This implies that Lloyd-Jones considers Paul, among all the apostles, the best biblical model of apostolic preaching for preachers to imitate today. Lloyd-Jones especially relies on 1 Corinthians 2:4–5 and 1 Thessalonians 1:5 as key verses in Paul's letters to explain apostolic preaching. His sermon "Not in Word Only," preached at Knox Presbyterian Church in Toronto in 1967, expounds 1 Thessalonians 1:5 to show extensively what apostolic preaching is and that it is composed of two things: the message and the power of the Spirit within it. The sermon reads as follows:

---

99. Lloyd-Jones, *Preaching and Preachers*, 92–95.

100. Lloyd-Jones, *Preaching and Preachers*, 95.

> Very well, let's look at these two things together because the Apostle tells us that there are two things. ... The first thing is the message that was preached. "Our Gospel came unto you not in word only," that is the message. But there was this other factor, "not in word only, but also in power, and in the Holy Ghost, and in much assurance." Now there are the two things: the message and the power of the Spirit upon it! That is to be seen in the Apostles. It is to be seen equally in the people who believed the message and became members of the Christian Church.[101]

The message of apostolic preaching means the sermon—the first element of true preaching reviewed earlier—is expository in its form and doctrinal in its content. However, according to 1 Thessalonians 1:5, Lloyd-Jones argues, even though preaching the essential doctrines (message) is absolutely necessary for true preaching, it will be useless if there is no power of the Spirit at work in the message. In "Not in Word Only," his discussion continues on this point:

> The Apostle [Paul] said that it came not in word only, but also in power, and in the Holy Ghost, and in much assurance. I want to emphasize this as much as the other. ... Orthodoxy is absolutely essential. ... But orthodoxy alone is not enough. A church can be perfectly orthodox and at the same time perfectly dead and perfectly useless. The Apostolic message was orthodox but there was something else. "Our Gospel came not unto you in word only but also in power, and in the Holy Ghost, and in much assurance." What is he talking about? He is talking primarily about himself as he preached to them. He says, "You know when I preached to you, I knew that it was not merely I, Paul, that was speaking. I knew that the Spirit was using me. I knew that I had got the power of the Holy Ghost. I knew that he had clothed himself upon me. I knew that I was nothing but the vehicle, the channel, the instrument. I knew that I was being used. I was preaching with much assurance. I knew something was happening, I knew that he was working in you." You see the Apostle always relied on the power of the Holy Spirit. It is not enough that we be certain of our message. We

101. Sargent, *Sacred Anointing*, 263.

> must be equally careful about our methods, and the Apostle's method was—trusting the Holy Spirit.[102]

For Lloyd-Jones, the basis of apostolic preaching is relying on the power of the Spirit. It is for the preacher to preach under the influence of the Holy Spirit, being used by the Spirit and becoming his channel through whom the power of the Spirit works. Lloyd-Jones defines this as the unction or anointing of the Spirit, which is the same idea as that of Spirit baptism:

> What is this [unction]? It is the Holy Spirit falling upon the preacher in a special manner. It is an access of power. It is God giving power, and enabling, through the Spirit, to the preacher in order that he may do this work in a manner that lifts it up beyond the efforts and endeavors of man to a position in which the preacher is being used by the Spirit and becomes the channel through whom the Spirit works.[103]

In short, to Lloyd-Jones, Spirit baptism is an indispensable element of the apostolic method. He argues that "our methods are as important as our message and we must not use the methods of the world." He states even that "the tragedy of the situation is that we think we need something new, whereas what we really need is this old, old Gospel preached in the old method and after the old, Apostolic manner."[104] Why is the method of relying on the Holy Spirit so important to true preaching? Lloyd-Jones is convinced that such statements of Paul in 1 Thessalonians 1:5 and 1 Corinthians 2:4–5 were Paul's theological and experiential confession: "Preaching is God's own act, not mine." Therefore, Lloyd-Jones believes that without God acting in preaching—working through the Holy Spirit—any human power, effort, knowledge, skills, method, and organization turn out to be ineffective.

As stated earlier, Lloyd-Jones was interested in how Spirit baptism on a preacher affected the act of preaching and the effect on the listeners by the preaching under the influence of the Spirit. For Lloyd-Jones, Spirit baptism provided a preacher with such a full assurance of salvation and of God's redemptive love that it led the preacher to preach the gospel with divine power and authority. Lloyd-Jones does not explain in detail how

102. Sargent, *Sacred Anointing*, 273–74.

103. Lloyd-Jones, *Preaching and Preachers*, 305.

104. Sargent, *Sacred Anointing*, 262, 274.

the experience of assurance (sealing) relates to empowerment for preaching (unction). Nonetheless, in his mind these two experiences are closely connected. Just as the main purpose of Spirit baptism is to give Christians (including preachers) full assurance of salvation, so it makes the preaching of salvation effective by the power of the Holy Spirit.

Lloyd-Jones regards Spirit baptism on a preacher as an experience of the love of God shed abroad in the preacher's heart, as Romans 5:5 states: "the love of God is shed abroad in our hearts by the Holy Ghost which is given unto us" (KJV). Consequently, he implies that there is a mystical connection between the deep experiences of God's love in a preacher's heart and being granted divine authority and power to preach, since this happened to the disciples on the day of Pentecost as well as to such powerful preachers as John Wesley, George Whitefield, Howell Harris, and Charles Spurgeon (1834–1892). As a good example of the connection between Spirit baptism and a preacher's experience of God's love, Lloyd-Jones refers to D. L. Moody's experience:

> I kept on crying all the time that God would fill me with His Spirit. Well, one day, in the city of New York—oh, what a day!—I cannot describe it, I seldom refer to it; it is almost too sacred an experience to name. Paul had an experience of which he never spoke for fourteen years. I can only say that God revealed Himself to me, and *I had such an experience of His love* that I had to ask him to stay his hand.[105]

According to Lloyd-Jones, other great evangelists of the eighteenth century who had similar experiences did not understand God's redemptive love and forgiveness in only an intellectual or superficial sense but came to know it experientially by becoming newly aware of the sealing of the Spirit in their hearts. The profound experience of God's redemptive love and forgiveness inflamed their hearts to offer their lives in sacrificial service to Christ and the gospel. Along these lines, the lack of a clear distinction between assurance and unction should itself be regarded as an original aspect of Lloyd-Jones's homiletics since in his view the experience of personal assurance and empowerment for preaching are alternative expressions of the same divine power.

105. Moody and Fitt, *Shorter Life of D. L. Moody*, 63; Lloyd-Jones, *Joy Unspeakable*, 80; emphasis added.

Moreover, Lloyd-Jones argues that Spirit baptism leads a preacher not only to be filled with compassion but also to be aflame with zeal for souls. In his lecture "Howell Harris and Revival," Lloyd-Jones points to Harris's crucial experience of Spirit baptism as a good example. Claiming that the experience of Spirit baptism transformed Harris into an effective evangelist, he states: "It is from that moment that this man began to be the flaming Evangelist. ... As a result of this experience, he felt a compassion for souls and a sorrow for all people who were in sin. It was this experience which led to his evangelistic activity."[106] As Lloyd-Jones asserts, what Harris himself saw when preaching in London in 1742 is enough to illustrate his powerful preaching ministry accompanied by his zeal for souls. Harris describes this event as follows:

> Prepared things to go to Wales—& talked with another simple woman full of fire & Zeal & Love & simplicity. I felt my soul in a flame & c. so went to Preach p[as]t 6 to p[as]t 8—full of the Lord in Praying I was drawn out most Powerfully & for all the Ministers & c.—preached on acts 3 ult. Part—repent & c.—that your Sins may be blotted out when the Times of Refreshing from the Lord shall come & c.—had such uncommon power from first to Last that I could hardly contain my self—now my voice was lifted up to some Purpose—sure the Lord came here tonight to feed His Lambs & to own me among them—I could not help now lifting up my hands & beating the Pulpit and pointing to Christ in Glory—crying to them come on come on.[107]

When Lloyd-Jones discusses Whitefield's effective preaching ministry, he makes a similar claim: that Spirit baptism"will give us a sorrow for souls and a concern for souls, and give us the zeal, and enable us to preach with power and conviction to all classes and kinds of men" as Whitefield experienced."[108]

It is worthwhile to note that Lloyd-Jones implies that Spirit baptism actually brings about the essential elements of the act of preaching, not only zeal, compassion, and power but also authority, freedom, liveliness, warmth, urgency, and pathos. Consequently, for him, if Spirit baptism does not exist in the act of preaching, it cannot be true preaching, even if the sermon itself is

106. Lloyd-Jones, *Puritans*, 286–91.

107. Nuttall, *Howell Harris*, 16–17.

108. Lloyd-Jones, *Puritans*, 127.

perfect in its exegetical and doctrinal content. Spirit baptism is an indispensable element of true preaching. As such, when Lloyd-Jones defines preaching as "logic on fire," "logic" refers to the message ("not in word only"); "on fire" refers to the power of the Spirit ("but also in power") that affects both a preacher and the preacher's act of preaching. Based on Paul's statement in 1 Thessalonians 1:5, Lloyd-Jones argues that "true preaching consists of both these elements combined in their right portions—the sermon, and the act of preaching. This 'act,' in addition to the sermon. That is true preaching."[109] In his lecture "Demonstration of the Spirit and of the Power," Lloyd-Jones describes how Spirit baptism affects the preacher's consciousness and the act of preaching:

> How do we recognise this [the power of the Spirit] when it happens? Let me try to answer. The first indication is in the preacher's own consciousness. "Our gospel came not unto you in word only," says Paul, "but also in power and the Holy Ghost, and much assurance." Who knew the assurance? Paul himself. He knew something was happening, he was aware of it. You cannot be filled with the Spirit without knowing it. He had "much assurance." He knew he was clothed with power and authority. How does one know it? It gives clarity of thought, clarity of speech, ease of utterance, a great sense of authority and confidence as you are preaching, an awareness of a power not your own thrilling through the whole of your being, and an indescribable sense of joy. You are a man "possessed," you are taken hold of, and taken up. I like to put it like this—and I know of nothing on earth that is comparable to this feeling—that when this happens you have a feeling that you are not actually doing the preaching, you are looking on. You are looking on at yourself in amazement as this is happening. It is not your effort; you are just the instrument, the channel, the vehicle: and the Spirit is using you, and you are looking on in great enjoyment and astonishment. There is nothing that is in any way comparable to this. This is what the preacher himself is aware of.[110]

---

109. Lloyd-Jones, *Preaching and Preachers*, 96.
110. Lloyd-Jones, *Preaching and Preachers*, 324.

What, for Lloyd-Jones, are the effects on the listeners of preaching under the influence of the Spirit? First, they also sense immediately as they listen to the sermon that something extraordinary is happening. Such preaching in the power of the Spirit brings about conviction and conversion among listeners. Lloyd-Jones addresses this point in his sermon "Not in Word Only":

> It is the Holy Spirit alone that can convict of sin. It is he alone that can enlighten the darkened human mind. It is he alone that can give a man life anew. And, as Paul was preaching in the power of the Spirit, the Spirit was working powerfully in them and [the Thessalonians] received the word. ... These men were born again. The Spirit had done his work and they turned to God from idols, they left the idols, they left the world, they left their sin. They entered into the life of Christ and took their place in the Christian Church and everybody saw it and everybody talked about it. And you know, they not only began but they went on with it.[111]

Lloyd-Jones further asserts that one of the significant roles of the Holy Spirit is not only to enlighten listeners' minds and understanding to see truths clearly, but also to lead listeners to sense those truths deeply in their hearts. In "The Sense of His Presence," one of a series of sermons on the doctrine of Spirit baptism preached at the Westminster Chapel in 1964, he explains: "What the Holy Spirit does is to make real to us the thing which we have believed by faith, the things of which we have had but a kind of indirect certainty only. The Holy Spirit makes these things immediately real."[112] In the same vein, Lloyd-Jones claims when the Holy Spirit comes down on people they "begin to have an awareness of spiritual things and clear views of them such as they have never had before."[113] He discusses this in "Expecting Revival," one of a series of sermons on revival delivered in 1959 to celebrate the centenary year of the British revival in 1859:

> They suddenly become conscious of this presence and of this power, and the first effect, is that spiritual things become realities. They have heard all these things before, they may have heard them a thousand

111. Sargent, *Sacred Anointing*, 208–9.
112. Lloyd-Jones, *Joy Unspeakable*, 85.
113. Lloyd-Jones, *Revival*, 100.

> times and indeed many thousand times, but what they testify is this: "You know, the whole thing suddenly became clear to me. I was suddenly illuminated, things that I was so familiar with stood out in letters of gold, as it were. I understood. I saw it all in a way that I had never done in the whole of my life." That is what they say. The Holy Spirit enlightens the mind and the understanding. They begin not only to see these things clearly but to feel their power.[114]

Through the work of the Spirit, he argues, the truths that people experientially come to realize are as follows: (1) "the glory and the holiness of God"; (2) "a deep and a terrible sense of sin, and an awful feeling of guilt"; and (3) "the love of God and of the Lord Jesus Christ and especially of his death upon the cross."[115] In the same sermon, he says:

> At last they see [the love of God and his Son's death on the cross]. Oh, they had always believed it theoretically and they had stayed to a communion service, but they had never felt anything, it had never truly become real for them. They had believed it, yes, they were honestly trusting to it, but they had never felt its power, they had never known what it was to be melted by it, to be broken by it. They had never known what it was to weep with a sense of unworthiness and then of love and joy as they realized that "God so loved the world, that he gave his only begotten Son, that whosever believeth in him should not perish, but have everlasting life." Suddenly it all becomes real to them and they are given to know that the Son of God has loved *them* and has given himself for *them*. It becomes an individual and a personal matter: "He died for *me*, even *my* sins are forgiven," and peace comes into their hearts; joy enters into them and they are lost in love and in a sense of praise of God the Father, God the Son, and God the Holy Spirit.[116]

In short, Lloyd-Jones believes that without the working of the Holy Spirit the message cannot lead listeners to experience it deeply in their hearts. Thus, his apostolic preaching requires that the message and the power of

---

114. Lloyd-Jones, *Revival*, 101.

115. Lloyd-Jones, *Revival*, 101–2.

116. Lloyd-Jones, *Revival*, 102; emphasis added.

the Spirit be united, as discussed by Paul in both 1 Thessalonians 1:5 and 1 Corinthians 2:4–5.

Taking all these things into account, Lloyd-Jones boldly declares, "John Calvin always needs George Whitefield." In this statement, Calvin stands for the message (orthodoxy), while Whitefield stands for "the power of the Spirit upon it" (Spirit baptism). What Lloyd-Jones intends to emphasize is that the sermon alone is not enough; it must be delivered in a demonstration of the Spirit and of power, that is, Spirit baptism. As Lloyd-Jones states: "Orthodoxy is essential, but orthodoxy alone has never produced a revival."[117] Even when he speaks of true preaching, his main concern is for revival. The reason he pays so much attention to the apostolic method of preaching is that he believes that "this is God's way in all revivals and reformations."[118]

More importantly, while studying not only the history of the church but also the Scriptures, Lloyd-Jones came to be convinced that Spirit baptism can be repeated many times, as illustrated specifically in the book of Acts. For him, what happened on Pentecost in Acts was not a "once and for all" event that cannot be repeated. On the contrary, he asserts that whenever revival has taken place, the church returns to the originating event that is described in Acts 2. He states, "Every time the Church is thus revived ... she is going back to something that happened before, rediscovering it, and finding the ancient supply." For him, the ancient supply is "the power of the Spirit," which is still available "if only we will go to it and go for it."[119] Consequently, he firmly believes that the possibility of powerful preaching like that of the apostles is open to all ministers today since "the ancient supply" is still available for the present day. On this point, Tony Sargent summarizes Lloyd-Jones's conviction regarding Spirit baptism as follows:

> He believed passionately that Apostolic power for preaching the Gospel is still available within God's sovereignty today. The Acts depicts the Church with preachers on fire; preachers who are given a great boldness and authority. In a word, they had unction [Spirit baptism]. This alone accounts for their astonishing success, which

117. Lloyd-Jones, *Puritans*, 126.

118. Sargent, *Sacred Anointing*, 275.

119. Lloyd-Jones, *Revival*, 28, 32, 199.

has been repeated in periods when the Spirit of God has been poured out upon the Church. The supply can still be tapped.[120]

THE INFLUENCE OF REVIVAL THEOLOGY AND LLOYD-JONES'S VISION FOR TRUE PREACHING

As confirmed in the previous chapter, Lloyd-Jones's understanding of Spirit baptism was significantly influenced by revival theology in the Reformed tradition, in particular the Calvinistic pneumatic school. His conviction regarding the necessity of Spirit baptism in true preaching, or apostolic preaching, should be understood as another proof of his being influenced by the old Calvinistic understanding of revival. Such influence can be well documented by the fact that belief in the connection between preaching and revival, as well as in the necessity of outpouring of the Spirit on preachers for revival, is commonly found in the writings of Puritans and Calvinistic Methodists in the seventeenth and eighteenth century.

As also discussed in the previous chapter, the Puritans who adhered to old Calvinistic revival theology held a common belief that a significant harbinger of revival was for the Spirit to be poured out on preachers with a great effect. As a result, their preaching, renewed by the Spirit, would have a much greater effect on people than ever before. The Spirit on preachers, they agreed, equipped them with a holy zeal, compassion, boldness, authority, and power. These Puritans sought earnestly for the great outpouring of the Spirit on both preachers and their preaching ministries since they felt keenly that without the act of God through his Spirit preaching the Reformed doctrines alone could not produce reformation or revival.

For instance, John Howe, an English Puritan in the seventeenth century, argued that during a gracious season, when the Spirit was poured out with a great outflow, preachers would have such a large share of the Spirit that people would hear "much other kind of sermons ... than you are wont to do nowadays," and "souls will surely be dealt with at another kind of rate." Howe also states, "Sure there will be a larger share, that will come even to the part of ministers, when such an effusion of the Spirit shall be as is here [in Ezek 39:29] signified: that they shall know how to speak to better purpose,

120. Sargent, *Sacred Anointing*, 77.

with more compassion and sense, with more seriousness, with more authority and allurement, than we now find we can."[121]

Solomon Stoddard, New England Puritan, is another who shared this conviction. In his sermon on Luke 4:18–19, "The Benefit of Gospel," he states: "Sometimes religion is in a withering condition but there are means that are serviceable for the reviving of it. And this is one special means, when the ministers have the Spirit of the Lord upon them. The Spirit of the Lord must be poured out upon the people, else religion will not revive. But when the Spirit is upon ministers, it is a very hopeful sign." He then answers an important question: "How does the Spirit's being upon ministers conduce to the reviving of religion?" First, he argues, "The Spirit gives them a zeal for God's glory and the salvation of souls." For him, "a holy zeal" in preachers makes them "prepared to declare the Word of God powerfully" by inflaming their hearts and making their message more effective. Also, it leads them to be "filled with courage to dispense the Word of God faithfully,"[122] not neglecting what they should preach or speaking too tenderly.

Second, Stoddard suggests that "if the Spirit be upon ministers, that gives them understanding and wisdom for their work." For him, "understanding and wisdom" is concerned with "men's iniquities." The Spirit upon preachers, he believed, helped their preaching to convince listeners of their iniquities so as to direct them to Christ: "God by his Spirit, enables ministers so to lay open the deceitfulness of their hearts, that they are brought to know themselves. ... God helps ministers to unravel their hearts, and so he leads them into an understanding of themselves." Stoddard concludes this sermon with an exhortation that the people of God should pray for their ministers since "if the Spirit rest upon them, that is a preparation for the reviving of religion."[123]

William Cooper, another New England Puritan, held the same view on the connection between preaching and revival. While witnessing the First Great Awakening taking place in New England, Cooper stated that it was surely the realization of what his predecessors noted above had anticipated for so long: "A number of preachers have appeared among us, to whom God has given such a large measure of his Spirit. ... They preach the Gospel of the

121. Howe, *Outpouring of the Holy Spirit*, 77; emphasis added.

122. Stoddard, *Efficacy of the Fear of Hell*, 34–35, 37–38.

123. Stoddard, *Efficacy of the Fear of Hell*, 39, 42, 53.

grace of God from place to place *with uncommon zeal and assiduity*."[124] Their message was the essential Reformed doctrines; their preaching manner was "not enticing words of man's wisdom" (1 Cor 2:4), but rather "His word in their mouths has been as a fire and as a hammer that breaketh the rock in pieces." The Spirit upon preachers, Cooper testified, led their hearts to be warmed with "an ardent love to Christ and souls" that animated their labors for the glory of God.[125]

The Welsh Calvinistic Methodists' understanding of revival and their writings on the subject also provided Lloyd-Jones with rich resources regarding the close connection between revival and preaching as well as regarding unusual anointings of the Spirit on ordinary preachers and the extraordinary effects of their preaching on listeners. For instance, the description by William Williams of Swansea regarding a succession of revivals that happened in 1779, 1791, and 1818 in Wales affirms that at the beginning of most revivals there were sudden outpourings of the power of the Holy Spirit on preachers. As a result, they preached in a completely different way from usual in their power, affections, and expressions; the audience also immediately sensed the difference and the presence of God in their act of preaching so that they underwent a great change through preaching individually and collectively. Here is a good example that Williams introduces concerning a Welsh revival in 1818, sparked through Richard Williams's (1802–1842) preaching:

> Richard Williams stood on a bench in the kitchen; in front of him was a square table, and on the top of that a small round one, doing duty as a reading-desk. He introduced the service in the usual way, but with more than usual fervor and unction, and the subject of his discourse was, "Coming to Christ." He had a sermon in his mind, and one with which he was perfectly familiar, for he had frequently preached it before, but when he had spoken for about a quarter of an hour he lost it quite, and began to say things that he had never thought of. It was not his own thoughts that he spoke now, and those which he uttered were not expressed in his usual style, nor with his usual voice. He felt that some one "was speaking through him," and for some time he was in doubt whether it was he himself that was preaching, or

124. Edwards, *Great Awakening*, 218; emphasis added.

125. Edwards, *Great Awakening*, 218.

> whether he was listening to another. The giddy ones that were talking in the parlor and outside became conscious that there was something unusual going on, and rushed into the kitchen with one accord. There they stood spell-bound and awe-struck, listening to the mighty words. Not one uttered a voice. No one wept. The feeling of awe upon every one present was too great for shouts, and even for tears; and when, at the close, the preacher gave out a hymn, no one was able to sing. The congregation separated in silence, and every one went his way to his own home, thinking, and afraid. What was it? It could not have been anything else than this which has been written, "The Holy Ghost fell on all them which heard the Word."[126]

Likewise, distinguishing the sermon and the act of preaching, Lloyd-Jones emphasizes the extraordinary work of the Spirit on the preacher and the preacher's act of preaching, even if he follows the Reformed tradition in addressing the ordinary work of the Spirit in preaching, such as with the Spirit's illuminating work on the preacher and the listener. The distinctiveness of Lloyd-Jones's homiletics is that it reflects the influence of Reformed revival theology, but is also formed within the matrix of his research and aspiration for revival. If his homiletics has its roots in pneumatology,[127] then at the root of the pneumatology is his understanding of and craving for revival.

More importantly, Lloyd-Jones discovered the ideal model of true preaching (or apostolic preaching)—theology on fire—in the history of the powerful preaching ministry of Calvinistic Methodist preachers such as Whitefield, Rowland, and Harris, who were active during the eighteenth-century revivals, rather than in Puritan preaching in the seventeenth century. Regarding Puritan preaching, as John Coffey points out, Lloyd-Jones is "always somewhat ambivalent."[128] Though he highly acclaims its expository and doctrinal emphases, he regards Puritans as "primarily teachers, ... not preachers."[129] He perceives the influence of Scholasticism in seventeenth-century Puritans

---

126. Williams, *Welsh Calvinistic Methodism*, 158–59.

127. Sargent, *Sacred Anointing*, xii.

128. Coffey, "Lloyd-Jones and the Protestant Past," 315.

129. Lloyd-Jones, *Knowing the Times*, 269. Lloyd-Jones's high appreciation for Puritan preaching is well reflected in his lecture "Preaching," delivered at the Westminster Conference in 1977 (*Puritans*, 372–89).

while estimating that they lack the freedom of the Spirit, spontaneity, and emotion. On the contrary, he views the combination between the Reformed doctrine (theology/light/mind) and the power of the Spirit (on fire/heat/heart) in the eighteenth-century Calvinistic Methodists' preaching as well-balanced. Preaching that holds this ideal combination, he believes, is the essence of the apostolic preaching to which the New Testament testifies and of which the church as well as the world is in the most need. He argues that in Edwards, too, there exists "the ideal combination—the great doctrines with the fire of the Spirit upon them." Therefore, for Lloyd-Jones, Edwards should be called a Calvinistic Methodist even though he was a Congregationalist.[130]

Lloyd-Jones exhorts preachers to continue their "regular work of preaching the gospel in all its fulness, in all its wholeness, after the manner of Puritan preaching,"[131] but never forgets to insist that they must constantly expect and seek the same outpouring of the Spirit in their preaching ministry as appeared in eighteenth-century revivals. As in his proposition "John Calvin always needs George Whitefield," Lloyd-Jones believed that while building on expository and doctrinal preaching after the Puritan manner, the powerful outpouring of the Spirit that the Calvinistic Methodist preachers enjoyed in their preaching ministry should be regarded as true preaching.

130. Lloyd-Jones, *Puritans*, 13, 205, 350, 368.

131. Lloyd-Jones, *Puritans*, 20.

8

EXEGETICAL CRITIQUES AND THEOLOGICAL EVALUATION

As stated earlier, Lloyd-Jones's doctrine of Spirit baptism and his conviction about the necessity of Spirit baptism in true preaching are rooted in both a particular interpretation of key texts and the history of the church. His consistent method for validating his assertions concerning Spirit baptism was to provide first a scriptural foundation and then the historical precedents to support it. For him, the interpretation of the biblical texts always took priority over the historical evidence. Also, as explored in chapter 4, Lloyd-Jones's interpretation of Spirit baptism in the New Testament was one of the most significant factors that contributed to his conviction on this matter. Therefore, it will be helpful to review his interpretation of the key texts in the New Testament related to Spirit baptism—Ephesians 1:13–14 and Romans 8:15–16—to evaluate the interpretive principles he employed.

This chapter will argue that even though Lloyd-Jones's consistent method was to present a biblical foundation first and then the historical evidence to support it, his personal experience, his studies of the history of revival (including the biographies and the journals of the saints), and his aspiration for a great awakening influenced his interpretation of the texts in question. Most of all, his exegetical work on these texts reflected his intention to suggest not only a biblical diagnosis but also an effective remedy already tested during periods of revival to overcome the malaise of believism from which contemporary churches suffered. These factors led Lloyd-Jones to interpret the texts differently from Puritans and the Reformed tradition, although it cannot be denied that their theological sources influenced his understanding in many ways. This chapter, therefore, will confirm that Lloyd-Jones's exegetical work was also formed in the matrix of his studies and longing for revival, as we found in the previous chapter regarding his homiletic.

EPHESIANS 1:13–14

Ephesians 1:13–14 is the core text for Lloyd-Jones's teaching on the sealing of the Spirit. It has been a focus for exegetical debate as to whether the verses refer to a conversion experience or a postconversion experience.[1] Lloyd-Jones's intensive exegetical work on the text can be found in his expository sermons on the verses preached in 1955 and published in *God's Ultimate Purpose* and "The Sealing of the Spirit," preached in 1965 and published in *Joy Unspeakable*. Even though there exists a decade-long gap between these sermons, there is little difference in their content and argument. On both occasions, Lloyd-Jones, as noted in chapter 4, takes the translation of the KJV, "in whom also after that ye believed, ye were sealed with that Holy Spirit of promise," as theologically correct though not literally accurate, arguing that there exists a sharp distinction and an interval between the initial experience of believing and a subsequent experience of being sealed by the Holy Spirit.

It should be noted that at the Fourth International Conference of Evangelical Students, held in 1939, Lloyd-Jones argued that there was no time interval between the point of believing and the sealing of the Spirit. In his address at the conference, published later under the title *Christ Our Sanctification*, Lloyd-Jones opposes the idea that "sanctification can be received in one act or action quite as definitely and in precisely the same way as justification was received."[2] He presents Acts 19:2 a passage that seems to support the wrong idea; he accepts the rendering of the Revised Version, rather than the Authorized Version, to dispute the idea:

> There are certain passages that seem to suggest it. One is the famous question put by Paul to certain people in Ephesus (recorded in Acts 19:2): "Have ye received the Holy Ghost since ye believed? [KJV]." But a mere perusal of the reading of the Revised Version at this point settles the matter at once—"Did ye receive the Holy Ghost when ye

1. "In whom ye also trusted, after that ye heard the word of truth, the gospel of your salvation: in whom also after that ye believed, ye were sealed with that holy Spirit of promise, which is the earnest of our inheritance until the redemption of the purchased possession, unto the praise of his glory." Ἐν ᾧ καὶ ὑμεῖς, ἀκούσαντες τὸν λόγον τῆς ἀληθείας, τὸ εὐαγγέλιον τῆς σωτηρίας ὑμῶν, ἐν ᾧ καὶ πιστεύσαντες ἐσφραγίσθητε τῷ πνεύματι τῆς ἐπαγγελίας τῷ ἁγίῳ, ὅς ἐστιν ἀρραβὼν τῆς κληρονομίας ἡμῶν, εἰς ἀπολύτρωσιν τῆς περιποιήσεως, εἰς ἔπαινον τῆς δόξης αὐτοῦ (NA[28]).

2. Lloyd-Jones, *Christ Our Sanctification*, 12.

> believed?" That is quite sufficient without our proceeding to consider the peculiar position of those Ephesian disciples.[3]

From this statement, we can see that initially Lloyd-Jones thought that faith and receiving the Spirit (or the sealing of the Spirit) were not separate. However, in 1955, in his sermon "Sealed with the Spirit," he confesses he was wrong to claim that there was no time difference between the two, asserting instead that the sealing of the Spirit is a postconversion experience:

> I confess that at one time I myself fell into error on the matter. A little booklet bearing my name, entitled *Christ Our Sanctification*, includes the argument that if we but follow the Revised Version instead of the Authorized Version we shall see that there is no time interval between the believing and sealing. I confess my former error. Actually I fell into it because I was concerned to show that sanctification is not an experience which is to be received after justification. This I still assert. But I was mistaken at that time with regard to the "sealing," as I proceed to show.[4]

As will be discussed later, finding out what happened between 1939 and 1955 that caused Lloyd-Jones to change his view is very important for understanding how his interpretation of Ephesians 1:13 differed from the Reformed position.

Returning to Lloyd-Jones's position from 1955 onward, to support his argument on an interval (or distinction) between believing and sealing of the Spirit, he quotes Charles Hodge's and Charles Simeon's statements in "The Sealing of the Spirit":

> Charles Hodge referring to this Authorized translation says, "This is more than a translation; it is an exposition of the original," and he is undoubtedly right. What he means is this: though, perhaps, they [KJV translators] should not have actually said "after that ye believed" they really were expounding the original Greek. These men were great Greek scholars and they translated it like this. They knew all about the exact meaning, but they were anxious to help the readers. So in

3. Lloyd-Jones, *Christ Our Sanctification*, 13.
4. Lloyd-Jones, *God's Ultimate Purpose*, 252.

> order to help them, they "expound" rather than translate at this point. "Whatever is meant by sealing," says Charles Hodge, "it is something which follows faith." Now that is the important point.
>
> Or take Charles Simeon with regard to this same statement. Referring to the sealing of the Spirit he says, "This was vouchsafed to many of the saints at Ephesus"—notice he does not say all of them. And then he continues, "There shall always be some in the Church who possess and enjoy it. ... This higher state of sanctification and assurance is reserved for those who 'after having believed' have maintained a close walk with God."[5]

Then Lloyd-Jones suggests a scriptural foundation for his argument from various cases in Acts: the disciples on Pentecost (Acts 2), the Samaritan converts (Acts 8), Saul (Acts 9), Cornelius (Acts 10, 11, 15), and the Ephesian disciples (Acts 19). According to Lloyd-Jones, all cases unveil an obvious interval since all of them had already been regenerated when they were "sealed" by the Holy Spirit.[6] Also, he argues, all these occasions in Acts prove that the sealing of the Spirit is something experiential.[7] For instance, he pinpoints how unscriptural it is to claim that the sealing of the Spirit on the disciples on the day of Pentecost in Acts 2 was unconscious:

> The Apostles were as men who appeared to be filled with new wine; they were in a state of ecstasy. They were rejoicing, they were praising God; they were moved, their hearts were ravished; they experienced things which they had never felt or known before. They were transformed, and were so different that you can scarcely recognize them as the same Peter and James and John and the rest as they once were. Not experimental! Nothing can be more experimental; it is the height of Christian experience.[8]

Lloyd-Jones's understanding of the sealing of the Spirit as a conscious experience is reflected in his contextual approach to Ephesians 1:13. According to Lloyd-Jones, the apostle Paul deals in this verse with an experiential aspect

---

5. Lloyd-Jones, *Joy Unspeakable*, 149–50.
6. Lloyd-Jones, *God's Ultimate Purpose*, 250–54; *Joy Unspeakable*, 150–54.
7. Lloyd-Jones, *God's Ultimate Purpose*, 267.
8. Lloyd-Jones, *God's Ultimate Purpose*, 269–70.

such as assurance and enjoyment regarding what he already stated previously in the first chapter:

> The Apostle has already dealt with the matter of our being in Christ and in the Church in this very chapter [Eph 1]. He started by saying "Blessed be the God and Father of our Lord Jesus Christ, who hath blessed us with all spiritual blessings in Christ: according as he hath chosen us in him before the foundation of the world." The term "predestination," which we have considered in verse 5 and again in verse 11—"In whom also we have obtained an inheritance, being predestinated according to the purpose of him ..."—again emphasizes that same aspect. But here [v. 13] the Apostle has turned to the experiential aspect, telling us that we, Jews and Gentiles, are inheritors together. He certainly returns here to something he has said already, for he is telling us of a further blessing above and beyond what he has previously mentioned.[9]

For Lloyd-Jones, the sealing of the Spirit here is to lead already-converted Christians to be more deeply assured of their possession of an eternal inheritance, their sonship, and God's redemptive love experientially, rather than in some unconscious manner. Such sealing by the Spirit, Lloyd-Jones argues, is "a direct and immediate testimony borne by the Holy Spirit to us":

> It does not mean that we hear any audible voice, or that we see some vision. Generally it comes as the result of the Spirit illuminating certain statements of Scripture, certain promises, certain assurances. He brings them to me with power and they speak to me, and I am certain of them. These things become luminously clear to me and I am as certain that I am a child of God as that I am alive. This is something which happens to us in such a manner that we not only believe in general that all who are Christians are children of God, but the Holy Spirit tells me in particular that I am a child of God.[10]

To support his argument regarding the immediate and direct aspect of the sealing, Lloyd-Jones draws from Thomas Goodwin and John Wesley. From

9. Lloyd-Jones, *God's Ultimate Purpose*, 268.
10. Lloyd-Jones, *God's Ultimate Purpose*, 274.

Goodwin, Lloyd-Jones quotes the following comment: "There is a light that cometh and overpowereth a man's soul and assureth him that God is his and he is God's, and that God loveth him from everlasting. ... It is a light beyond the light of ordinary faith. ... It is the next thing to heaven; you can have no more, until you come thither."[11] Then, from Wesley, Lloyd-Jones quotes: "It is something immediate and direct, not the result of reflection or argumentation. ... There may be foretastes of joy and peace, of love, and these not delusive but really from God long before we have the witness in ourselves."[12]

Lloyd-Jones argues that there exists "a great richness in the exposition of our present theme [the sealing of the Spirit]" in the history of the church. Then, he names of Goodwin, Owen, Hodge, Simeon, Wesley, and Whitefield, all of whom, he claims, were in support of his argument that the sealing with the Spirit is obviously experiential.[13] However, it should be noted that there existed a disagreement between Goodwin and Owen with regard to the interpretation of the sealing of the Spirit in Ephesians 1:13. Goodwin interpreted the sealing as an extraordinary action of the Spirit: "a second work of grace giving an immediate assurance of salvation."[14] On the other hand, Owen argued that the sealing was the Spirit himself, clearly stating, "The effects of this sealing are gracious operations of the Holy Spirit in and upon believers but the sealing itself is the communication of the Spirit unto us."[15] Thus Owen took a different position from Lloyd-Jones on this matter. Edwards's interpretation of the sealing of the Spirit also shows an obviously different position from Goodwin as well as Lloyd-Jones. Edwards understood the sealing of the Spirit as "the vital, gracious, sanctifying communication and influence of the Spirit,"[16] rather than as an immediate work of the Spirit. In *Religious Affections*, he states:

> And when the Scripture speaks of the seal of the Spirit, it is an expression which properly denotes, not an immediate voice or suggestion, but some work or effect of the Spirit, that is left as a divine mark upon

11. Goodwin, *Exposition on Ephesians*, 233, 236; Lloyd-Jones, *God's Ultimate Purpose*, 274–75.
12. Wesley, *Bicentennial Edition of Works* 1:95–100; Lloyd-Jones, *God's Ultimate Purpose*, 275.
13. Lloyd-Jones, *God's Ultimate Purpose*, 271.
14. Ferguson, "John Owen and the Doctrine," 123.
15. Owen, *Works of John Owen* 4:400.
16. Edwards, *Religious Affections*, 237.

> the soul, to be an evidence, by which God's children might be known. The seals of princes were the distinguishing marks of princes: and thus God's seal is spoken of as God's mark, Revelation 7:3. "Hurt not the earth, neither the sea, nor the trees, till we have sealed the servants of our God in their foreheads"; together with Ezekiel 9:4, "Set a mark upon the foreheads of the men that sigh and cry for all the abominations that are done in the midst thereof." When God sets his seal on a man's heart by his Spirit, there is some holy stamp, some image impressed and left upon the heart by the Spirit, as by the seal upon the wax. And this holy stamp, or impressed image, exhibiting clear evidence to the conscience, that the subject of it is the child of God, is the very thing which in Scripture is called the seal of the Spirit, and the witness, or evidence of the Spirit. And this image enstamped by the Spirit on God's children's hearts, is his own image: that is the evidence by which they are known to be God's children, that they have the image of their Father stamped upon their hearts by the spirit of adoption. ... And the saints are the jewels of Jesus Christ, the great potentate, who has the possession of the empire of the universe: and these jewels have his image enstamped upon them, by his royal signet, which is the Holy Spirit. And this is undoubtedly what the Scripture means by the seal of the Spirit; especially when it is enstamped in so fair and clear a manner, as to be plain to the eye of conscience; which is what the Scripture calls *our spirit* [Rom 8:16]. This is, truly an effect that is spiritual, supernatural, and divine. This is, in itself, of a holy nature, being a communication of the divine nature and beauty. That kind of influence of the Spirit which gives and leaves this stamp upon the heart, is such that no natural man can be the subject of anything of the like nature with it. This is the highest sort of witness of the Spirit, which it is possible the soul should be the subject of.[17]

In short, for both Owen and Edwards, the essence of the sealing of the Spirit was not any immediate or extraordinary work of the Spirit but was to be understood rather in terms of the indwelling of the Spirit and his sanctifying influence in a believer.

---

17. Edwards, *Religious Affections*, 232–33.

Lloyd-Jones's exegetical work on Ephesians 1:13 is closely connected with his conviction of the necessity of Spirit baptism in true preaching. He is assured that power to preach comes from the preacher's assurance; the sealing of the Spirit brings the preacher the highest form of assurance of salvation and God's love:

> If we are uncertain, doubtful and hesitant, our witness is going to be affected. If we are uncertain about the word of God, as to what is true and what is not true, or if I am uncertain about my relationship to him and the truth of these things in my case, I shall, as we have seen, be an advocate, not a witness. But when a man is baptized with the Spirit or sealed with the Spirit, he knows; the Spirit is the certainty. That leads not only to certainty in the individual, it leads to power. It must do. It is when we are certain, that we speak with authority and power.[18]

So far, we have explored Lloyd-Jones's exegetical work on Ephesians 1:13, focusing on his sermons that deal intensively with the verse and the doctrine of the sealing of the Spirit. The most controversial issue here is whether his interpretation of the sealing of the Spirit as a subsequent experience after believing has any grammatical foundation. Lloyd-Jones himself did not elaborate on the grammatical foundation for his interpretation. In his sermon "Sealed with the Spirit," he states only:

> It is generally agreed that the Epistle does not say: "In whom also believing ye are sealed with the Holy Spirit." The word is in the past tense; it is not "as you believed" or "when you believed," it is at the very least, "having believed." The Revised Version suggests the past, "having also believed, ye were sealed with the holy Spirit of promise"; and I suggest that even the phrase "having believed" suggests that these two things are not identical, and that the sealing does not immediately follow the act of belief.[19]

Additionally, in his sermon "The Sealing of the Spirit," he states:

> They [KJV translators] should not have actually said: "after that ye believed." The better translation is "believing," or "having believed."

18. Lloyd-Jones, *Joy Unspeakable*, 157.
19. Lloyd-Jones, *God's Ultimate Purpose*, 249.

> You can take it in both ways. "In whom also believing, ye were sealed with that Holy Spirit of promise"; or again, "Who having believed ..." Now both those translations are correct and the authorities are divided between the two. But this does not make any difference at all to the meaning. What the apostle is saying is this: you also having heard the message of the truth of the gospel, you have believed it, you have received it, and believing (or having believed) ye were sealed with the Holy Spirit of promise. So that it leaves the meaning exactly the same. It is presumed and taken for granted that they have believed, they were already believers when they were sealed.[20]

Subsequently, however, his position inspired controversy over the exegesis of Ephesians 1:13, particularly regarding the grammatical interpretation of the aorist participle πιστεύσαντες and its relation to the main verb, ἐσφραγίσθητε, which is also aorist.

The key to interpreting this passage lies in the temporal relationship between the verb and the participle. In *Baptism with the Spirit*, Michael Eaton argues that "the aorist participle refers to something that is prior to the action of the main verb."[21] As a basis for his argument, he cites E. de Witt Burton, who asserts that the aorist participle "is most frequently used of an action antecedent in time to the action of the main verb."[22] Therefore, Eaton concludes, "It is by no means *necessary* to take the aorist tense in Ephesians 1:13 as synchronous with the main verb."[23] Read in this manner, Paul appears to indicate that sealing by the Holy Spirit is subsequent to the believer's profession of faith, as indicated for example by the NASB translation, "having also believed, you were sealed in Him with the Holy Spirit of promise."

Conversely, in *The Spirit of Promise*, Donald Macleod objects to this position, asserting that "Greek tenses have to do primarily not with the time of the action (past, present, or future) but with the state of the action (complete, incomplete, or indefinite)." The aorist, he argues, is "the tense of indefinite action." He refers to A. T. Robertson, who claims that the aorist is

20. Lloyd-Jones, *Joy Unspeakable*, 149.
21. Eaton, *Baptism with the Spirit*, 234–35.
22. Burton, *Syntax of the Moods and Tenses*, 63.
23. Eaton, *Baptism with the Spirit*, 235; emphasis mine.

"simple action without representing it either as completed or incompleted."[24] Although Macleod does not make the statement, Robertson argues that if the aorist participle is used with a main verb that is aorist, the action is "specially likely to be coincident."[25]

Furthermore, Macleod presents the phrase ἀποκριθεὶς εἶπεν ("Jesus answered and said"), a frequent expression in the Gospels,[26] as obvious evidence of "the unwisdom of deducing from the aorist participle in Ephesians 1:13 that there is a clear interval between believing and being sealed." He explains as follows: "'Ἀποκριθεὶς (answering) is an aorist participle exactly similar to πιστεύσαντες (believing) in Eph 1:13. Yet it would be absurd to say that the Lord's saying was subsequent to the Lord's answering; And even more absurd to hold that it was possible to have answered without having said." Macleod concludes that faith logically precedes justification, but this does not mean that there is an interval between the two. Likewise, believing logically precedes being sealed, but it does not necessarily indicate that there exists a distance in time between the two.[27]

D. A. Carson supports Macleod's position, suggesting that "adverbial participles modifying verbs refer, in many occurrences, to action that is concurrent with that of the finite verb."[28] Craig S. Keener also objects to interpreting sealing as subsequent to believing the gospel due to a grammatical pattern—an aorist participle preceding an aorist main verb—since there exist too many instances where this interpretation is not logically possible. As an example, he suggests Ephesians 1:20 (ἣν ἐνήργησεν ἐν τῷ χριστῷ, ἐγείρας αὐτὸν ἐκ τῶν νεκρῶν, καὶ ἐκάθισεν ἐν δεξιᾷ αὐτοῦ ἐν τοῖς ἐπουρανίοις), which contains a similar grammatical construction. In this case, he argues, "it cannot imply subsequence because if it did, it would mean that God exerted his mighty power in Christ *after* resurrecting him, rather than by resurrecting him."[29]

Stanley Porter's study focusing on the aorist participle in Paul's epistles provides an opportunity to reexamine Ephesians 1:13, along with the sealing of the Spirit, through recent Greek grammar research. In *Verbal Aspect in the*

---

24. Macleod, *Spirit of Promise*, 50.
25. Robertson, *Grammar of the Greek New Testament*, 1114.
26. For instance, Matt 4:4; 12:39, 48; 13:11, 37; 15:3, 13.
27. Macleod, *Spirit of Promise*, 50.
28. Carson, *Showing the Spirit*, 247.
29. Keener, *Gift and Giver*, 155.

Greek of the New Testament, with Reference to Tense and Mood, Porter states, "Of the approximately 120 Aorist Participles found in relation to a main verb (in Paul's letters), approximately 78 precede and 42 follow the main verb, with those preceding showing a definite tendency toward antecedent action and those following showing a definite tendency toward coincidental action." As he explains, this study concentrates first on "the aorist participles found in relation to a main verb"[30] in Paul's letters. Unlike the previous explanations by Burton and Robertson, Porter's examination of the data reveals that there is a tendency for temporal meaning to differ—"antecedent action" or "coincidental action"—depending on whether the aorist participle is situated before or after the main verb. Intriguingly, in Ephesians 1:13, the aorist participle πιστεύσαντες precedes the main verb ἐσφραγίσθητε.[31] This means that Porter's study supports the argument that "believing" is reasonably understood as antecedent to "being sealed" since aorist participles preceding the main verb show "a definite tendency toward antecedent action."

When these various views on the aorist participle found in Ephesians 1:13 are compared, Porter's research is the most persuasive since he not only analyzes all of the aorist participles used by Paul, but he also examines the difference of temporal inference according to the position of the aorist participle in relation to the main verb. Porter's analysis provides a grammatical foundation for Lloyd-Jones's interpretation on Ephesians 1:13 that the sealing of the Spirit takes place after believing the gospel.

Nonetheless, some scholars, such as James Dunn and Gordon Fee, argue that while acknowledging the grammatical foundation for interpreting sealing as subsequent to believing, Paul's intended meaning, as indicated by the context, should be considered weightier than the grammatical structure when interpreting the verse. According to the context, believing and sealing of the Spirit are not separated events but are coincidental. Dunn argues:

> The aorist participle does in fact usually express antecedent action, but it is the context, not the grammatical form, which determines this. And the context here indicates that we should take the two verbs

30. Porter, *Verbal Aspect*, 383–84.

31. In the case of Eph 1:20, which Keener suggests as an example to reject interpreting "sealing" as occurring after believing the gospel in Eph 1:13, the aorist participle is situated after the main verb. According to Porter's study, therefore, this syntactic ordering means that the two actions are coincident.

> ["having believed" and "you were sealed"] as the two sides of the one event: it is when they believed that God sealed them with the Spirit. As in Gal 3:2, the step of faith is met by the gift of the Spirit.[32]

Dunn explains the whole section of Ephesians 1:3–14 as one sentence, arguing that "the blessings with which the individual is blessed when he becomes a Christian, that is, when he comes to be ἐν Χριστῷ," is based on verse 3, in particular the phrase ἐν Χριστῷ. The chief of these blessings, Dunn argues, is the gift of the Holy Spirit since "the whole sentence moves forward majestically to the climax of vv. 13f."[33]

Fee also argues that the aorist participle ("having believed") shows the logical precedence over the main verb ("you were sealed"), rather than implying a temporal interval; Paul's intention is to say that Christians in Ephesus, including gentile believers, received the Holy Spirit when they believed:

> That the aorist participle intends something antecedent to the main verb need not be doubted; but the two verbs have nothing to do with separate and distinct experiences of faith. Rather, the one ("having believed [in Christ]") logically precedes the other ("you were sealed"): but from Paul's perspective these are two sides of the same coin, thus "attendant circumstance." There is simply nothing in the context, nor anything inherent in this bit of grammar, that would cause one to think that Paul intends to refer here to two distinct experiences. The argument, in fact, has to do with the reality that these Gentiles in becoming believers in Christ also received the promised Holy Spirit, thus indicating that they too are God's own possession. Arguments

32. Dunn, *Baptism in the Holy Spirit*, 159.

33. Dunn, *Baptism in the Holy Spirit*, 159. For reference, Macleod takes the same position. He argues that Lloyd-Jones's interpretation is not supported by the context: "This whole section of Ephesians [Eph 1] is dominated by the statement in verse three that God has blessed us with all spiritual blessings. It is very difficult, so soon after such a statement, to claim that some Christians lack a particular blessing, especially one of such importance that the expositor can say, 'It is one of the most vital of all New Testament doctrines with respect to revival and reawakening in the Christian church.' Can we honestly say that we have been blessed with all spiritual blessings when we have not yet been sealed with the Spirit? Indeed, is it not the very purpose of what follows verse three to expound the meaning of all spiritual blessings? These include election, adoption, and redemption. Are we to break off there and say that the sealing belongs to a different order of thought—that is not part of the all spiritual blessings enjoyed by all believers but something quite distinct experienced only by some and perhaps only by a few?" (*Spirit of Promise*, 50–51).

about individual Christian experience are therefore beside Paul's point.[34]

Both Dunn and Fee suggest that the sealing of the Spirit in Ephesians 1:13 refers to the Holy Spirit himself, who is given when one believes in the gospel, rather than indicating an experience of the Spirit subsequent to regeneration.

The Reformed position on the sealing of the Spirit in Ephesians 1:13, which places more emphasis on the contextual meaning than the grammatical interpretation regarding the two verbs (πιστεύσαντες and ἐσφραγίσθητε), is to regard the sealing of the Spirit as the Holy Spirit himself, who is received at the moment of believing.[35] As stated earlier, Lloyd-Jones held this Reformed view until 1939. Our concern is what led him to deviate from the Reformed position in his understanding of the sealing, which may in turn have influenced his interpretation of the text.

As the most convincing reason for the change, we can consider Lloyd-Jones's extraordinary experiences of the Holy Spirit in 1949, already discussed in chapter 3. In the summer of that year, he was overwhelmed twice by an experience of a consciousness of God's nearness and the outpouring of God's love unto his heart. Murray evaluates the impact of these experiences on Lloyd-Jones: "The experiences of that year contributed to a deepening of his appreciation of what happens to the church in a time of revival, namely, that there is an overwhelming sense of God's love and a full assurance of salvation, accompanied by awe and joy and praise." Murray continues, "Those experiences also clarified his conviction that what happens to many in a time of revival may happen to individual Christians at other periods." In short, Lloyd-Jones's personal experiences in 1949 convinced him that "those experiences of the Spirit which mark many lives in times of revival are essentially the same in their nature as those which may be known by individuals at other times."[36] In "How Revival Comes," one of the series of sermons on revival in 1959, Lloyd-Jones expresses the same conviction:

> While I am thus, mainly, dealing with the Church in general and with the need for revival in the Church, obviously at the same time it is a

34. Fee, *God's Empowering Presence*, 670.
35. Kaiser, "Baptism in the Holy Spirit," 32.
36. Murray, David Martyn Lloyd-Jones: The *Fight of Faith*, 380, 381, 383.

> perfect message for the individual. What a revival really means is, of course, something happening at one and the same time to a number of individuals. But there is no need for us to wait until revival comes to have individual experiences. So, all that we shall be considering has an immediate and direct application to any individual who may be in the condition that I am about to describe.[37]

For Lloyd-Jones, there is little difference in nature between revival and baptism with the Spirit. He regards revival as a large number of people being baptized with the Spirit simultaneously. Thus, his doctrine of Spirit baptism should be understood as an individualized version of his revival doctrine. As a basis for this, as discussed in chapter 3, the general characteristics of Spirit baptism he suggests—an exceptional work of the Spirit, assurance of salvation, the sovereignty of God, repeatability, authority, and power—are in essence identical with the characteristics of revival he proposes. Both of them deal with "a question, primarily, of the enjoyment of a full assurance of salvation" and "sudden and sovereign manifestations of His love."[38] From the overwhelming experiences in 1949, Lloyd-Jones believed that he had the same kind of revival (Spirit baptism) experiences; they must have been an important motive for him to shape his doctrine of Spirit baptism as a personalized version of revival.

From this point of view, for Lloyd-Jones there was no difference between the argument that one need not seek revival (outpouring of the Spirit) insofar as Pentecost was a once-for-all event and the claim that one need not to seek baptism with the Spirit since one was baptized with the Spirit when one was regenerated. To him, both arguments were serious sins and errors that effectively quenched the Holy Spirit since they discouraged individual Christians as well as the church from praying for more outpourings of the Spirit. In his mind, the Pentecost–revival relation could be replaced with a regeneration–Spirit baptism relation. In this regard, Ian Randall argues: "The passion with which Lloyd-Jones expressed himself on this issue [baptism with the Spirit] cannot be understood without recognizing the close link he made with revival. … Those who denied that individuals needed this

37. Lloyd-Jones, *Revival*, 149.
38. Murray, David Martyn Lloyd-Jones: The *Fight of Faith*, 383.

baptism were inevitably, for him, questioning the need for revival itself."[39] Accordingly, for Lloyd-Jones, proving that baptism with the Spirit was a post-regeneration experience was as important as proving that there could be more revivals after Pentecost. His interpretation of Ephesians 1:13 therefore should be regarded as his exegetical attempt to demonstrate from the New Testament that the sealing (baptism) of the Spirit was an experience of the outpouring of the Spirit subsequent to regeneration, as he himself experienced in 1949. One can argue that Lloyd-Jones's personal experiences and his aspiration for individual Christians to seek and experience personal revivals (Spirit baptism) influenced him to interpret the verse in a different way from the Reformed camp.

It is evident throughout Lloyd-Jones's sermons on Ephesians 1:13 that his main concern was to distinguish the sealing of the Spirit from regeneration in order for Christians to seek further outpourings of the Spirit individually, which, he believed, were experienced collectively in times of revival. As Lloyd-Jones commenced a series of expositions on Ephesians 1:13 in 1955, he stated, "It [the sealing of the Spirit] is one of the most vital of all the New Testament doctrines with respect to revival and reawakening in the Christian Church." In "The Nature of Sealing [1]," one of the sermons in this series, Lloyd-Jones considers the sealing of the Spirit and revival ("a quickening in the Church among God's people") to be synonymous, emphasizing the necessity of a right doctrine of the sealing for Christians to experience it.[40] From this perspective, he argues:

> The story of the Church through the centuries shows that every revival has come as the result of a quickening in the Church among God's people. Revival starts in the Church and spreads outwards. A lifeless and moribund church never achieves anything of lasting value, but when something happens in the Church the world hears about it; its curiosity is aroused, and as on the Day of Pentecost, it begins to ask what certain phenomena signify. Such is the history of every revival; it is God's way of working. He quickens His Church and His people first.[41]

---

39. Randall, "Lloyd-Jones and Revival," 99–100.
40. Lloyd-Jones, *God's Ultimate Purpose*, 244, 255–56.
41. Lloyd-Jones, *God's Ultimate Purpose*, 255.

Therefore, we can conclude that Lloyd-Jones's own experiences of the Spirit and his conviction regarding the need for revival, either individually or collectively, influenced him to interpret Ephesians 1:13 to say that there exists a time interval between believing and sealing of the Spirit.

ROMANS 8:15–16

Romans 8:15–16 is another important text for Lloyd-Jones's doctrine of baptism with the Spirit (or full assurance of salvation), as is evident in the sixteen consecutive sermons he preached on these two verses in his series on Romans.[42] The reason this text is so important in his doctrine of Spirit baptism is that he views it as dealing with an incremental series of experiences (the Spirit of bondage prior to the Spirit of adoption, and the Spirit of adoption prior to the witness of the Spirit) in the life of believer related to baptism with the Spirit. The following section will demonstrate that his developmental understanding of Romans 8:15–16 is different from the standard Puritan position at some points, even though considerable Puritan influence can be found in his interpretation. Lloyd-Jones's distinct position on the text, as is the case with his interpretation on Ephesians 1:13–14, comes from his reading of the biographies of the saints and the history of revival as well as from his longing for contemporary Christians to enjoy the great experience of revival.

In Romans 8:15–16, the apostle Paul, describing the new life in the Holy Spirit that is allowed the believer as the result of Christ's saving work, discusses the contrast between the "spirit of bondage" and the "spirit of adoption." The first challenge Lloyd-Jones has to face as he interprets these verses is how to understand the term *πνεῦμα*, which appears twice in verse 15. He rejects the interpretation that both instances of *πνεῦμα* refer to merely a disposition or feeling. He also disagrees with the KJV translation ("For ye have not received the spirit of bondage again to fear; but ye have received the Spirit of adoption, whereby we cry, Abba, Father"), which interprets the

42. In Lloyd-Jones, *Romans: The Sons of God*, sermons 16–30 are devoted to Rom 8:15–16. "For ye have not received the spirit of bondage again to fear; but ye have received the Spirit of adoption, whereby we cry, Abba, Father. The Spirit itself beareth witness with our spirit, that we are the children of God." *οὐ γὰρ ἐλάβετε πνεῦμα δουλείας πάλιν εἰς φόβον ἀλλ' ἐλάβετε πνεῦμα υἱοθεσίας ἐν ᾧ κράζομεν· αββα ὁ πατήρ. αὐτὸ τὸ πνεῦμα συμμαρτυρεῖ τῷ πνεύματι ἡμῶν ὅτι ἐσμὲν τέκνα θεοῦ* (NA[28]).

first instance as a disposition or feeling ("the spirit") and the latter as the Holy Spirit ("the Spirit").[43]

Lloyd-Jones's position is that both instances of πνεῦμα should be viewed as referring to the Holy Spirit. With the KJV, he agrees that the term πνεῦμα in the phrase πνεῦμα υἱοθεσίας should be interpreted as the Holy Spirit. Lloyd-Jones argues that this interpretation is supported by Paul's statement in Galatians 4:6: "And because ye are sons, God hath sent forth the Spirit of his Son into your hearts, crying, Abba, Father." Thus, in the sixteenth sermon from *Romans: The Sons of God*, he argues, "it is the Holy Spirit, the Spirit of God's Son, who is sent into our hearts, and thereby leads us to cry out, 'Abba, Father.'"[44] However, he disagrees with those who translate πνεῦμα in the phrase πνεῦμα δουλείας as "the spirit of slavery," including the KJV translators. Those who support this interpretation[45] argue that the Holy Spirit cannot be described as "the Spirit of bondage" since 2 Corinthians 3:17 ("Now the Lord is that Spirit: and where the Spirit of the Lord is, there is liberty") demonstrates that the Holy Spirit is the Spirit of liberty. Therefore, they understand this verse as intending to show the contrast between the preconversion state ("the spirit of bondage") and the conversion state ("the Spirit of adoption").[46]

On the contrary, Lloyd-Jones argues that even if the Holy Spirit is the Spirit of freedom, the Spirit "starts by producing a spirit of bondage and of fear" to attain the ultimate goal of freedom. In other words, he understands that "the spirit of bondage and fear" is also given by the work of the Holy Spirit; that is, "'the spirit of bondage and fear' always precedes the 'Spirit of adoption.'" In his view, an unconverted person cannot have a spirit of fear without the work of the Holy Spirit. This position is closely linked to his interpretation of the man of Romans 7 in Romans 7:7–25. He regards the man in Romans 7 as not regenerate but "in this preliminary stage, under conviction of sin as the result of the Spirit's work."[47] He states:

---

43. Lloyd-Jones, *Romans: The Sons of God*, 197.

44. Lloyd-Jones, *Romans: The Sons of God*, 198.

45. Lloyd-Jones does not identify any interpreter to support this position in the sermon but simply refers to them as a "school" (Lloyd-Jones, *Romans: The Sons of God*, 198).

46. Lloyd-Jones, *Romans: The Sons of God*, 198.

47. Lloyd-Jones, *Romans: The Sons of God*, 202, 205, 207.

> [The man of Rom 7:7–25] has been awakened to the true nature of the law, and he realizes that he is not only in a state of bondage, but also in a state of the utmost danger. He is under condemnation; and he cannot deliver himself from the guilt of sin, nor from the power of sin. He would give anything if he could but do so; but he cannot. So he is left in a state of bondage and of fear.[48]

In short, Lloyd-Jones considers the man of Romans 7 as in a state of bondage and of fear as the result of the Spirit's work; he believes that the man's state shows exactly what it means to receive "the spirit of bondage to fear" in Romans 8:15. As such, he understands "the spirit of bondage and fear" as a state in the preliminary stage of conviction of sin under the law through the work of the Spirit.

It should be noted that Lloyd-Jones's position that the Holy Spirit produces "the spirit of bondage and fear" first before bringing about "the spirit of adoption" is a particularly Lutheran perspective that derives from the theology of Martin Luther (1483–1546) himself. Luther regarded the work of God (or gospel) as twofold—proper and alien:

> The proper office of the gospel is to proclaim the proper work of God, i.e., grace, through which the Father of mercies freely gives to all men peace, righteousness and truth, mitigating all his wrath. … But the strange work of the gospel is to prepare a people perfect for the Lord, that is, to make manifest sins and pronounce guilty those who were righteous in their own eyes by declaring that all men are sinners and devoid of the grace of God. … So the gospel sounds exceedingly harsh in its alien tones, and yet this must be done, in order that it may be able to sound with its own proper tones.[49]

Likewise, Luther believed that God produces conviction of sin in sinners through the gospel before proclaiming forgiveness of sins and transforming them into believers.

Although it ultimately derives from Luther's theology, Lloyd-Jones states that his interpretation that both instances of πνεῦμα in verse 15 refer to the Holy Spirit and that the Spirit of bondage precedes the Spirit of adoption in

48. Lloyd-Jones, *Romans: The Sons of God*, 205.

49. Luther, *Sermons 2*, in *Luther's Works* 52:20.

Christians' experience can be found in some Puritans, such as John Preston, Thomas Horton, and Goodwin.[50] For instance, for Goodwin, Romans 8:15 shows that the Holy Spirit not only witnesses sonship in the believer but also witnesses bondage to sin and death; the Spirit of bondage precedes the Spirit of adoption:

> God the Holy Ghost ... hath a peculiar office assigned him, which therefore must needs be necessary, as appears by that title given him, Rom 8:15, "the Spirit of bondage"; and as such he is received ere he becomes a "Spirit of adoption." ... The Holy Ghost is a Spirit of bondage in conversion only; and in that it is said "to fear again," it implies it was once received. The office of which Spirit appears by the opposite effect of the same Spirit as he is called "the Spirit of adoption," which is to witness adoption and sonship, as the other is to witness our slavery and bondage to sin and death.[51]

Richard Sibbes, a Puritan who significantly influenced Lloyd-Jones, also held this interpretation of the verse, arguing for "the order that the Spirit of God keeps. Ere it comforts, it shakes and makes us fear."[52] In his sermon "The Witness of Salvation," dealing with Romans 8:15–16, Sibbes states:

> The first work then of the Comforter is to put a man in fear. Further, hence is shewed, that until this Spirit doth work this fear, a man doth not fear. The heart holds out. The obstinacy is so great, that if hell gates were open, a man will not yield till then that the Spirit worketh it. So St John speaks of the Comforter, that "when he comes, he will convince or reprove the world of sin," John 16:8; that is, he will convince and shew a man that he is but a bondman; and so he makes us to fear. No man must think this strange, that God deals with men at first in this harsh manner, as it were to kill them, ere he make them alive; nor be discouraged, as if God had cast them off for ever as none of his; for this bondage and spirit of fear is a work of God's Spirit, and

50. Lloyd-Jones, *Romans: The Sons of God*, 203.
51. Goodwin, *Work of the Holy Ghost*, in *Works* 6:363.
52. Sibbes, "Witness of Salvation," in *Works* 7:370.

> a preparative to the rest. But it is but a common work, and therefore, unless more follow it, it can afford us no comfort.[53]

This strand of Puritan theology that emphasized the conscious experience of the conviction of sin by the work of the Spirit—the Spirit of bondage—as the preliminary stage for saving faith is typically referred to as "preparationism." Eaton argues that Puritan preparationism much influenced Lloyd-Jones's understanding of Romans 8:15.[54]

Nonetheless, it is noteworthy that Lloyd-Jones's interpretation of the man in Romans 7 as not regenerate but being in a state of bondage and fear as the result of the Spirit's work, while relating "man" in Romans 7 to "the spirit of bondage to fear" in Romans 8:15, deviates from the Puritan tradition, which interpreted the man as regenerate.[55] Eaton points out:

> He [Lloyd-Jones] related the "Spirit of bondage" to the description in Romans 7:14–25 of a person delighting in the Law but failing to keep it and so crying out, "O wretched man that I am!" In this respect Lloyd-Jones was departing from the common Puritan exegesis of Romans 7:14–25 which followed Calvin and Luther in understanding this section of Romans to be a description of the Christian's struggle against sin, a struggle which continues even in the most mature Christian.[56]

Lloyd-Jones himself reveals the difference in an appendix to *Romans: The Law: Its Functions and Limits* (his expository sermons on Rom 7:1–8:4) as follows: "What is surprising to me is that Perkins and other Puritans ... when they actually comment on Romans 7 regard it as being a description of the regenerate man."[57] Gootjes points out that Lloyd-Jones's position on the man in Rom 7 is similar to that of John Wesley. Wesley also interpreted the man in Romans 7 as referring to a person who was neither unregenerate nor regenerate, but who came to know the law and realized his sin through the

53. Sibbes, "Witness of Salvation," 370.
54. Eaton, *Baptism with the Spirit*, 205.
55. Eaton, *Baptism with the Spirit*, 205.
56. Eaton, *Baptism with the Spirit*, 205.
57. Lloyd-Jones, *Romans: The Law*, 358.

work of the Holy Spirit.[58] For instance, in his explanatory notes on Romans 7:7,[59] Wesley states:

> The character here assumed is that of a man, first ignorant of the law, then under it, and sincerely, but ineffectually, striving to serve God. To have spoken this of himself, or any true believer, would have been foreign to the whole scope of his discourse; nay, utterly contrary thereto, as well as to what is expressly asserted, Rom 8:2.[60]

Eaton explains that Lloyd-Jones's different interpretation of "man" in Romans 7 from the usual Puritan exegesis can be attributed to his understanding of conversion as a process.[61] Lloyd-Jones's distinctive interpretation, as Eaton indicates, reflects his conviction regarding an order of salvation, in particular as related to conversion. Lloyd-Jones believed that it was necessary for one to be for some time under the conviction of sin by the work of the Spirit before coming to enjoy full salvation in Christ. Our main concern here is to find out what led him to this conviction, on the assumption that it influenced his interpretation of both Romans 7:14–25 and 8:15.

We should note that Lloyd-Jones identifies instances in the biographies of saints and the history of revivals as abundant evidence to support his interpretation of both texts as well as his conviction regarding the process of conversion. With respect to biographies of the saints, Lloyd-Jones presents John Bunyan's (1628–1688) conversion experience, which lasted eighteen months, as an example of being in the spirit of bondage or of the man in Romans 7. For instance, in his twentieth sermon in *Romans: The Law: Its Functions and Limits*, Lloyd-Jones states:

> We argued that chapter 7 [of Romans] is nothing but a hypothetical, imaginary picture painted by the Apostle of a man who sees the complete hopelessness of salvation by the Law. Or else we may say that it is the picture of a man who is actually under a very deep conviction of sin. I would suggest that in John Bunyan's *Grace Abounding*

58. Gootjes, *성령으로의 세례*, 181–82.

59. "What shall we say then? Is the law sin? God forbid. Nay, I had not known sin, but by the law: for I had not known lust, except the law had said, Thou shalt not covet."

60. Wesley, *Explanatory Notes*, 227.

61. Eaton, *Baptism with the Spirit*, 207.

> we have a picture which is very reminiscent of this. Bunyan spent eighteen months in an agony of conviction of sin and repentance. He saw the spirituality of the Law and the truth about himself, but he had not seen anymore; he had not seen the way of deliverance, the way of escape.[62]

Also, Lloyd-Jones argues that when one reads the history of any of the great revivals, one can find the same case as Bunyan on a great scale.[63] In the sermon quoted above, he introduces a reawakening that took place in Scotland in 1630, ignited by John Livingstone's (1603–1672) sermon:

> Take for instance the great event at Kirk-of-Shotts in Scotland in 1630. As the result of the sermon preached by John Livingstone on that notable Monday morning there were many people who were in an agony of conviction as described perfectly in the second section of Romans chapter 7. Some remained in that state for hours, some for days, and some for weeks. They felt utterly lost. They saw the spirituality of the Law, they saw their own utter failure and the uselessness of all their own efforts. They could not find release and relief. There they were, groaning, some literally lying under the hedgerows, others knocking at the door of the minister in the early hours of the morning, crying for the relief which they could not find. That, it seems to me, is the position described so perfectly by the Apostle Paul in Romans 7:13–25. It is a very early manifestation of spiritual life; but is no more than that—conviction but not conversion.[64]

In his sixteenth sermon in *Romans: The Sons of God* (another of his expository sermons on Rom 8:5–17), Lloyd-Jones suggests that the first work of the Spirit in the period of revival is to produce a spirit of bondage in people's hearts:

> When the Spirit of God comes down in revival His first work invariably is to humble people, to convict them profoundly of sin, to make them feel utterly and completely hopeless. This happens to people

62. Lloyd-Jones, *Romans: The Law*, 261. Also, in his sixteenth sermon in *Romans: The Sons of God*, Lloyd-Jones suggests Bunyan's case as an example of being in a state of "the spirit of bondage" (202).

63. Lloyd-Jones, *Romans: The Sons of God*, 202.

64. Lloyd-Jones, *Romans: The Law*, 262.

> who had never felt such a thing before. A great spirit of conviction possesses them, they groan in agony, and may fall to the ground in torment. That is a "spirit of bondage" and "a spirit of fear." They feel that nothing can be done for them, and this is the result of the outpouring of the Holy Spirit.[65]

Likewise, Lloyd-Jones suggests biographies of the saints and the history of revival as the ground for the validity of his interpretation of Romans 7:14–25 and 8:15. From this fact, we can assume that his reading of Christian experience and the history of revivals shaped his assurance regarding an order of salvation: the conviction of sin by the work of the Spirit comes first, before conversion or saving faith. His position on the man in Romans 7, as distinct from the common Puritan tradition and emphasizing the necessity of conviction of sin before conversion, shows that his studies of the history of revival played a significant role in his interpretation of "the spirit of bondage" in Romans 8:15, too.

After addressing the issue of "the spirit of bondage," Lloyd-Jones explains the meaning of "the Spirit of adoption (πνεῦμα υἱοθεσίας)." First, he opposes the position that the Spirit of adoption should be understood as merely "the result of our being led by the Spirit, a kind of deduction we draw by applying the tests to ourselves,"[66] as verse 14 states earlier: "For as many as are led by the Spirit of God, they are the sons of God." He does not regard verses 15 and 16 as an extension or repetition of verse 14, but as "a definite gradation and progress here, leading to a climax."[67] In this context, he argues, the Spirit

65. Lloyd-Jones, *Romans: The Sons of God*, 202.

66. Lloyd-Jones, *Romans: The Sons of God*, 235. In his sermon on Rom 8:14, Lloyd-Jones suggests ten practical tests to examine whether one is being led by the Spirit: having a spiritual outlook on life, desiring to live to God's glory, longing for a greater knowledge of God, concern about one's lack of love of God, increasing awareness of sin within, grieving for committing a sin, becoming sensitive to sin and evil, desiring righteousness and holiness, mortifying the deeds of the body, and manifesting the fruit of the Spirit (183–93).

67. Lloyd-Jones, *Romans: The Sons of God*, 235. By contrast, Edwards interprets Rom 8:14–16 as integrated rather than as developmental. In *Religious Affections*, he argues: "And indeed the Apostle, when in that, Romans 8:16, he speaks of the Spirit's bearing witness with our spirit, that we are the children of God, does sufficiently explain himself, if his words were but attended to. What is here expressed, is connected with the two preceding verses, as resulting from what the Apostle had said there, as every reader may see. … Here, what the Apostle says, if we take it together, plainly shows, that what he has respect to, when he speaks of the Spirit's giving us witness or evidence that we are God's children; is his dwelling in us, and leading us, as a spirit of adoption, or spirit of a child, disposing us to behave towards God as to a Father. This

of adoption who leads one to the desire to cry "Abba, Father" is not in the realm of intellectual arguments or explanations, but essentially belongs to the realm of "feeling and subjectivity, and emotions."[68]

According to Lloyd-Jones, the Aramaic word "Abba" was a familiar word used by a little child when calling the child's father, like "Papa" and "Dad"; this expression was not allowed by slaves among Jews. In Mark 14:36 ("Abba, Father, all things are possible unto thee; take away this cup from me"), Jesus himself uses this expression in the most distressing moment in the garden of Gethsemane. Lloyd-Jones argues that God wants his children to use the same word in their prayers with assurance. He concludes, "That is the very cry, the Apostle tells us, that comes out of the heart of the one who realizes that he has been adopted as a child of God."[69] Lloyd-Jones explains the word "cry" (κράζω) as "a loud cry expressing deep emotion ... fervency, earnestness, and importunity."[70] He summarizes what these expressions together imply:

> Each of these expressions—"cry," "Abba," "Father"—conveys the idea that we are speaking to Someone whom we know. He is not merely a God in whom we believe intellectually, theologically, theoretically, doctrinally only. All this is possible to one who is not a child of God at all. I have repeatedly told you that there is such a thing as a mere intellectual assent to truth. There is a purely academic kind of belief. The Apostle does not mean that! He has chosen terms which preclude such a meaning, and he insists upon this further emphasis.[71]

For Lloyd-Jones, the first type of assurance of salvation, which he calls assurance through deduction, can be found in Romans 8:14, whereas the Spirit of adoption in verse 15 is the second type of assurance, at a higher level

---

is the witness or evidence the Apostle speaks of, that we are children, that we have the spirit of children, or spirit of adoption. And what is that, but the spirit of love? There are two kinds of spirits the Apostle speaks of, the spirit of a slave, or the spirit of bondage, that is fear; and the spirit of a child, or spirit of adoption, and that is love. The Apostle says, we hadn't received the spirit of bondage, or of slaves, which is a spirit of fear; but we have received the more ingenuous noble spirit of children, a spirit of love, which naturally disposes us to go to God, as children to a father, and behave towards God as children. And this is the evidence or witness which the Spirit of God gives us that we are children. This is the plain sense of the Apostle" (237–38).

68. Lloyd-Jones, *Romans: The Sons of God*, 235.

69. Lloyd-Jones, *Romans: The Sons of God*, 240–41.

70. Lloyd-Jones, *Romans: The Sons of God*, 241.

71. Lloyd-Jones, *Romans: The Sons of God*, 241–42.

than the first one. He explains that the Spirit of adoption is a part of Spirit baptism but is only a preliminary stage or experience. The witness of the Spirit in verse 16 ("The Spirit itself beareth witness with our spirit, that we are the children of God"), the third type and the highest level of assurance, is "the most vital and essential part" of baptism with the Spirit. To sum up, although the "Spirit of adoption" and the "witness of the Spirit" are different aspects of baptism with the Spirit,[72] the latter is not only more important but is also the essence of Spirit baptism.

Lloyd-Jones takes note of the expression "the Holy Spirit himself (αὐτὸ τὸ πνεῦμα)" in verse 16. In verse 15, it is Christians who are telling God that "we love him," whereas in verse 16 it is God, through the Holy Spirit, telling Christians that "he loves us." Also, the testimony of the Holy Spirit himself, Lloyd-Jones argues, is given directly to Christians' spirits "in the most unmistakable manner":[73]

> The Apostle chose to put it in this way: "The Spirit Himself beareth witness." Why did he not simply say: "The Spirit beareth witness," or "The Spirit also beareth witness with our spirit"? He deliberately said "The Spirit Himself beareth witness with our spirit," as if to safeguard us against the very errors we have considered and to make it clear to us that he is not concerned here with the witness of the "work" of the Spirit in us but with the Person of the Spirit Himself witnessing to us, and with our spirits—which is a very different thing. We have already seen, in verse 14, what the work of the Spirit is, and that it is a "witness." We have seen in verse 15, still more strikingly, that it is when the Spirit comes into our hearts that we in our own spirits have the Spirit of adoption. That again is part of the work of the Spirit. But here, Paul emphasizes that he is not dealing with such work of the Spirit, but with what the Spirit Himself does directly.[74]

To support his argument, Lloyd-Jones quotes a commentary on Romans 8:16 by Scottish theologian Robert Haldane (1764–1842), asserting that this

72. Lloyd-Jones, *Romans: The Sons of God*, 273, 300.
73. Lloyd-Jones, *Romans: The Sons of God*, 302.
74. Lloyd-Jones, *Romans: The Sons of God*, 299–300.

witness of the Spirit is different from the fruits of the Holy Spirit;[75] it is the direct witness given by the Spirit himself to the believer's heart. Lloyd-Jones quotes:

> What we learn, therefore, from it is, that the Holy Spirit testifies to our spirit in a distinct and immediate testimony, and also with our spirit in a concurrent testimony. This testimony, although it cannot be explained, is nevertheless felt by the believer; it is felt by him, too, in its variations, as sometimes stronger and more palpable, and at other times more feeble and less discernible. … This witnessing of the Spirit to the believer's spirit, communicating consolation, is never His first work, but is consequent on His other work of renovation. He first gives faith, and then seals. "After that ye believed ye were sealed with that Holy Spirit of promise." He also witnesseth with our spirit, generously shining on His own promises, making them clear, assuring us of their truth, enabling our spirit to embrace them and to discover our interest in them.[76]

Lloyd-Jones believed that the witness of the Spirit was a distinct and direct testimony of the Spirit that took place after regeneration; it was another description of the sealing of the Spirit indicated in Ephesians 1:13. Consequently, he concludes, on the basis of Romans 8:15–16 and Ephesians 1:13, that baptism with the Spirit rarely occurs at the time of conversion; rather, there is an interval between regeneration and Spirit baptism.[77]

It should be noted that Lloyd-Jones's incremental reading of Romans 8:15–16 differs from that of such Puritans as Sibbes and Goodwin, whom Lloyd-Jones follows with respect to the doctrine of assurance. Sibbes and Goodwin did not regard "the Spirit of adoption" in verse 15 as the experience of receiving assurance of salvation (or sealing of the Spirit), nor as a form of assurance lower than "the witness of the Spirit" in verse 16. Sibbes understood verse 16 as an explanation regarding one's obtaining a better estate by

75. Lloyd-Jones, *Romans: The Sons of God*, 294. Haldane states: "It is not merely the fruits of the Holy Spirit in the lives of believers which afford this testimony, but the Spirit Himself, by imparting filial confidence, inspires it in the heart" (*Exposition of the Epistle to the Romans*, 362).

76. Haldane, *Exposition of the Epistle to the Romans*, 363; Lloyd-Jones, *Romans: The Sons of God*, 295.

77. Lloyd-Jones, *Romans: The Sons of God*, 317, 324.

receiving "the Spirit of adoption" in verse 15. Then he found two witnesses in verse 16: "the witness of our spirit" and "the witness of God's Spirit with our spirit," which conjointly testify to one's sonship:

> The apostle tells them, they may thank God the spirit of fear thus came, that hereafter they might partake of the Spirit of adoption to fear no more. He stirs them up, as it were, to be thankful, because now they had obtained a better state. Why, what estate? A very high one: ver. 16, "The Spirit itself beareth witnesseth with our spirit, that we are the children of God." The thing is then to know ourselves to be the children of God. There must be sound evidences. Here then are two set down, whose testimony cannot fail. ... 1. The witness of our spirit. 2. The witness of God's Spirit with our spirit.[78]

Likewise, Sibbes's exegetical work on the text shows that the Spirit's immediate sealing to give Christians a full assurance was confined to "the witness of God's Spirit with our spirit" in verse 16. In fact, the main text for Sibbes and Goodwin to explain the degrees of assurance of salvation was 1 John 5:8 ("And there are three that bear witness in earth, the Spirit, and the water, and the blood: and these three agree in one"), rather than Romans 8:15–16.[79] According to Sibbes, the witness of the blood, the lowest form of assurance, came from faith in the death of Christ. The witness of the water, the second form of assurance, came from the marks of sanctification in one's life. The witness of the Spirit, the highest level of assurance, came from the sealing of the Spirit. For Sibbes, both testimonies of blood and water belong to "the witness of our spirit" in Romans 8:16 and are indirect and deductive. The testimony of the Holy Spirit belongs to "the witness of the Spirit with our spirit" in the same verse, which is direct and immediate.[80]

From this comparison between Puritans and Lloyd-Jones, we can see that Lloyd-Jones's developmental reading of Romans 8:15–16 (the Spirit of bondage prior to the Spirit of adoption, and the Spirit of adoption prior to the witness of the Spirit), in particular the interpretation of "the Spirit of adoption," is idiosyncratic, even though Lloyd-Jones ultimately follows their position on

78. Sibbes, "Witness of Salvation," 376.

79. Sibbes, "Witness of Salvation," 370; Goodwin, *Exposition on Ephesians*, 207.

80. Sibbes, *Fountain Sealed*, 439–40; Sibbes, "Witness of Salvation," 377.

the different levels of assurance of salvation as well as their emphasis on the immediate witness of the Spirit. Our main concern is to discover what led to Lloyd-Jones's peculiar interpretation since he holds to an incremental understanding of the text that is distinct from the Puritans, whose doctrine of assurance Lloyd-Jones also follows. As in the case of Lloyd-Jones's interpretation of "the Spirit of bondage," I argue, his studies of the biographies or journals of preachers and the history of revival influenced him to interpret the text in this way.

Lloyd-Jones describes the Spirit of adoption as follows: "This is subjective; it is a feeling, and not a question of a man persuading himself, or deducing it from the Scriptures, but an elemental feeling within, something that has been poured in by the Spirit, leading a man to cry 'Abba, Father.'" Importantly, for Lloyd-Jones, the Spirit of adoption as a postconversion experience is not what every Christian receives and enjoys, even though, he believes, "most of the early Christians, if not all, had full assurance of salvation [the Spirit of adoption], the reason being that in New Testament times the Holy Spirit had been poured forth in unusual profusion."[81] Nonetheless, he argues that during times of revival, numerous Christians also received and enjoyed the Spirit of adoption:

> Now as most of the New Testament Epistles were written to such people, it is not surprising that they were written on the assumption that their recipients had all had the great experience which leads to this "Spirit of adoption." ... It is quite clear that the early Church was in this exalted condition in respect of experience, a condition which has not persisted, alas, in the subsequent history of the Christian Church, but which, as I say, is repeated from time to time during an awakening or a period of revival.[82]

In particular, Lloyd-Jones's specific examples of the Spirit of adoption were obtained by his reading the journals of great evangelists in the eighteenth century such as Whitefield, Harris, and Wesley. In his twenty-first sermon in *Romans: The Sons of God*, expounding Romans 8:15, Lloyd-Jones

81. Lloyd-Jones, *Romans: The Sons of God*, 248–49.
82. Lloyd-Jones, *Romans: The Sons of God*, 249.

suggests Whitefield and Wesley as examples of receiving the Spirit of adoption.[83] Also, as we reviewed in chapters 3–5, Lloyd-Jones believes that Whitefield's and Harris's descriptions of their experiences exactly portray what his understanding of the Spirit of adoption looks like, apart from the debate over whether these experiences were conversion or postconversion experiences.

We should note that Lloyd-Jones's attention to and emphasis on an experience of the Spirit of adoption was closely connected with his concern for the malaise of believism ("taking it by faith") and as a result the superficiality that he diagnosed as prevalent in the churches of his day. For Lloyd-Jones, the popular teaching of "taking it by faith" is "the greatest single hindrance to a true and deep experience of 'the Spirit of adoption whereby we cry, Abba, Father.'" Also, he argues, it discourages Christians from examining themselves since self-examination in this teaching implies a lack of faith.[84] In the twenty-second sermon in *Romans: The Sons of God*, expounding Romans 8:15, Lloyd-Jones insists that one needs to pursue the experience of "crying, Abba, Father" as Whitefield enjoyed, abandoning the false teaching of "taking it by faith" that confines one in a state of superficiality:

> Most serious thinkers will agree that the main trouble in the Church today—I am speaking of evangelical churches in particular at this point—is the appalling superficiality. This is made very clear as we read the biographies of men who have lived in past centuries. Take, for example, the Journals of George Whitefield; read that man's experiences of the love of God and of Christ, and his love to them. How superficial most of us are by contrast! Why? Because we think we have "taken it by faith"; and so do not examine ourselves. But what do we really have? Have we ever really cried "Abba, Father" with a cry coming up from the depths of our being? That is what we should be saying; that is what the Spirit can enable us to say. Any teaching which prevents us from examining and searching ourselves, testing and proving ourselves, condemning our own superficiality, and from seeking for something bigger and deeper is of necessity condemned. And such is the invariable effect of the teaching which tells us to "take

83. Lloyd-Jones, *Romans: The Sons of God*, 271.

84. Lloyd-Jones, *Romans: The Sons of God*, 277.

it by faith and not to worry about our feelings," and to thank God for it, because we have taken it, and assume that all is well.[85]

It is noteworthy that Lloyd-Jones always attempts to prove the validity of his exegetical work on Romans 8:15–16 by appealing to the history of revival and individual Christians' spiritual experiences. Furthermore, he presents the content (or doctrine) extracted from his exegetical results as not only a diagnosis but also as a remedy for the troubles from which the church suffers. Accordingly, Lloyd-Jones's incremental interpretation of the text should be considered his exegetical attempt to suggest a biblical remedy, which he believes has been proved effective in the times of revival, to overcome the ills of believism and general superficiality in the church. In keeping with what many Christians experienced during times of revival, Lloyd-Jones longed for contemporary Christians to experience the love of God through the outpouring of the Spirit—the Spirit of adoption—by which believers who remained assured of their salvation only by deduction (the lowest level of assurance) could cry out, "Abba, Father," filled with joy from full assurance of their salvation. Furthermore, Lloyd-Jones wanted to see them go further, not being content with the experience of the Spirit of adoption alone but seeking the highest level of assurance that came from the direct witness of the Spirit to their hearts.

So far, we have explored Lloyd-Jones's exegetical work on Ephesians 1:13–14 and Romans 8:15–16. Analyzing his exegetical work on these two core texts related to his doctrine of Spirit baptism indicates that he holds different interpretations from the Reformed or the Puritan position, although he relies on their theological sources in many respects. As we discovered, this difference seems attributable to factors such as his personal experience of Spirit baptism, his readings of the biographies (or journals) of the saints and the history of revival, and his lifelong aspiration for a great outpouring of the Spirit. In one sense, he proposes the interpretive principle to provide a biblical foundation first and then to provide the historical evidence for that interpretation. However, his convictions and aspirations concerning revival as well as his intention to suggest a biblical diagnosis and remedy for contemporary churches, informed and developed by his research on the

85. Lloyd-Jones, *Romans: The Sons of God*, 278.

history of revival, provide a framework for his interpretation of these texts. Therefore, we can affirm that his exegetical work was also formed in the matrix of his studies and aspirations for revival, just as we found in the previous chapter that his homiletics had its roots in his understanding of and craving for revival.

9

—

CONCLUSIONS AND IMPLICATIONS

This book argues that Lloyd-Jones's position on Spirit baptism should be considered a reappropriation of an older doctrine regarding assurance of salvation and revival that prevailed within the Reformed tradition from the sixteenth until the mid-nineteenth centuries, rather than as a novel view or as identical to contemporary Pentecostal or charismatic doctrines. Before looking at the implications of Lloyd-Jones's doctrine of Spirit baptism for the contemporary church and homiletics, I will summarize the main contents of the study.

In the first chapter, by analyzing Lloyd-Jones's sermons and lectures we surveyed the general characteristics of Spirit baptism as Lloyd-Jones understood it. In his view, first, baptism with the Spirit is a subsequent experience of an exceptional work of the Spirit that is distinct from regeneration. Second, the event of Spirit baptism furnishes the believer with a full assurance of salvation. Third, baptism with the Spirit is entirely dependent on the sovereignty of God. Fourth, it can be repeated many times. Fifth, it simultaneously brings both preacher and congregation a sense of authority. Sixth, it provides preachers with the enormous power of the Holy Spirit. In the chapter, we affirmed that Lloyd-Jones's doctrine of Spirit baptism is closely associated with his understanding of true preaching. Lloyd-Jones was convinced that baptism with the Spirit was obligatory for efficacy in the ministry of preaching since it provided a preacher with authority and power from on high, leading the preacher to become the channel through whom the Holy Spirit could work.

In chapter 2, we found that even though Lloyd-Jones's understanding of Spirit baptism shares features in common with the Pentecostal position, such as being a postconversion experience, being an empowerment for witness and service, and providing the evidence for the present existence of the gifts of the Holy Spirit, there exists a considerable difference between the two. First, Lloyd-Jones objects to the Pentecostal insistence on glossolalia as an initial physical evidence of Spirit baptism. Second, he opposes the Pentecostal stance that baptism of the Spirit is given through the laying on of hands due to his belief that the blessing is only given according to the sovereignty of God. Third, he does not regard Spirit baptism as a once-for-all crisis experience, as Pentecostals typically assert. We concluded that a substantial difference between the two stems from the Reformed origin of Lloyd-Jones's stance. His doctrine of baptism with the Spirit originates from the old Reformed doctrine regarding assurance of salvation and revival.

Before examining the Reformed roots of his doctrine of Spirit baptism, we explored in chapters 3–4 the probable key factors that contributed to Lloyd-Jones's doctrine of Spirit baptism, such as his upbringing as a Welsh Calvinistic Methodist, his personal experiences of the Holy Spirit, his interpretation of Spirit baptism in the New Testament, and the history and theology of revival in the eighteenth century. We concluded that the most significant factor among them was his background growing up under the influence of Welsh Calvinistic Methodism and his appreciation of eighteenth-century revivals. Lloyd-Jones's understanding and craving for revival, in particular the revival of Calvinistic Methodism in the eighteenth century, was the matrix through which he developed his view of the doctrine of Spirit baptism.

Chapter 5 suggested that the two main axes of Lloyd-Jones's doctrine of Spirit baptism, assurance and revival, originated from the Reformed tradition as it developed from the sixteenth until the mid-nineteenth centuries. However, we also found a notable deviation from Reformed theology in reintroducing the doctrine of assurance, in that he acknowledges the possibility of the immediate work of the Spirit without means of the scriptural word. His distinctive position demonstrates that his doctrine of Spirit baptism was formed and developed in the context of his understanding of and aspiration for revival, since he believed that in the course of revival the immediate works of the Holy Spirit were commonly found. Also, his distinctive position indicates that his doctrine of Spirit baptism is a reflective reappropriation of older doctrines in the circumstances of the twentieth century in which he lived, rather than simple repetition of their original substance. Lloyd-Jones suggests the doctrine of Spirit baptism as an effective remedy for cold intellectualism, which he regards as the greatest danger threatening the life of evangelical churches. His diagnosis of the contemporary church led him to be more open to the possibility of the immediate work of the Spirit apart from the context of reading or hearing the proclamation of God's word, exhorting Christians to seek a more direct and experiential certainty of their salvation and sonship.

In chapter 6, focusing on Lloyd-Jones's homiletics, we investigated the intimate relationship between his homiletics and Spirit baptism. We found that his approach to homiletics was also inherited from the old Reformed tradition in general and from English Puritans and Jonathan Edwards in particular, in that it was expository in method, doctrinal in content, and experiential in goal. However, his emphasis on the necessity of Spirit baptism in preaching distinguished his homiletics from other forms of Reformed preaching. Lloyd-Jones's unique understanding of preaching was the result of being influenced by the old Calvinistic revival theology and by his interest in and research on the history of revival. Lloyd-Jones established his distinctive homiletics, which is closely related to the experience of Spirit baptism on a preacher and the listeners, based on his study of the extraordinary work of the Spirit and in particular of powerful preaching ministries during periods of revival. Above all, with his discovery of what he came to regard as true preaching—logic on fire—in the history of the eighteenth-century Calvinistic Methodists, he believed that what the Christian church as well as the world in his day most direly needed was this kind of preaching.

In chapter 7, reviewing Lloyd-Jones's exegetical work on the key texts related to Spirit baptism (Eph 1:13–14 and Rom 8:15–16), we found that he offered interpretations of these texts that differed from either the Reformed or Puritan positions, although he relied on their theological sources in many respects. In the case of Ephesians 1:13–14, Lloyd-Jones understood the sealing of the Spirit as a postconversion event, contrary to the Reformed position, which regards it as identical to regeneration. Concerning Romans 8:15–16, we found that Lloyd-Jones's developmental reading of the text (the Spirit of bondage prior to the Spirit of adoption, and the Spirit of adoption to the witness of the Spirit), in particular his interpretation of "the Spirit of adoption," is different from the Puritans' understanding. This difference is attributable to such factors as his personal experience of the Holy Spirit, his readings of the biographies (or journals) of the saints and the history of revival, and his lifelong aspiration for a great outpouring of the Spirit. In terms of methodology, he maintained the principle of first indicating the biblical basis for his proposed interpretation and only then turning to historical evidence for further support. Even so, his prior convictions and aspirations concerning revival as well as his intention to suggest a biblical diagnosis and remedy for contemporary churches, shaped and developed by his research into the history of revival, provided a framework for interpretation when he approached these texts. Therefore, we affirmed that we could find the matrix of his studies and aspiration for revival in his exegetical work, which we identified in his homiletics.

To sum up, Lloyd-Jones's understanding of Spirit baptism stems from the Reformed doctrine related to assurance of salvation and revival that was propagated from the sixteenth to the nineteenth centuries, rather than being indebted to Pentecostal or charismatic doctrines. At the same time, his doctrine of Spirit baptism is a thoughtful reappropriation of the older doctrines within the context of his own day rather than a simple repetition of their original content. His doctrine was shaped, on the one hand, by Puritan spirituality and Welsh revivalism, and, on the other hand, by his personal experience of the Spirit, which served to confirm the doctrinal views he had gained from these earlier sources. Most of all, his avid reading of the history of revival and his lifelong aspiration for revival was the matrix in which his doctrine of Spirit baptism was formed and developed; this same matrix influenced his homiletics as well as his exegetical work. As confirmed, this conceptual background ultimately led his doctrine of Spirit baptism, his understanding of true preaching, and his interpretation of the key texts related to Spirit baptism to be distinguished from the Reformed tradition. It encouraged Lloyd-Jones to place more emphasis on the extraordinary works of the Spirit, including the immediate work of the Spirit and the experiential aspect of assurance. Lloyd-Jones's doctrine of Spirit baptism has its roots in his revival theology and his fervent longing for revival.

An urgent need for baptism with the Spirit—outpouring of the Spirit or revival—was Lloyd-Jones's own lifelong spiritual burden. In his sermon "A Burden for Revival," a sermon on the subject of revival to commemorate the centenary of the Welsh revival of 1859, Lloyd-Jones describes the burden for the recovery of Zion in Isaiah's heart:

> The (devastated) condition of Zion has become his one concern, the passion of his life, the one thing about which he always speaks. It has become a burden upon his spirit. And that is how revivals have always begun. God has put a burden in this way upon somebody, upon one man, perhaps, or upon a number of men—the number does not matter. You might say that a man develops a kind of one-track mind, it is all he talks about: "I will take no rest, I will not hold my peace." He is speaking about it [the recovery of Zion, revival], telling people about it, exhorting people to consider it. Thus, I say, God begins to move. That was the truth about the prophet Isaiah.[1]

Lloyd-Jones himself, like the prophet Isaiah, shouldering the burden of the supreme need of revival in the church from the beginning to the end of his ministry, continued to preach about it with undiminishing passion, to exhort people to consider it gravely, and to pray for it earnestly. That was the essence of Lloyd-Jones's preaching.

For Lloyd-Jones, Murray argues, the great danger of contemporary churches was "to attempt to do God's work without the energizing power of the Spirit." In particular, Lloyd-Jones was troubled to observe the absence of any expectation in preachers that "God may work in an extraordinary and remarkable way"[2] in their preaching ministry. Lloyd-Jones's desire for preachers to know extraordinary power in their preaching is closely related to the homiletical implications of his doctrine of Spirit baptism. Today's churches in Europe, the United States, Canada, and South Korea are suffering from a steady decline in numbers and diminishing influence over the world. For instance, almost half of all Canadians did not attend a worship service (Catholic or Protestant) in 2008, a figure that jumped more than twofold compared to 1986.[3] This is not just a matter of numbers or church growth but is a matter of spiritual change and growth. The steady decline in numbers reflects the diminishing transformative power of preaching due in part to ignorance of the work of the Spirit in the ministry of preaching. If preaching, as God's ordained way to gather the elect from the world and to build up their faith as the body of Christ, would recover its efficacy through

1. Lloyd-Jones, *Revival*, 257–58.
2. Murray, *David Martyn Lloyd-Jones: The Fight of Faith*, 386–87.
3. Eagle, "Changing Patterns of Attendance," 200.

the work of the Holy Spirit, it would bring about a steady flow of conversion, transformation, and spiritual growth, as designed by God.

In this situation, Lloyd-Jones's conviction regarding the necessity of baptism of the Spirit in the ministry of preaching encourages preachers to seek a more in-depth experience of God's glory, holiness, power, and eternal love toward them through experiential work of the Spirit, not content with their intellectual or superficial knowledge of God. The great preachers of the eighteenth and nineteenth centuries, such as Wesley, Whitefield, Harris, and Spurgeon, did not understand God's redemptive love and forgiveness of their sin in only an intellectual sense. All of them had the profound experience of the Spirit to lead them to become experientially aware of God's redemptive love and forgiveness. They experienced God's glory, presence, and mighty power repeatedly. Lloyd-Jones also had such profound experiences of the Spirit. Therefore, seeking these same experiences of the Spirit that the great evangelists had, preachers should yearn to enjoy full assurance in their salvation and the love of God, and be filled with boldness, freedom, authority, and power, all of which come from on high, in their preaching ministries.

Lloyd-Jones's stress on the necessity of Spirit baptism in preaching intends to acknowledge that a preacher as a human agent is fundamentally insufficient to do the task of preaching. Michael Knowles argues that preachers should realize their "fundamental inability to effect the kinds of spiritual change for which we and our congregation long"; they should be convinced of "a corollary need for reliance on the unconstrained and uncontrollable power of God"[4] for their preaching task. As Lloyd-Jones argues, "Without believing in and knowing something of the power of the Spirit, it [preaching] is a heart-breaking task," and only the power of the Holy Spirit makes it possible to achieve the spiritual transformation of listeners through preaching. To be filled with the Spirit again by experiencing the outpouring of the Spirit empowers preaching to become God's own act because it enables a preacher to "become the channel through whom the Holy Spirit works,"[5] clothing the preacher with authority and power from on high so as to authenticate the truth of the word. Lloyd-Jones preached that "the greatest need of the hour,

4. Knowles, *Of Seeds and the People of God*, 111.

5. Lloyd-Jones, *Preaching and Preachers*, 305, 315.

as I see it, it is a mighty outpouring of the Spirit of God to authenticate, to prove, the truth of this one and only message."[6]

The most urgent need for preachers now is to return to "the ancient supply," baptism of the Spirit, aspiring to experience God's eternal love as the true source of spiritual "fire" and the new-covenant power to sustain their lives and in their preaching ministries, rather than searching for cutting-edge methodologies and new messages. Facing the current situation of declining churches, preachers need to be filled with God's love and power over and over to overcome the staggering challenges in front of them through experiencing baptism with the Spirit. Lloyd-Jones's conviction regarding the necessity of Spirit baptism still tells us of the urgent need to expect and to pray for the extraordinary work of the Holy Spirit in the ministry of preaching, not just to be content with the usual work of the Spirit, while seeking above all to expound Scripture itself.

---

6. Sargent, *Sacred Anointing*, 276–77.

BIBLIOGRAPHY

—

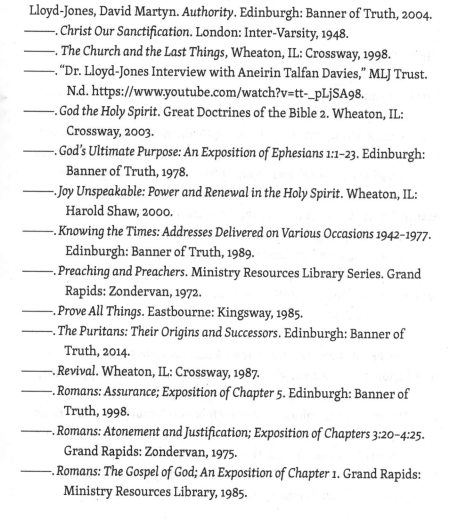

PRIMARY SOURCES

Lloyd-Jones, David Martyn. *Authority*. Edinburgh: Banner of Truth, 2004.

———. *Christ Our Sanctification*. London: Inter-Varsity, 1948.

———. *The Church and the Last Things*, Wheaton, IL: Crossway, 1998.

———. "Dr. Lloyd-Jones Interview with Aneirin Talfan Davies," MLJ Trust. N.d. https://www.youtube.com/watch?v=tt-_pLjSA98.

———. *God the Holy Spirit*. Great Doctrines of the Bible 2. Wheaton, IL: Crossway, 2003.

———. *God's Ultimate Purpose: An Exposition of Ephesians 1:1–23*. Edinburgh: Banner of Truth, 1978.

———. *Joy Unspeakable: Power and Renewal in the Holy Spirit*. Wheaton, IL: Harold Shaw, 2000.

———. *Knowing the Times: Addresses Delivered on Various Occasions 1942–1977*. Edinburgh: Banner of Truth, 1989.

———. *Preaching and Preachers*. Ministry Resources Library Series. Grand Rapids: Zondervan, 1972.

———. *Prove All Things*. Eastbourne: Kingsway, 1985.

———. *The Puritans: Their Origins and Successors*. Edinburgh: Banner of Truth, 2014.

———. *Revival*. Wheaton, IL: Crossway, 1987.

———. *Romans: Assurance; Exposition of Chapter 5*. Edinburgh: Banner of Truth, 1998.

———. *Romans: Atonement and Justification; Exposition of Chapters 3:20–4:25*. Grand Rapids: Zondervan, 1975.

———. *Romans: The Gospel of God; An Exposition of Chapter 1*. Grand Rapids: Ministry Resources Library, 1985.

———. *Romans: The Law: Its Functions and Limits; An Exposition of Chapters 7:1–8:4*. Grand Rapids: Zondervan, 1979.

———. *Romans: The Sons of God, 8:3–17*. Carlisle, PA: Banner of Truth, 1995.

———. *Spiritual Blessing: The Path to True Happiness*. Eastbourne: Kingsway, 1999.

———. *Spiritual Depression: Its Causes and Cure*. Grand Rapids: Eerdmans, 1965.

———. *Unsearchable Riches of Christ: An Exposition of Ephesians 3:1–21*. Edinburgh: Banner of Truth, 1991.

SECONDARY SOURCES

Allison, Gregg R. *Historical Theology: An Introduction to Christian Doctrine*. Grand Rapids: Zondervan, 2011.

Ames, William. *The Marrow of Theology*. Translated and edited by John D. Eusden. Grand Rapids: Baker, 1968.

Atherstone, Andrew, David Ceri Jones, and William Kay. "Lloyd-Jones and the Charismatic Controversy." Pages 114–55 in *Engaging with Martyn Lloyd-Jones: The Life and Legacy of "the Doctor,"* edited by Andrew Atherstone and David Ceri Jones. Nottingham: Inter-Varsity, 2011.

Barbee, David M. "The Allurer of the Soul: The Holy Spirit in Puritan Preaching." Pages 111–24 in *The Holy Spirit and the Christian Life: Historical, Interdisciplinary, and Renewal Perspectives*. New York: Palgrave Macmillan, 2014.

Baxter, Richard. *Five Disputations of Church-Government, and Worship*. London: R. W., 1659.

Bayne, Paul. *An Entire Commentary Upon the Whole Epistle of the Apostle Paul to the Ephesians*. London: Davies & Mortlock, 1658.

Bebbington, David W. *Evangelicalism in Modern Britain: A History from the 1730s to the 1980s*. London: Routledge, 1989.

———. "Revival and Enlightenment in Eighteenth-Century England." Pages 17–41 in *Modern Christian Revivals*, edited by Edith L. Blumhofer and Randall Balmer. Urbana: University of Illinois Press, 1993.

Beeke, Joel R. *The Quest for Full Assurance: The Legacy of Calvin and His Successors*. Edinburgh: Banner of Truth, 1999.

———. "William Perkins and His Greatest Case of Conscience: 'How a Man May Know Whether He Be the Child of God, or No.'" *Calvin Theology Journal* 41 (2006): 255–77.

Beeke, Joel R., and Mark Jones. *A Puritan Theology: Doctrine for Life*. Kindle ed. Grand Rapids: Reformation Heritage, 2013.

Beeke, Joel R., and Randall J. Pederson. *Meet the Puritans*. Grand Rapids: Reformation Heritage, 2006.

Bennett, Richard. *The Early Life of Howell Harris*. Edinburgh: Banner of Truth, 1962.

Berkhof, Louis. *The Assurance of Faith*. Kindle ed. Reprint, Louisville: GLH, 2018.

Brauer, Jerald C. "The Nature of English Puritanism: Reflections on the Nature of English Puritanism." *Church History* 23 (1954): 99–108.

Brencher, John Frederick. "David Martyn Lloyd-Jones 1899–1981 and Twentieth-Century Evangelicalism." PhD diss., University of Sheffield, 1997.

Brooks, Thomas. *The Works of Thomas Brooks*. Edited by A. Grosart. 6 vols. London: Nichol, 1861–1866.

Bruner, Frederick Dale. *A Theology of the Holy Spirit: The Pentecostal Experience and the New Testament Witness*. Eugene, OR: Wipf & Stock, 1997.

Buchanan, James. *The Office and Work of the Holy Spirit*. 6th ed. New York: Carter, 1847.

Burton, Ernest DeWitt. *Syntax of the Moods and Tenses in New Testament Greek*. 3rd ed. Edinburgh: T&T Clark, 1973.

Caldwell, Robert W., III. *Theologies of the American Revivalists: From Whitefield to Finney*. Downers Grove, IL: InterVarsity, 2017.

Carson, D. A. *Showing the Spirit: A Theological Exposition of 1 Corinthians 12–14*. Kindle ed. Grand Rapids: Baker Books, 2019.

Catherwood, Christopher. "Afterword." Pages 265–79 in *Martyn Lloyd-Jones: Chosen by God*, edited by Christopher Catherwood. Westchester, IL: Crossway, 1988.

Catherwood, Frederick, and Elizabeth Catherwood. *Martyn Lloyd-Jones: The Man and His Books*. Bryntirion, Wales: Evangelical Library of Wales, 1984.

Cherry, Conrad. *The Theology of Jonathan Edwards: A Reappraisal*. Bloomington: Indiana University Press, 1990.

Coffey, John. "Lloyd-Jones and the Protestant Past." Pages 293–325 in *Engaging with Martyn Lloyd-Jones: The Life and Legacy of "the Doctor,"* edited by Andrew Atherstone and David Ceri Jones. Nottingham, UK: Inter-Varsity, 2011.

Crawford, Michael J. *Seasons of Grace: Colonial New England's Revival Tradition in Its British Context*. Religion in America. New York: Oxford University Press, 1991.

Dallimore, Arnold A. *George Whitefield: The Life and Times of the Great Evangelist of the Eighteenth-Century Revival*. Edinburgh: Banner of Truth, 1970.

Davies, Horton. "Elizabethan Puritan Preaching." *Worship* 44.2 (1970): 101.

———. *The Worship of the English Puritans*. London: Dacre, 1948.

———. *Worship and Theology in England, vol. 1*. Princeton: Princeton University Press, 1961.

Dayton, Donald W. *Theological Roots of Pentecostalism*. Studies in Evangelicalism 5. Grand Rapids: Francis Asbury, 1987.

Dever, Mark. *The Affectionate Theology of Richard Sibbes*. Kindle ed. A Long Line of Godly Men Profile Series. Orlando, FL: Reformation Trust, 2017.

———. *Richard Sibbes: Puritanism and Calvinism in Late Elizabethan and Early Stuart England*. Macon, GA: Mercer University Press, 2000.

Downame, John. *The Christian Warfare*. Norwood, NJ: Johnson, 1974.

Dunn, James D. G. *Baptism in the Holy Spirit: A Re-examination of the New Testament Teaching on the Gift of the Spirit in Relation to Pentecostalism Today*. Studies in Biblical Theology 15. London: SCM, 1970.

Durham, James. *A Learned and Complete Commentary upon the Book of the Revelation*. Glasgow: Spencer, 1788.

Eagle, David E. "Changing Patterns of Attendance at Religious Services in Canada, 1986–2008." *Journal for the Scientific Study of Religion* 50 (2011): 187–200.

Eaton, Michael A. *Baptism with the Spirit: The Teaching of Martyn Lloyd-Jones*. Downers Grove, IL: InterVarsity, 1989.

Edwards, Jonathan. *The Works of Jonathan Edwards*. Edited by Kenneth P. Minkema et al. 26 vols. New Haven: Yale University Press, 1957–2009.
Elton, Edward. *The Triumph of a True Christian Described*. London: Field for Mylburne, 1623.
Evans, Eifion. *Daniel Rowland and the Great Evangelical Awakening in Wales*. Edinburgh: Banner of Truth Trust, 1995.
———. "'The Power of Heaven in the Word of Life': Welsh Calvinistic Methodism and Revival." In *Pentecostal Outpourings: Revival and the Reformed Tradition*, edited by Robert Davis Smart et al., 3–28. Grand Rapids: Reformation Heritage, 2016.
Eveson, Philip H. *Travel with Martyn Lloyd-Jones: In the Footsteps of the Distinguished Welsh Evangelist, Pastor and Theologian*. Leominster: Day One, 2004.
Fee, Gordon D. *God's Empowering Presence: The Holy Spirit in the Letters of Paul*. Grand Rapids: Baker Books, 1994.
Ferguson, Sinclair B. "Evangelical Ministry: The Puritan Contribution." Pages 263–80 in *The Compromised Church: The Present Evangelical Crisis*, edited by John H. Armstrong. Wheaton, IL: Crossway, 1988.
———. "John Owen and the Doctrine of the Holy Spirit." Pages 101–29 in *John Owen: The Man and His Theology*, edited by Robert W. Oliver. Darlington, UK: Evangelical, 2002.
Finney, Charles G. *Lectures on Revivals of Religion*. Cambridge: Harvard University Press, 2013.
———. *Memoirs of Rev. Charles G. Finney*. New York: Barnes, 1876.
Flavel, John. *The Character of an Evangelical Pastor, Drawn by Christ*. London: Rutt, 1814.
———. *A Treatise of the Soul of Man*. London: J. D. for Parkhurst, 1698.
———. *The Whole Works of John Flavel*. 6 vols. London: Baynes and Son, 1820.
Fleming, Robert. *The Fulfilling of the Scripture*. 7th ed. Glasgow: Smith, 1753.
Goodwin, Thomas. *The Works of Thomas Goodwin, D.D.* Edited by John C. Miller. 12 vols. Edinburgh: Nichol, 1861–1867.
Gootjes, N. H. *성령으로의 세례와 신자의 체험*. [The Baptism with the Spirit and the Believer's Experience.] Seoul: Reformed Company for Faith Action, 1989.

Greenham, Richard. *The Works of the Reverend and Faithful Servant of Jesus Christ M. Richard Greenham*. London: Kingston, 1599.

Guthrie, William. *The Christian's Great Interest; Or the Trial of a Saving Interest in Christ, and the Way to Attain It*. Philadelphia: Presbyterian Board of Publication, 1825.

Haldane, Robert. *Exposition of the Epistle to the Romans*. 9th ed. Edinburgh: Oliphant, 1874.

Haller, William. *The Rise of Puritanism*. Philadelphia: University of Pennsylvania Press, 1972.

Harris, Howell. *A Brief Account of the Life of Howell Harris, Esq; Extracted from Papers Written by Himself. To Which Is Added a Concise Collection of His Letters from the Year 1738, to 1772*. Trevecka, UK, 1791.

Haykin, Michael A. G. *Jonathan Edwards: The Holy Spirit in Revival*. Darlington, UK: Evangelical, 2006.

———. *The Revived Puritan: The Spirituality of George Whitefield*. Dundas, ON: Joshua, 2000.

Heath, Gordon L. *Doing Church History: A User-Friendly Introduction to Researching the History of Christianity*. Toronto: Clements, 2008.

Heitzenrater, Richard P. *Mirror and Memory: Reflections on Early Methodism*. Nashville: Kingswood, 1989.

Hopkins, Samuel. *The Works of Samuel Hopkins: With a Memoir of His Life and Character*. 3 vols. Boston: Doctrinal Tract and Book Society, 1854.

Horton, Thomas. *Forty-six Sermons Upon the Whole Eighth Chapter of the Epistle of the Apostle Paul to the Romans*. London: Maxwell for Parkhurst, 1674.

Howe, John. *The Outpouring of the Holy Spirit; Or, the Prosperous State of the Christian Interest Before the End of Time, By a Plentiful Effusion of the Holy Spirit*. London: Religious Tract Society, 1835.

Hughes, Hugh J. *Life of Howell Harris: The Welsh Reformer*. Newport, UK: Jones, 1892.

Jones, David Ceri. "'A Glorious Morn'?: Methodism and the Rise of Evangelicalism in Wales, 1735–62." Pages 97–114 in *British Evangelical Identities Past and Present*, edited by Mark Smith. Milton Keynes: Paternoster, 2008.

Jones, David Ceri, Boyd Stanley Schlenther, and Eryn Mant White. *The*

Elect Methodists: Calvinistic Methodism in England and Wales, 1735–1811. Cardiff: University of Wales Press, 2012.

Jones, R. Tudur. *Grym y Gair a Fflam y Ffydd*. Bangor, UK: Cyhoeddiadua'r Gair, 1998.

Jung, Keun-Doo. "An Evaluation of the Principles and Methods of the Preaching of D. M. Lloyd-Jones." ThD diss., Potchefstroom University, 1986.

Kaiser, Walter C., Jr. "The Baptism in the Holy Spirit as the Promise of the Father: A Reformed Perspective." Pages 15–46 in *Perspectives on Spirit Baptism: Five Views*, edited by Chad Owen Brand. Nashville: B&H, 2004.

Kay, William K. "Martyn Lloyd-Jones's Influence on Pentecostalism and Neo-Pentecostalism in the UK." *Journal of Pentecostal Theology* 22 (2013): 275–94.

Keener, Craig S. *Gift & Giver: The Holy Spirit for Today*. Grand Rapids: Baker Academic, 2001.

Keddie, Gordon J. "'Unfallible Certenty of the Pardon of Sinne and Life Everlasting': The Doctrine of Assurance in the Theology of William Perkins (1558–1602)." *Evangelical Quarterly* 48.4 (1976): 230–44.

Knott, John Ray. *The Sword of the Spirit: Puritan Responses to the Bible*. Chicago: University of Chicago Press, 1980.

Knowles, Michael P. *Of Seeds and the People of God: Preaching as Parable, Crucifixion, and Testimony*. Eugene, OR: Cascade, 2015.

Kurian, George Thomas, and Mark A. Lamport, eds. *Encyclopedia of Christianity in the United States*. 5 vols. Lanham, MD: Rowman & Littlefield, 2016.

Laud, William. *The Works of the Most Reverend Father in God, William Laud, Sometime Lord Archbishop of Canterbury*. Edited by William Scott and James Bliss. 7 vols. Oxford: Parker, 1847–1860.

Lawson, Steven J. *The Passionate Preaching of Martyn Lloyd-Jones*. Sanford, FL: Reformation Trust, 2016.

Lewis, Peter. *The Genius of Puritanism*. Morgan, PA: Soli Deo Gloria, 2001.

Lloyd-Jones, Bethan. *Memories of Sandfields*. Edinburgh: Banner of Truth, 2008.

Lovelace, Richard. "Edwards' Theology." *Christian History* 8 (1985): 22–25.

Luther, Martin. *Sermons 2 Luther's Works*. Edited by Hans J. Hillderbrand. Vol 52, *Luther's Works*. St. Louis: Concordia, 1974.

Macleod, Donald. *The Spirit of Promise*. Fearn, UK: Christian Focus, 1986.

MacLure, Millar. *Paul's Cross Sermons, 1534–1642*. Toronto: University of Toronto Press, 1958.

Macpherson, John, ed. *The Westminster Confession of Faith*. 2nd ed. Edinburgh: T&T Clark, 1882.

Masters, Peter. "Opening the Door to Charismatic Teaching." *The Sword and Trowel* 2 (1988): 24–35.

Mather, Cotton. *Magnalia Christi Americana, Or, the Ecclesiastical History of New-England; From Its First Planting, in the Year 1620, Unto the Year of Our Lord 1698*. Hartford, CT: Andrus and Son, 1855.

Maton, Thomas. *The Complete Works of Thomas Manton*. 22 vols. London: Nisbet, 1870–1875.

McClymond, Michael J., and Gerald R. McDermott. *The Theology of Jonathan Edwards*. New York: Oxford University Press, 2012.

Menzies, William W., and Stanley M. Horton. *Bible Doctrines: A Pentecostal Perspective*. Kindle ed. Springfield, MO: Gospel Publishing House, 2012.

Moody, Paul Dwight, and Arthur Percy Fitt. *The Shorter Life of D. L. Moody*. Chicago: Bible Institute Colportage, 1900.

Murray, Iain H. *D. Martyn Lloyd-Jones: Letters 1919–1981*. Edinburgh: Banner of Truth, 1994.

———. *David Martyn Lloyd-Jones: The Fight of Faith, 1939–1981*. Edinburgh: Banner of Truth, 2009.

———. *David Martyn Lloyd-Jones: The First Forty Years, 1899–1939*. Edinburgh: Banner of Truth, 2012.

———. *Jonathan Edwards: A New Biography*. Edinburgh: Banner of Truth, 1987.

———. *The Life of Martyn Lloyd-Jones 1899–1981*. Edinburgh: Banner of Truth, 2013.

———. *Lloyd-Jones: Messenger of Grace*. Edinburgh: Banner of Truth, 2008.

———. *Pentecost Today?: The Biblical Basis for Understanding Revival*. Edinburgh: Banner of Truth, 1998.

———. *Revival and Revivalism: The Making and Marring of American Evangelicalism 1750–1858*. Edinburgh: Banner of Truth, 1994.

New, John F. H. *Anglican and Puritan: The Basis of Their Opposition, 1558–1640*. Stanford, CA: Stanford University Press, 1964.

Nuttall, Geoffrey Fillingham. *The Holy Spirit in Puritan Faith and Experience*. Chicago: University of Chicago Press, 1992.

———. *Howel Harris, 1714–1773: The Last Enthusiast*. Cardiff: University of Wales Press, 1965.

O'Donnell, Matthew Brook. "Two Opposing Views on Baptism with/by the Holy Spirit and of 1 Corinthians 12:13: Can Grammatical Investigation Bring Clarity?" Pages 331–36 in *Baptism, the New Testament and the Church: Historical and Contemporary Studies in Honour of R. E. O. White*, edited by Stanley E. Porter and Anthony R. Cross. Journal for the Study of the New Testament Supplement Series 171. Sheffield: Sheffield Academic, 1999.

Owen, John. *A Memoir of the Rev. Daniel Rowlands*. London: Seeley and Burnside, 1840.

———. *Of Communion with God the Father, Son and Holy Ghost*. 1657. Reprint, Edinburgh: Banner of Truth, 1965.

———. *The Works of John Owen*. Edited by William H. Goold. 24 vols. London: Johnstone & Hunter, 1850–1853.

Packer, James I. "David Martyn Lloyd-Jones." Pages 109–23 in *Chosen Vessels: Portraits of Ten Outstanding Christian Men*, edited by Charles Turner, 109–23. Ann Arbor, MI: Vine, 1985.

———. *A Quest for Godliness: The Puritan Vision of the Christian Life*. Wheaton, IL: Crossway, 2010.

———. "The Witness of the Spirit: The Puritan Preaching." Pages 334–542 in *Puritan Papers*, vol. 1, 1956–1959, edited by J. I. Packer, locs. Kindle ed. Phillipsburg, NJ: P&R, 2000.

Palma, Anthony D. *The Holy Spirit: A Pentecostal Perspective*. Kindle ed. Springfield, MO: Gospel Publishing House, 2001.

Park, Wan-Chul. "Integration of Mind and Heart in the Preaching of Jonathan Edwards." *Journal of Reformed Theology* 24 (2006): 211–45.

———. "The Integration of the Word and Experience in the Preaching of David Martyn Lloyd-Jones." *Journal of Reformed Theology* 24 (2006): 517–78.

Pearlman, Myer. *The Heavenly Gift: Studies in the Work of the Holy Spirit*. Springfield, MO: Gospel Publishing House, 1935.

———. *Knowing the Doctrines of the Bible*. Kindle edition.Springfield, MO: Gospel Publishing House, 1981.

Perkins, William. *The Art of Prophesying*. Kindle ed. Reprint, Pavlik, 2012.

———. *The Work of William Perkins*. Edited by Ian Breward. Appleford, UK: Courtenay, 1970.

Pettit, Norman. *The Heart Prepared: Grace and Conversion in Puritan Spiritual Life*. Yale Publications in American Studies 11. New Haven: Yale University Press, 1966.

Piper, John. "A Passion for Christ-Exalting Power." Desiring God, January 2016. http://www.desiringgod.org/messages/a-passion-for-christ-exalting-power.

Porter, Stanley E. *Verbal Aspect in the Greek of the New Testament: With Reference to Tense and Mood*. Studies in Biblical Greek 1. New York: Lang, 1993.

Powicke, Frederick James. *A Life of the Reverend Richard Baxter, 1615–1691*. London: Cape, 1924.

Preston, John. *The New Covenant, or the Saints Portion: A Treatise Unfolding the All-Sufficiencie of God, Man's Uprightness, and the Covenant of Grace*. 10th ed. London: I. D. for Bourne, 1637.

Randall, Ian M. "Lloyd-Jones and Revival." Pages 91–113 in *Engaging with Martyn Lloyd-Jones: The Life and Legacy of "the Doctor,"* edited by Andrew Atherstone and David Ceri Jones. Nottingham, UK: Inter-Varsity, 2011.

———. "Martyn Lloyd-Jones and Methodist Spirituality." *Wesley Methodist Studies* 5 (2013): 97–122.

Rast, Lawrence R., Jr. "Jonathan Edwards on Justification by Faith." *Concordia Theological Quarterly* 72 (2008): 347–62.

Robertson, A. T. *A Grammar of the Greek New Testament in the Light of Historical Research*. 3rd ed. London: Hodder & Stoughton, 1919.

Robinson, Matthew. *Logic on Fire: The Life and Legacy of Dr. Martyn Lloyd-Jones*. DVD. New Albany, MS: Media Gratiae, 2015.

Ryken, Leland. *Worldly Saints: The Puritans as They Really Were*. Grand Rapids: Academie, 1986.

Sargent, Tony. *The Sacred Anointing: The Preaching of Dr. Martyn Lloyd-Jones*. Wheaton, IL: Crossway, 1994.

Schaefer, Paul R., Jr. *The Spiritual Brotherhood: Cambridge Puritans and the*

Nature of Christian Piety. Kindle ed. Grand Rapids: Reformation Heritage, 2011.

Sibbes, Richard. *The Complete Works of Richard Sibbes*. Edited by Alexander Ballach Grosart. 7 vols. Edinburgh: Nichol, 1862.

Smart, Robert Davis. *Jonathan Edwards's Apologetic for the Great Awakening*. Grand Rapids: Reformation Heritage, 2011.

Smeaton, George. *Doctrine of the Holy Spirit*. Edinburgh: T&T Clark, 1882.

Smith, John E. *Jonathan Edwards: Puritan, Preacher, Philosopher*. Notre Dame, IN: University of Notre Dame Press, 1992.

Smith, Timothy L. "How John Fletcher Became the Theologian of Wesleyan Perfectionism 1770–1776." *Wesleyan Theological Journal* 15 (1980): 68–87.

Stoddard, Solomon. *The Efficacy of the Fear of Hell to Restrain Men from Sin*. Boston: Fleet, 1713.

Stott, John. *Baptism and Fullness: The Work of the Holy Spirit*. Downers Grove, IL: InterVarsity, 2006.

Strype, John. *The History of the Life and Acts of Edmund Grindal, the First Bishop of London*. London: J. S. M. A., 1710.

Sweeney, Douglas A. *Jonathan Edwards and the Ministry of the Word*. Downers Grove, IL: InterVarsity, 2009.

Thomas, I. D. E. *The Golden Treasury of Puritan Quotations*. Chicago: Moody, 1975.

Tomkins, Stephen. *John Wesley: A Biography*. Grand Rapids: Eerdmans, 2003.

Torrey, R. A. *The Person and Work of the Holy Spirit: As Revealed in the Scriptures and in Personal Experience*. Kindle ed. Reprint, Cross Reach, 2016.

Turnbull, Ralph G. *Jonathan Edwards, the Preacher*. Grand Rapids: Baker, 1958.

Walton, Brad. *Jonathan Edwards, Religious Affections and the Puritan Analysis of True Piety, Spiritual Sensation and Heart Religion*. Lewiston, NY: Mellen, 2002.

Wesley, John. *The Bicentennial Edition of the Works of John Wesley*. Edited by Frank Baker and Richard P. Heitzenrater. 34 vols. Nashville: Abingdon, 1984–2003.

———. *Explanatory Notes upon The New Testament*. London: Wesleyan Conference Office, 1866.

———. *The Journal of John Wesley*. Edited by Percy Livingston Parker. Chicago: Moody, 1974.

———. *Sermons on Several Occasions, Vol. 1*. New York: Emory and Waugh, 1829.

———. *Wesley's Standard Sermons*. Edited by Edward H. Sugden. 4th ed. 2 vols. London: Epworth, 1956.

———. *The Works of the Reverend John Wesley, A.M.* Edited by John Emory. 7 vols. New York: Methodist Book Concern, 1839–1840.

White, Eryn M. "The Eighteenth-Century Evangelical Revival and Welsh Identity." In *British Evangelical Identities Past and Present*, edited by Mark Smith, 85–96. Milton Keynes: Paternoster, 2008.

———. "Revival and Renewal amongst the Eighteenth-Century Welsh Methodists." Pages 1–12 in *Revival, Renewal, and the Holy Spirit*. Edited by Dyfed Wyn Roberts. Milton Keynes: Paternoster, 2009.

Whitefield, George. *George Whitefield's Journals*. Edinburgh: Banner of Truth, 1978.

———. *Sermons on Important Subjects*. London: Fisher, 1841.

Williams, William. *Welsh Calvinistic Methodism: A Historical Sketch of the Presbyterian Church of Wales*. 2nd ed. London: Presbyterian Church of England, 1884.

Wise, S. F. "Sermon Literature and Canadian Intellectual History." Pages 79–97 in vol. 2 of *Pre-industrial Canada 1760–1849*. Readings in Canadian Social History. Toronto: McClelland and Stewart, 1982.

Yates, Arthur S. *The Doctrine of Assurance*. London: Epworth, 1952.

SUBJECT INDEX

—

SCRIPTURE INDEX

Old Testament

New Testament

GOD'S TIME FOR US
Barth's Reconciliation of Eternity & Time in Jesus Christ
JAMES J. CASSIDY
THE TRINITY & MARTIN LUTHER
Revised Edition
CHRISTINE HELMER
THE BEAUTY of THE LORD
Theology As Aesthetics
JONATHAN KING
RENDERING THE WORD in THEOLOGICAL HERMENEUTICS
Mapping Divine & Human Agency
MARK ALAN BOWALD
STUDIES IN HISTORICAL & SYSTEMATIC THEOLOGY
LEXHAM PRESS